| READING |

Basic   Intermediate   Advanced   Expert

| LISTENING |

Basic   Intermediate   Advanced   Expert

Informative passages

HACKERS APEX LISTENING includes informative and interesting listening passages on a variety of academic topics and everyday situations in a university setting.

Useful online study materials

HACKERS APEX LISTENING provides access to quality online study materials at HackersBook.com. These include streaming audio recordings of all passages accessible through QR codes in the book.

HACKERS
APEX LISTENING
for the TOEFL iBT®

Basic

Preface

Preface

Thank you for purchasing *HACKERS APEX LISTENING for the TOEFL iBT Basic*. The TOEFL iBT is a highly challenging exam, so it is important to select an effective study guide. All of us at Hackers Language Research Institute are confident that this publication will be an invaluable resource as you prepare for the TOEFL iBT.

HACKERS APEX LISTENING for the TOEFL iBT is a series of comprehensive study guides for students planning to take the TOEFL iBT or for those wanting to improve their general English listening skills. This series includes four books that progress in difficulty. Students can begin at the level that matches their current abilities and then move on to the higher ones. All of the books in this series provide step-by-step question-solving strategies for every TOEFL question type. These are based on thorough research and years of instructional experience. Each book also includes informative and interesting listening passages that enable students to improve their English listening skills and familiarize them with academic topics and spoken English used in everyday university settings. Furthermore, students will receive access to quality online study materials that are designed to help them get the most out of the books in this series. Key features of *HACKERS APEX LISTENING for the TOEFL iBT* books include:

- Detailed explanations and question-solving strategies for all TOEFL Listening question types
- A large number of high-quality TOEFL Listening passages and questions
- Two full-length TOEFL Listening tests
- Dictation exercises to enhance listening comprehension ability
- Vocabulary exercises to review essential vocabulary that appeared in the passages
- An answer book with complete scripts, Korean translations, and lists of key vocabulary
- Access to streaming audio recordings of all passages through QR codes
- Access to supplementary study materials online (www.HackersBook.com)

Thank you again for choosing *HACKERS APEX LISTENING for the TOEFL iBT Basic*, and we wish you all the best whether you are preparing to take the TOEFL iBT in the near future or simply hoping to develop your English listening skills overall.

Table of Contents

How to Use This Book — 6
About the TOEFL iBT — 8
NOTE-TAKING — 10

CHAPTER 01 — **Main Purpose/Topic** — 13
Example — 15
Listening Practice 1, 2, 3, 4 — 17
iBT Listening Test 1, 2 — 25
• Vocabulary Review — 32

CHAPTER 02 — **Detail** — 33
Example — 35
Listening Practice 1, 2, 3, 4 — 37
iBT Listening Test 1, 2 — 45
• Vocabulary Review — 52

CHAPTER 03 — **Function** — 53
Example — 55
Listening Practice 1, 2, 3, 4 — 57
iBT Listening Test 1, 2 — 65
• Vocabulary Review — 72

CHAPTER 04 — **Attitude** — 73
Example — 75
Listening Practice 1, 2, 3, 4 — 77
iBT Listening Test 1, 2 — 85
• Vocabulary Review — 92

HACKERS APEX LISTENING
for the TOEFL iBT
Basic

CHAPTER 05	**Organization**	93
	Example	95
	Listening Practice 1, 2, 3, 4	97
	iBT Listening Test 1, 2	105
	• Vocabulary Review	112

CHAPTER 06	**Connecting Contents**	113
	Example	115
	Listening Practice 1, 2, 3, 4	117
	iBT Listening Test 1, 2	125
	• Vocabulary Review	132

CHAPTER 07	**Inference**	133
	Example	135
	Listening Practice 1, 2, 3, 4	137
	iBT Listening Test 1, 2	145
	• Vocabulary Review	152

- **Actual Test 1**   154
- **Actual Test 2**   164

How to Use This Book

1. Understand the Question Type

Each chapter includes an Overview page that provides essential information about the featured question type and key strategies for answering it. Make sure you fully understand the strategies before moving on to the Example section, where you can apply the key strategies to short conversation and lecture passages with one question each.

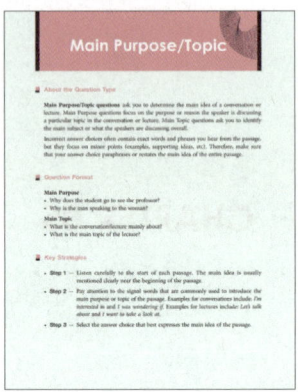

2. Improve Your Skills with Listening Practice Exercises

Each chapter includes four Listening Practice exercises, which consist of two conversation and two lecture passages. These will help you become more familiar with the featured question type, as well as other question types. Each exercise is accompanied by a dictation section so that you can enhance your listening comprehension ability.

3. Take the iBT Listening Tests

Each chapter includes two iBT Listening Tests, which consist of longer conversation and lecture passages with 4 to 5 questions each that are similar to those that appear on the TOEFL iBT. Taking these tests will enable you to improve your listening comprehension skills and prepare for the TOEFL iBT.

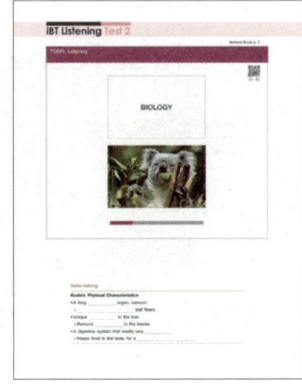

4 Review Essential Vocabulary

At the end of each chapter is a Vocabulary Review, which includes questions on essential vocabulary from the chapter. You will be able to easily memorize the vocabulary words through various types of questions.

5 Evaluate Your Progress with Actual Tests

The book includes two Actual Tests, which are full-length listening tests that include passages and questions that closely match what appears on the TOEFL iBT. They provide an excellent opportunity to apply the skills you have learned and evaluate your progress.

6 Check the Answer Book

The Answer Book specifies the correct answer choice for all questions and provides complete scripts and Korean translations of all passages and questions. It also includes a list of key vocabulary words from each passage with definitions.

About the TOEFL iBT

What Is the TOEFL iBT?

The TOEFL (Test of English as a Foreign Language) iBT (Internet-Based test) includes Reading, Listening, Speaking, and Writing sections to comprehensively assess English ability. Although most tasks require the application of only one of these skills, some require the use of two or more. The TOEFL iBT is designed to measure a student's capacity to use and understand English at a university level and is, therefore, much more difficult than many other English proficiency tests.

TOEFL iBT Structure

Section	No. of passages and questions	Time (min.)	Score	Notable Features
Reading	• 2 Passages • 10 Questions/Passage	36	30	• Each passage is approximately 700 words long.
Listening	• 2 Conversations • 5 Questions/Conversation • 3 Lectures • 6 Questions/Lecture	41	30	• Speakers have various accents, including American, British, Australian, etc.
Speaking	• 1 Independent Task • 3 Integrated Tasks	17	30	• Independent Task asks you to state your opinion about a specific topic. • Integrated Tasks ask you to provide a response based on reading and listening content.
Writing	• 1 Integrated Task • 1 Academic Discussion Task	35	30	• Integrated Task asks you to provide a response based on reading and listening content. • Academic Discussion Task asks you to state your opinion about a specific topic in an online classroom.

Total Time: Approximately 2 hours / Total Score: 120

TOEFL iBT Listening Section

The TOEFL iBT Listening Section largely consists of conversations and lectures. Conversations mainly take place in university settings, and lectures discuss topics from different academic fields covered in university lectures. Note-taking is allowed while listening to conversations and lectures. Therefore, the ability to listen, understand, and organize information is more important than relying on memory. The test consists of 2 Parts with either 11 or 17 questions. Each Part has 1 conversation and 1 to 2 lectures.

TOEFL iBT Listening Question Types

Question Type	Description
Main Purpose/Topic	Choose the answer choice that best represents the main idea of the conversation or lecture.
Detail	Choose the answer choice that corresponds to specific information or important details introduced in the conversation or lecture.
Function	Choose the answer choice that best describes the underlying function or purpose of a speaker's specific statement.
Attitude	Choose the answer choice that best represents the speaker's attitude or opinion regarding a specific matter.
Organization	Choose the answer choice that best describes the overall organization of the passage or the relationship between ideas in the passage.
Connecting Contents	Choose the answer choices that correspond to related ideas clearly stated in the passage.
Inference	Choose the answer choice that can be inferred based on relevant information in the passage.

NOTE-TAKING

Strategies for Note-taking

1. **Write down the main idea using key words.**
   Listen carefully to the beginning of the conversation or lecture. Write down the main idea in a short sentence or phrase using key words.

2. **Organize information into subtopics and categories.**
   Identify the subtopics and organize the information into groups or categories. Listen for signal words (First of all, Secondly, Now, Later, Then, Another, etc.) used to introduce subtopics.

3. **Write down the supporting details.**
   Write down the supporting details for each subtopic or category. Especially for lectures, it is good to take notes according to how the lecturer gives supporting details. For example, the lecturer may give the definition of a term, compare two or more ideas, or give a list of important items.

4. **Do not try to write down everything.**
   Make your notes brief and do not try to write down every single word. Include only essential key words. It is also helpful to use symbols and abbreviations of your own.

Note-taking Example

Script

> P: Today we are going to continue our discussion on the differences between mammals and reptiles. One of the key traits that distinguish these two types of animals is the way that they control their body temperatures. I'm sure you have all heard the expressions "hot-blooded" and "cold-blooded," right? Well, it's actually a bit more complicated than that. Basically, mammals rely on their ability to burn fats and sugars to generate heat as required. In contrast, reptiles depend on external factors, such as the sun, to warm their bodies, or cold water to cool them. OK... Let's look at these functions in a bit more detail.

Note

diffs. bet. mammals & reptiles: way they ctrl. body temp.	— *Main Topic*
1. mammals: burn fat & sugar → heat	— *Type 1*
2. reptiles: ext. factors	— *Type 2*
e.g. sun → warm	
e.g. cold water → cool	*Examples of Type 2*

Common Symbols and Abbreviations

The key to note-taking is writing down only the essential information of the conversation or lecture. Using symbols and abbreviations will allow you to make your notes brief and accurate. With symbols and abbreviations, you can write down more information in a quick and efficient way. Below are some commonly used symbols and abbreviations.

1. Symbols

Symbols can save you time and increase the amount of information you write down about a passage.

=	equals; to be	K	1,000	X	not, no
+	and; plus	&	and	/	per, each
>	more than	∴	therefore/so	/day	per day
<	less than	←	from	/h	per hour
↑	increase	@	at	/w	per week
↓	decrease	#	number (of)	∵	because

2. Abbreviations

There are several methods to make abbreviations, but make sure to keep your method consistent. Here are some ways to make abbreviations.

- Omit latter part: European → Eu
- Omit vowels: movement → mvmt
- Omit middle letters: government → govt

e.g.	for example	usu.	usually	info.	information
prob.	problem	w/	with	sum.	summary
ppl	people	cf.	compare	psych.	psychology
rsn.	reason	c.	century	Qs	questions
etc.	and so on	max.	maximum	pics	pictures
i.e.	that is; in other words	min.	minimum	w/o	without
intro.	introduction	fr.	from	vs	versus
concl.	conclusion	tech	technology	ea.	each
b.f.	before	reg	regular	btw	by the way

www.HackersBook.com

HACKERS APEX LISTENING
for the TOEFL iBT
Basic

CHAPTER 01

Main Purpose/Topic

Main Purpose/Topic

About the Question Type

Main Purpose/Topic questions ask you to determine the main idea of a conversation or lecture. Main Purpose questions focus on the purpose or reason the speaker is discussing a particular topic in the conversation or lecture. Main Topic questions ask you to identify the main subject or what the speakers are discussing overall.

Incorrect answer choices often contain exact words and phrases you hear from the passage, but they focus on minor points (examples, supporting ideas, etc.). Therefore, make sure that your answer choice paraphrases or restates the main idea of the entire passage.

Question Format

Main Purpose
- Why does the student go to see the professor?
- Why is the man speaking to the woman?

Main Topic
- What is the conversation/lecture mainly about?
- What is the main topic of the lecture?

Key Strategies

- **Step 1** — Listen carefully to the start of each passage. The main idea is usually mentioned clearly near the beginning of the passage.

- **Step 2** — Pay attention to the signal words that are commonly used to introduce the main purpose or topic of the passage. Examples for conversations include: *I'm interested in* and *I was wondering if*. Examples for lectures include: *Let's talk about* and *I want to take a look at*.

- **Step 3** — Select the answer choice that best expresses the main idea of the passage.

Example

A. Listen to a conversation between a student and a professor.

Note-taking

Student's Problem
Needs help choosing the _____ of the _____

Professor's Suggestion
Decide what you are going to _____ _____
e.g. Development of the air force and the _____

Why does the student go to see the professor?

(A) To get information about a test
(B) To change the topic of his presentation
(C) To arrange an interview with an expert
(D) To ask for advice about the subject of his paper

B. Listen to part of a lecture in a biology class.

Note-taking

Raccoons' Paws
- Extremely _____ paws
- Used to tell whether something is _____ to eat
- _____ on the food makes them wet.
  → Improves the sense of touch

What is the main topic of the lecture?

(A) How animals hunt for food
(B) How animals depend on their senses
(C) Why raccoons wet their food
(D) Why raccoons hold objects in their paws

CHAPTER 01 | Main Purpose/Topic   **15**

Dictation

Answer Book p. 2

Listen again and fill in the blanks.

A.

S: Professor Adams, I need your help _____ _____ _____ of my paper. I would like to write about World War II, but there is _____ _____. Do you have any advice for me?

P: Um, it's a good topic, but I think you have to decide what you are going to _____ _____. For instance, what do you _____ _____ _____ about World War II?

S: Well, my grandfather was a pilot at that time, so I _____ _____ _____ about the air force during World War II.

P: That's interesting. Hmm... You could write about how the air force evolved during the war and _____ _____ _____ _____. You can interview your grandfather about that, too.

S: That's great! I _____ _____ _____ _____.

P: No problem. _____ _____ _____.

B.

P: All of us, whether human or animal, _____ _____ our senses every day. We use our eyes to see, our tongues to taste, and so on... In animals, some senses are _____ _____ _____. Um, for example... Dogs have powerful noses, and bats have sensitive ears. But what about raccoons? Raccoons like to _____ _____ _____, and this has something to do with _____ _____ _____ _____. Raccoons have extremely sensitive paws. So, the raccoon uses its paws to _____ _____ about different objects. In this way, it can tell _____ _____ _____ _____ _____ to eat. Now, when a raccoon washes its food, the moisture on the food _____ _____ _____ _____. For raccoons, moisture improves their sense of touch.

Listening Practice 1

Answer Book p. 3

Listen to a conversation between a student and a student activities office employee.

Note-taking

Student's Question
How do I enter the campus _____ _____?

Application Procedure
1. Choose the _____ application on the website
2. Fill in the form and _____ it
3. Upload a scan of a _____ _____

---

1 Why does the student visit the student activities office?

(A) He needs a new password for a website.
(B) He wants to get tickets for a concert.
(C) He does not know how to enter a competition.
(D) He cannot decide which concert to attend.

2 What does the student say about his band?

(A) It has entered many competitions.
(B) It has never performed in public before.
(C) It is popular on campus.
(D) It has played together for several years.

3 According to the employee, what does the student need to provide?

(A) A schedule of show times
(B) A letter of recommendation
(C) A recording of his music
(D) A scan of his student ID

Dictation

Answer Book p. 3

Listen again and fill in the blanks.

M: Hello. Are you busy?

W: _____ _____ _____. How can I help you?

M: I have some questions about the, uh, music contest. I heard there will be _____ _____ on campus, but I'm not sure _____ _____ _____.

W: Actually, you _____ _____ _____ _____ _____. I can give you the link. Are you _____ _____ the solo or group competition?

M: Group. I'm in a band, and, um, we _____ _____ _____ for around three years now.

W: OK. Then, on the website, just choose the group application. _____ _____ _____ _____, and submit it. Oh, and you must also _____ that you are a student here.

M: How can I do that?

W: _____ _____ _____ is to scan your student ID. Then, just upload it with the application.

M: Oh, I understand. Is there anything else I should know?

W: Well, I _____ _____ _____ an hour or two before the contest. It's always _____ _____ _____ _____.

M: OK. I'll do that. Thanks for the advice!

Listening Practice 2

Listen to part of a lecture in a music history class.

Note-taking

Early 1500s ~ 1700s
- 1500s: Violins with three strings → _____ strings
- 1600s ~ 1700s: Stradivari created the _____ design.

19th Century
Modern _____, chin and shoulder _____

1. What is the main purpose of the lecture?

   (A) To discuss Renaissance arts culture
   (B) To explain the history of the violin
   (C) To illustrate the importance of music in Italy
   (D) To explore the life of a famous violinist

2. What does the professor say about Antonio Stradivari?

   (A) He figured out the perfect design for a violin.
   (B) He started the first successful violin business.
   (C) He added a chin rest and shoulder rest to the violin.
   (D) He made millions of dollars in his lifetime.

3. According to the professor, what was the result of the invention of the modern bow?

   (A) Violins produced a louder sound.
   (B) Performers could play for a longer time.
   (C) Musicians could hold the violin more easily.
   (D) Performances were more exciting to watch.

Dictation

Answer Book p. 4

C1_P2_D

Listen again and fill in the blanks.

P: As we've discussed, the Renaissance was a period of _____ _____ in Italy. The country's arts culture was thriving as many wealthy people _____ _____ _____, including music... Soon, um, Italy became famous for _____ _____ _____. In particular, it became known as the place where the violin was _____ _____ _____.
The violin was not the first stringed instrument in Italy... but it became _____ _____ _____. We can see pictures of violins in paintings from around 1530. At this time, violins were _____ _____ _____ _____ _____. Then, after around 1550, a fourth string was added. This is how violins look today.
Now, making violins was a family business, so many famous brands were _____ _____ _____. The most famous of all was Stradivari. Antonio Stradivari created the perfect violin design in the late 1600s and early 1700s. Uh, he discovered _____ _____ _____ _____ _____ for the best sound, and his violins _____ _____ _____. He crafted around one thousand violins and hundreds of them still exist.

S: I've heard about them. Aren't they expensive?

P: Oh, yes. Stradivari violins are still considered _____ _____ _____ _____ _____ in the world, so they are worth millions of dollars.
Anyway... some helpful changes were made in the 19th century. For example, the modern bow was invented. Its _____, _____, and balance allowed musicians to play longer _____ _____ _____. Also, a chin rest and a shoulder rest were added to make the violin _____ _____ _____. With these new features, the modern violin was born.

Listening Practice 3

Listen to a conversation between a student and a professor.

Note-taking

Student's Problem

Visiting a _____ on the 26th
→ Cannot take next week's _____

Professor's Solution

- Go to the _____ by yourself before then
- Write a _____ _____ instead

---

1 What is the student's problem?

(A) She needs extra time to study for an exam.

(B) She has a class trip on the same day as an exam.

(C) She cannot think of a good essay topic.

(D) She missed the deadline for a writing contest.

2 What does the student say about next week's exam?

(A) She thinks it will be difficult.

(B) She is not prepared for it.

(C) She has studied a lot for it.

(D) She hopes it will be canceled.

3 What does the student have to do after visiting the museum?

(A) Take a quiz

(B) Make a speech

(C) Read a book

(D) Interview some artists

Dictation

Answer Book p. 5

Listen again and fill in the blanks.

P: Hi, Ashley. Um, _____ _____ _____ _____ today?

S: I have a problem that I'd like to ask you about.

P: Oh? What is it?

S: You see, my art class is visiting a museum on the 26th, and, uh, that's _____ _____ _____ _____ your exam.

P: I see... Does this mean you cannot _____ _____ _____ _____?

S: Well, uh, I'd like to take it. I've read all the books and done all the exercises, so I'm _____ _____ the exam. But, uh, I also have to _____ _____ _____ on one of the exhibits at the museum.

P: Well, can't you go to the exhibits _____ _____ before then?

S: I could, but our professor has _____ _____ _____ _____ for us. Some artists are going to talk about their work. I would _____ _____ _____ that.

P: I understand. Maybe there's something we can do. Hmm... How about writing a research paper _____ _____ taking the exam? I can _____ _____ _____ for you.

S: That would be great! Thank you, Professor.

Listening Practice 4

Answer Book p. 5

Listen to part of a lecture in a physiology class.

C1_P4

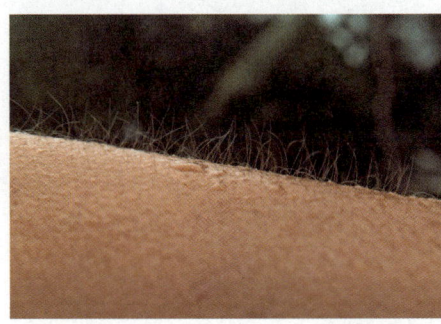

Note-taking

Goosebumps

: Small, _____ _____ on our skin

How They Happen

1. Nervous system sends _____ to tiny _____ under the skin.
2. Some parts of the skin _____ _____.

---

1 What is the main topic of the lecture?

(A) The characteristics of human skin
(B) Why people are afraid of the dark
(C) How and why goosebumps occur
(D) How animals react to danger

2 According to the professor, what happens in the body when it senses danger?

(A) The body begins to sweat.
(B) The brain works more quickly.
(C) Some muscles become relaxed.
(D) Some parts of the skin stick out.

3 According to the professor, how do goosebumps help animals stay warm?

(A) By changing the body temperature
(B) By forming a layer of air
(C) By producing more fur
(D) By blocking cold wind

Dictation

Listen again and fill in the blanks.

P: Imagine this... You're watching a scary movie in a dark room. Suddenly, you hear a strange sound. You become afraid. Your body _____ _____, and the hair on your skin _____ _____ _____ _____ _____ are goosebumps. But, what exactly are they, and how do they occur?

To begin with, goosebumps are _____, _____ _____ on our skin. They, uh, look like _____ _____ _____ _____ _____ after its feathers have been removed. That's why we call them "goose" bumps... Anyway, they _____ _____ _____ when we are cold, afraid, or even when we _____ _____ _____.

Um, but goosebumps happen _____ _____ _____. They're a natural response by the body to danger. What happens is that our nervous system _____ _____ to tiny muscles under the skin. This _____ _____ _____ _____ _____. Then, this makes other parts of the skin stick out.

This happens in animals, too. Um, think of how animals react when they're threatened... Cats are a good example. When cats sense danger, their fur puffs up. So, um, this _____ _____ _____ _____ than they actually are. Therefore, they are less likely to be attacked... Also, in animals with lots of fur or hair, goosebumps create _____ _____ _____ _____ _____ around the body. This _____ _____ _____ _____.

Goosebumps in humans, however, don't have these functions. Well, um, they did before, when our bodies had thick hair. But we lost the hair as we _____ _____ _____. Still, we get goosebumps just like our ancestors did.

iBT Listening Test 1

Answer Book p. 6

TOEFL Listening

Note-taking

Suggestion to Student

Work as an _____ on the professor's research project

Research Assistant's Work

- _____ some documents from German into English
- Work around two months over the _____ _____
- A paid position
  → Can pay for _____ without a problem

CHAPTER 01 | Main Purpose/Topic

1 Why does the professor ask to see the student?
   Ⓐ To offer a position on a project
   Ⓑ To recommend taking a summer class
   Ⓒ To ask an opinion on a recent lecture
   Ⓓ To give advice on a research paper

2 How does the professor typically choose an assistant for his project?
   Ⓐ By accepting applicants
   Ⓑ By asking other professors
   Ⓒ By uploading a post online
   Ⓓ By creating a list of names

3 According to the professor, what does the project include?
   Ⓐ Searching for information in the library
   Ⓑ Translating some documents
   Ⓒ Teaching English to German students
   Ⓓ Organizing some reading materials

4 What did the student originally plan to do during the summer vacation?
   Ⓐ She wanted to spend time on a hobby.
   Ⓑ She expected to work in a library.
   Ⓒ She was going to study abroad.
   Ⓓ She intended to make money for tuition.

Dictation

Answer Book p. 6

Listen again and fill in the blanks.

S: Hi, Professor Brown. I heard you _____ _____ _____ _____.

P: Oh, yes. I asked you to _____ _____ because... I would like you to _____ _____ as an assistant on my research project. Normally, I get applications from students for this, but I'd like to _____ _____ _____ for you.

S: _____ _____ _____... Um, what would I have to do, exactly?

P: Mostly, you'd be _____ _____ _____ from German into English. I know that your German is strong, so I think the work would _____ _____ _____.

S: Thanks. If I _____ _____ _____, how long would I have to work for the project?

P: The project will take around two months _____ _____ _____ _____.

S: Oh, _____ _____ _____, I'm not sure if I can... I need to work to earn money for _____ _____ during the summer break.

P: Well, this is a paid position. You would be able to _____ _____ _____ without a problem. Does that _____ _____ _____?

S: That's great to hear! I'll definitely think about it.

P: Okay, then. I really hope you can _____ _____ _____.

iBT Listening Test 2

TOEFL Listening

BIOLOGY

Note-taking

Koala's Physical Characteristics
- A long _____ organ; caecum
  → _____ _____ leaf fibers
- Unique _____ in the liver
  → Remove _____ in the leaves
- A digestive system that works very _____
  → Keeps food in the body for a _____ _____

1. What is the lecture mainly about?
   - Ⓐ Why the koala's habitat is under threat
   - Ⓑ How the koala interacts with its environment
   - Ⓒ Why the koala was introduced to Australia
   - Ⓓ How the koala gets its nutrition

2. According to the professor, where does the koala's name come from?
   - Ⓐ A local word for eucalyptus leaves
   - Ⓑ Its habit of hanging from trees
   - Ⓒ A sound that it makes while eating
   - Ⓓ Its ability to survive without water

3. According to the professor, which part of the koala has special functions?
   - Ⓐ Its body size
   - Ⓑ Its sharp claws
   - Ⓒ Its digestive system
   - Ⓓ Its sense of smell

4. According to the professor, why does the koala spend most of its days asleep?
   - Ⓐ It searches for food at night.
   - Ⓑ It absorbs little energy from its food.
   - Ⓒ It cannot see well in bright sunlight.
   - Ⓓ It needs to recover from eating toxic leaves.

Dictation

Answer Book p. 7

Listen again and fill in the blanks.

P: So, I'm sure you all know what a koala is, right? But, um, did you know it _____ _____ _____ _____ _____ in eucalyptus trees and eats the leaves of this tree? Today, I'm going to talk about the koala and _____ _____ _____ _____.
Both the koala and the eucalyptus tree _____ _____ _____ Australia... In fact, they _____ _____ over millions of years. Now, eucalyptus trees hold _____ _____...
When the koala eats the leaves, it _____ _____ of that moisture. This _____ _____ _____ _____ _____ for several days without coming down from the tree for water. Actually, the name koala _____ _____ _____ _____ _____ _____ that means "no water."
But still, eucalyptus leaves are _____ _____ _____... They are tough and contain _____ _____. This _____ _____ _____ _____, a poor source of energy, and even _____ _____ _____. So, many animals avoid eucalyptus leaves. For the koala, however, they are _____ _____ _____ _____. This is possible because of the special functions of _____ _____ _____. For instance, it has _____ _____ _____ _____ called the caecum that _____ _____ _____ _____. Also, its liver has _____ _____ that can _____ _____ in the leaves, which makes them _____ _____ _____. Lastly, the koala's digestive system _____ _____ _____, so it keeps food in its body for _____ _____ _____. This allows it to gain _____ _____ _____ _____ _____.

Even though the koala has _____ _____, it still gets _____ _____ from eucalyptus leaves... As a result, koalas sleep for _____ _____ _____ _____, often from 18 to 22 hours.

Vocabulary Review

Answer Book p. 8

A. Choose the correct word for each meaning.

| confirm | pleasure | gather | tough |

1. strong and difficult to break down: _____
2. to check that something is true: _____
3. to collect things or people together: _____
4. feeling of happiness and joy: _____

B. Fill in the blanks with the appropriate words or phrases from the box.

| function | depend on | support | emotion | remove |

5. Anger is often a strong _____ that you cannot control easily.
6. Entering words and numbers into the computer is the _____ of a keyboard.
7. Pets _____ their owners for food and water.
8. I have to _____ all the dust from the windows to make them clean.
9. Mary's parents _____ her dream.

C. Choose the closest meaning for each highlighted word or phrase.

10. The winner of the speech contest will get a prize.
    (A) information (B) document (C) competition (D) position

11. Emma has a unique fashion style that nobody can copy.
    (A) sensitive (B) special (C) tense (D) native

12. During summer break this year, my family will travel to California.
    (A) vacation (B) exhibit (C) moisture (D) exercise

13. All the pictures in the gallery were good, but, in particular, the last one was the most beautiful.
    (A) extremely (B) typically (C) basically (D) especially

14. The average Korean consumes more than 60 kilograms of rice in a year.
    (A) avoids (B) eats (C) suits (D) crafts

HACKERS APEX LISTENING
for the TOEFL iBT
Basic

CHAPTER 02

Detail

Detail

About the Question Type

Detail questions ask you to identify specific details or facts that are mentioned in a conversation or lecture.

Correct answers restate specific information explicitly mentioned in the passage. Incorrect answers contain new, contradictory, or irrelevant information. Some questions may require you to select more than one correct answer choice.

Question Format

- According to the conversation, what is ~?
- What does the professor say about ~?
- According to the professor, what are the reasons for ~? *Choose 2 answers*.
- What are the two examples the man gives of ~? *Choose 2 answers*.

Key Strategies

- **Step 1** — Identify the main topic and focus on important information supporting the main idea. For example, listen carefully for definitions, examples, reasons, results, and features.

- **Step 2** — Listen carefully for signal words that are commonly used to introduce supporting ideas. Some examples include: *For instance, To illustrate, That's because, As a result, Similarly,* and *On the other hand*.

- **Step 3** — Select the answer choice that best presents the information from the conversation or lecture. Remember, the correct answer often paraphrases information, or repeats it using different words.

Example

Answer Book p. 8

A. Listen to a conversation between a student and a physics department employee.

C2_ExA

Note-taking

Student's Problem
Looking for Jefferson Hall
→ Didn't get a _____ _____

Employee's Suggestion
Change your _____ _____ on the website
to get important _____ through texts

Why does the student need to update her phone number?

(A) She wants to register for an event.
(B) She has to receive important messages.
(C) She needs to submit class assignments.
(D) She has to call an employee for help.

Answer Book p. 8

B. Listen to part of a lecture in a history class.

C2_ExB

Note-taking

Egyptian Boats
• Light boats: Good for _____ and _____
  in shallow waters e.g. Skiff
• Large ships: Transported _____ _____
  and animals in deeper waters
• Others: Used for _____ ceremonies

According to the professor, what were the two functions of ancient Egyptian boats? *Choose 2 answers.*

(A) Attacking enemies
(B) Hunting and fishing
(C) Traveling to other countries
(D) Religious ceremonies

Dictation

Answer Book p. 8

Listen again and fill in the blanks.

A.

W: Excuse me. I'm hoping you can help. I think I'm lost. I'm _____ _____ Jefferson Hall because, um, _____ _____ _____ _____ an orientation there at 10 a.m.

M: Oh, Jefferson Hall is _____ _____ the library. Uh, didn't you get a text message from us? We _____ _____ to every student.

W: Uh, I never received it...

M: That's strange... Um, let me _____ _____ _____ on the school website... Is your phone number 555-9028?

W: That's _____ _____, actually. My phone number is 555-9628.

M: I see. I suggest you log in to your account and change it, then. We send _____ _____ _____ through texts.

W: All right, thank you. I'll do that right after _____ _____.

M: OK. And, uh, you should hurry if you want to get there on time.

B.

P: In the ancient world, many people _____ _____ _____ _____... In ancient Egypt, people lived near the Nile, a long and wide river. The Egyptians _____ _____ the Nile, so they created many boats for _____ _____.

One of them was called a skiff. It was a light boat made of thin pieces of wood that _____ _____ _____. The skiff's light weight _____ _____ _____ hunting and fishing in shallow waters.

The other kind of boat was a large ship. It could _____ _____ _____ and animals. So it was _____ _____ _____ _____ in deeper waters.

Now, the Egyptians also used boats for _____ _____. Uh, they used the boats to carry images of their gods between temples, or to transport the dead bodies of important leaders.

Listening Practice 1

Answer Book p. 9

Listen to a conversation between a student and a professor.

Note-taking

Student's Problem
Doesn't _____ the _____ very well

Professor's Solution
• Read some _____ _____
• Join a _____ _____ for the class

1 What is the student's problem?

   (A) She has trouble understanding a class.
   (B) She failed the midterm exam.
   (C) She does not know what books to read.
   (D) She needs more time to write a paper.

2 What does the professor say about his class?

   (A) It gives many reading materials.
   (B) It includes a discussion session.
   (C) It will be taught differently.
   (D) It has difficult content.

3 What does the professor offer the student?

   (A) A library card
   (B) A makeup quiz
   (C) A list of books
   (D) A group project

Dictation

Answer Book p. 9

Listen again and fill in the blanks.

S: Hello, Professor Carter. I think you _____ _____ _____ _____ your office in the last class.

P: Hi, Emily. I wanted to see how you are doing. Are you _____ _____ the midterm exam?

S: Well, I'm studying every day, but this class has been... um... difficult for me. Even though I study a lot, I _____ _____ _____ _____ very well.

P: I thought so... Well, your quiz score in the last class was low, but don't worry. The class is _____ _____, so it can be tough. Hmm... Do you want me to _____ _____ _____ for you?

S: Yes, that would be great! I really _____ _____ _____.

P: There are some _____ _____ you can read. Let me give you _____ _____ _____ _____... Here. I think you can find them in the library. Um, another option is _____ _____ _____. Many students are _____ _____ _____, so I'm sure you can find one for this class.

S: That's a great idea! Thanks for all your help, Professor.

Listening Practice 2

Answer Book p. 10

Listen to part of a lecture in an environmental science class.

Note-taking

Factors of Habitats
- _____ to move around
  e.g. Snow leopards need lots of _____.
- _____ e.g. Rabbits
- Food and _____
  e.g. A _____ for tigers

1 What is the main topic of the lecture?
   (A) How to protect wild animals
   (B) What animals like to eat
   (C) What makes a good habitat
   (D) How animals build their homes

2 According to the professor, what is true of snow leopards?
   (A) They live in large families.
   (B) They change homes often.
   (C) They keep large amounts of food.
   (D) They need lots of space.

3 What does the professor say about shelters?
   (A) They provide protection from danger outside.
   (B) They give animals a small space to move around.
   (C) They are usually found underground.
   (D) They last around one year before animals leave them.

Dictation

Answer Book p. 10

Listen again and fill in the blanks.

P: Imagine _____ _____ _____ ... It is probably warm, safe, and _____ _____ _____ that you need... Well, um, even animals need homes like these. They're called habitats, and today I'd like to tell you what they should _____ _____ .

A habitat is a place where an organism such as a plant or an animal lives. But now, a good habitat doesn't just provide _____ _____ _____ _____ . It also provides _____ _____ _____ . So it has to have four parts: space, shelter, food, and water.

Um, by space, I mean room _____ _____ _____ ... Some animals, like, uh, snow leopards need _____ _____ _____ . That way, they can find food, water, and other resources _____ _____ _____ _____ _____ other snow leopards...

For smaller animals, less space might be needed. So, squirrels don't need _____ _____ _____ _____ a snow leopard.

Let's move on to shelter now. Shelters provide animals a place to eat, sleep, and _____ _____ _____ . A good shelter should also provide _____ _____ _____ _____ or dangerous animals. So, uh, rabbits... They build their shelters underground. That way, they can be safe and hide from their predators.

Every habitat should also have _____ _____ _____ _____ . For example, tigers will _____ _____ in a jungle, where they can hunt for large animals and drink from a river... On the other hand, a city park might be _____ _____ _____ for squirrels. They can _____ _____ _____ _____ there, or drink water that collects on the ground.

Listening Practice 3

Answer Book p. 11

Listen to a conversation between a student and a facilities manager at the university.

Note-taking

Student's Problem
Needs a new place because the _____ work is too noisy

Student's Needs
- 40 members → Has to be _____
- A _____ and a stage

1 Why does the student talk to the manager?
   (A) To request a place to practice
   (B) To complain about noisy students
   (C) To borrow music equipment
   (D) To ask about a school competition

2 According to the student, what is the disadvantage of Gemma Hall?
   (A) It does not have a piano or a stage.
   (B) It shares the building with the science department.
   (C) It is too close to a construction area.
   (D) It is difficult to get there after class.

3 According to the student, what does the choir group require?
   (A) Better instruments
   (B) Extra practice time
   (C) A large space
   (D) A change in schedule

Dictation

Answer Book p. 11

Listen again and fill in the blanks.

W: Hi, Mr. Bowman. Could I _____ _____ _____?

M: Sure. What would you like to talk about?

W: Well... As you know, our choir group is _____ _____ _____ _____ next month. It's _____ _____ _____ for us, but I don't think we can practice in Gemma Hall anymore. We _____ _____ _____ _____.

M: Oh? What's the problem?

W: The construction work in the science department office is _____ _____. It's so distracting since we're in the next building. We can't _____ _____ _____!

M: OK, OK... Let me find you another place. Is there _____ _____ _____?

W: We have 40 members, so it _____ _____ _____ _____. We also need a piano and a stage.

M: All right. Is that it?

W: Oh, one more thing. We _____ _____ from 9 a.m. to noon. Everyone in the choir _____ _____ _____ _____ this schedule.

M: OK. _____ _____ _____ _____ before your practice tomorrow. I'll let you know what's available.

Listening Practice 4

Listen to part of a lecture in a biology class.

Note-taking

How Sperm Whales Make Sounds
The spermaceti, a special _____, makes various sounds.

Why Sperm Whales Make Sounds
- To hunt → Don't have good _____
- To _____ with each other

1. What is the main topic of the lecture?
   (A) The hunting of sperm whales
   (B) Characteristics of the largest whale species
   (C) Communication methods in marine mammals
   (D) The ways sperm whales use sound

2. Why does the sperm whale use clicking sounds when hunting prey?
   (A) It usually finds its prey in very deep water.
   (B) Its eyesight is not very good.
   (C) Its clicking noises do not travel long distances.
   (D) It swims slower than its prey.

3. What does the professor say about the language of sperm whales?
   (A) It usually contains random patterns.
   (B) Scientists are still trying to understand it.
   (C) It is different for each family of whales.
   (D) Researchers use it to talk to the whales.

Dictation

Answer Book p. 12

Listen again and fill in the blanks.

P: How many of you know the book *Moby Dick*? It's a classic, and its main character is a sperm whale. Sperm whales have _____ _____ _____. Today, we will learn about _____ _____ _____ _____.

But first, let's talk about several other characteristics of sperm whales. These whales have _____ _____ _____ of any animal. They also _____ _____ _____ any other marine mammal, and they use their sharp teeth to capture and hold squid, their favorite food...

Now, let's see how they make sounds. The huge head of a sperm whale contains _____ _____ _____ called the spermaceti. That's where the whale got its name. The spermaceti _____ _____ _____ thick, waxy oil. It can make _____ _____ for specific purposes. One is _____ _____ _____ clicking noises, which the whale produces for hunting. You see, the sperm whale does not have _____ _____, so it uses sound to find prey. When the clicking sound hits something, like squid in the water, the noise _____ _____ _____ _____. This way, the whale can know that something is there.

But scientists think _____ _____ _____ of sound is for communication with other sperm whales. They do not know exactly what the whales are saying yet. They believe, uh, sperm whales can send _____ _____ to each other. When they communicate, they use a language with regular patterns. They _____ _____ _____ to create different messages. But, uh, researchers are still _____ _____ _____ the sperm whale's messages. If they do, maybe one day we could talk to sperm whales with underwater speakers and microphones!

iBT Listening Test 1

TOEFL Listening

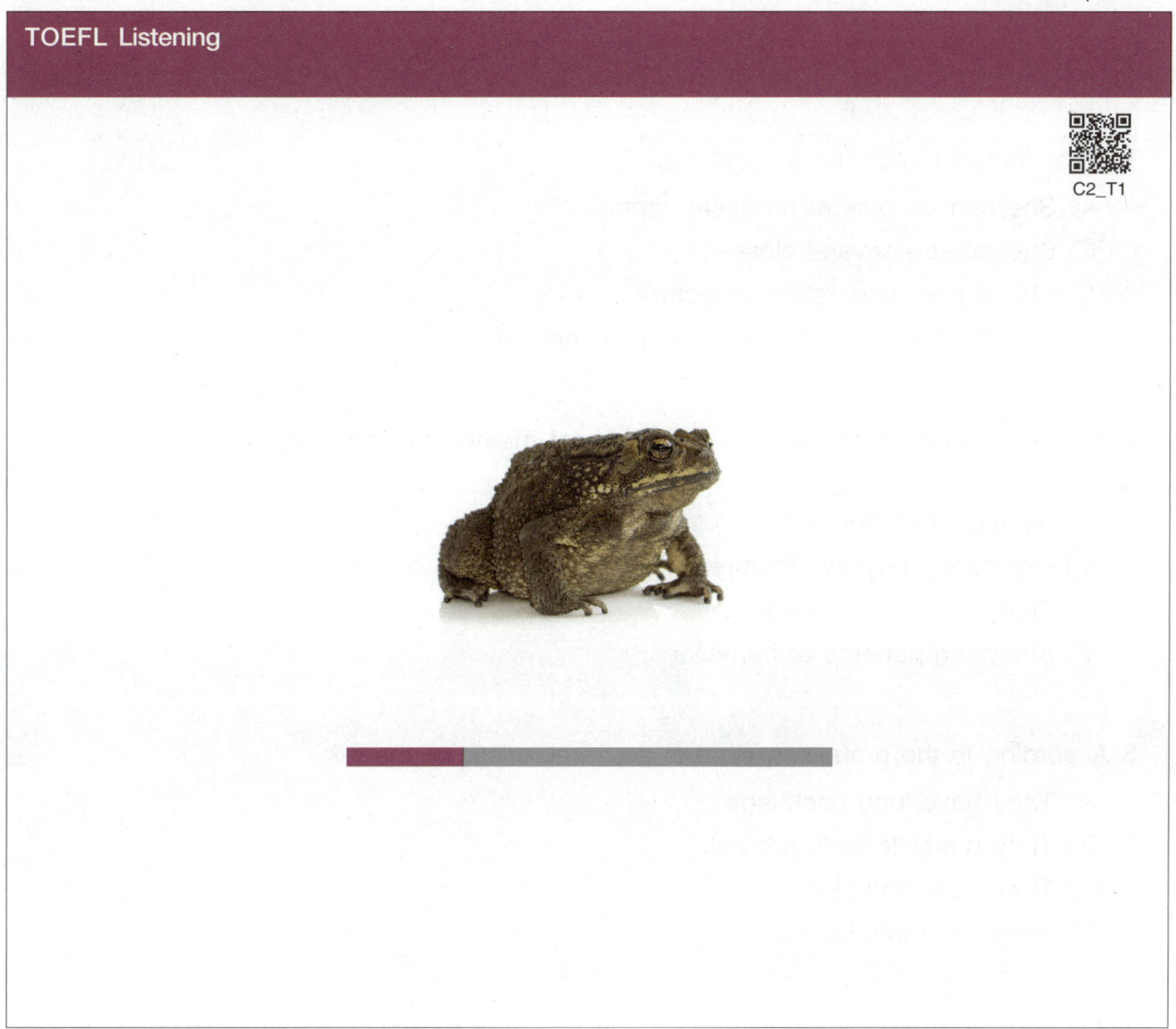

Note-taking

_____ between Frogs and Toads

• Physically
- Frogs: More _____, thinner and have stronger and longer _____
- Toads: A short and _____ body, short and _____ legs

• Skin
- Frogs: Smooth and _____
- Toads: Dry skin that feels thick and _____

1. What problem does the student have?
   Ⓐ She cannot think of an essay topic.
   Ⓑ She missed several classes.
   Ⓒ She did not understand a lecture.
   Ⓓ She got a poor grade on an assignment.

2. According to the professor, what is the best method to distinguish frogs from toads?
   Ⓐ Seeing what they eat
   Ⓑ Comparing physical features
   Ⓒ Studying living conditions
   Ⓓ Analyzing patterns of behavior

3. According to the professor, what is a characteristic of toads?
   Ⓐ They have long back legs.
   Ⓑ They prefer to walk around.
   Ⓒ They have soft skin.
   Ⓓ They have thin bodies.

4. According to the conversation, what is the reason frogs stay close to the water?
   Ⓐ They need to watch their eggs.
   Ⓑ They drink water more often than toads.
   Ⓒ Their skin can lose moisture very fast.
   Ⓓ Their main food lives underwater.

Dictation

Answer Book p. 13

Listen again and fill in the blanks.

S: Professor, do you have time to talk? I have some questions about yesterday's lecture...

P: Oh... It was the class on frogs and toads, right?

S: Yes. I'm still not sure about the _____ _____ _____ _____ _____.

P: Well, they _____ _____ _____ in many ways, like _____ _____ _____ or what they eat. Let's see... OK, the best way is to _____ _____ _____ _____ _____. In general, frogs _____ _____ _____. They are thinner and have stronger and longer back legs, so they can _____ _____.

S: So then, toads _____ _____ _____?

P: Pretty much. They've got _____ _____ _____ _____ _____, so they _____ _____ _____ _____. Their legs are also short and thick. And they like to walk around _____ _____.

S: I've got it. Anything else?

P: Another big difference is skin. If you look at a frog, its skin is _____ _____ _____. Frogs _____ _____ _____ the water. This is because they _____ _____ _____. Meanwhile, toads have dry skin that _____ _____ _____ _____.

S: I think I understand it better now. Thank you, Professor.

iBT Listening Test 2

TOEFL Listening

ARCHAEOLOGY

Note-taking

Mysteries of Stonehenge

Stonehenge: A _____ _____ in England, made up of 83 giant stones
- How It Was Built: Stones _____ _____ far away and are very heavy.
  → Would have required _____ _____ _____ to move them
- Why It Was Built: _____ of many ancient leaders and _____ _____ around Stonehenge
  → Was probably used as a _____ _____ for about 500 years

1. What is the main topic of the lecture?
   Ⓐ A new discovery at Stonehenge
   Ⓑ A famous architect who built Stonehenge
   Ⓒ An important monument in history
   Ⓓ An attraction that recently opened

2. According to the professor, what is a feature of Stonehenge?
   Ⓐ It has many stones that are in good condition.
   Ⓑ It consists of hundreds of stones.
   Ⓒ It has pieces in different positions.
   Ⓓ It includes round-shaped stones.

3. According to the professor, what is a clue about the purpose of Stonehenge?
   Ⓐ The year when it was built
   Ⓑ The direction that it faces
   Ⓒ The origin of its stones
   Ⓓ The bones found around it

Listen again to part of the lecture. Then answer the question.

4. Why does the professor say this:
   Ⓐ To emphasize that a monument was built long ago
   Ⓑ To indicate a lack of information about a construction
   Ⓒ To explain why some ideas have been criticized
   Ⓓ To imply that there are various theories

Dictation

Answer Book p. 14

Listen again and fill in the blanks.

P: Does anyone like _____ _____ _____? Then, you will be interested in learning about today's topic, _____ _____ _____ called Stonehenge.

Stonehenge is basically _____ _____ _____ which _____ _____ _____ Salisbury, England. There are 83 giant stones. Um, most of them are standing, while some are _____ _____ _____ _____ the standing stones. Together, the stones _____ _____ _____. Many of the stones are broken, and only _____ _____ _____ _____.

Scientists believe Stonehenge was built between 5,000 and 3,000 BC. _____ _____ _____ _____, people wonder how it was built. The stones _____ _____ _____ _____, and they're very heavy. Um, each stone weighs 25 tons _____ _____. That's about _____ _____ _____ _____ a large bus filled with people. _____ _____ _____ _____ how people could have moved them or _____ _____ on top of other stones. You know, at the time, _____ _____ _____ _____ yet, and people _____ _____ _____ made of wood and stone. It would have _____ _____ _____ to move the stones. But, um, we can _____ _____ _____ _____. There are _____ _____ _____ _____.

The purpose of Stonehenge is another mystery that we _____ _____ _____. But still, scientists have been able to _____ _____ _____. Researchers _____ _____ _____ around Stonehenge and analyzed them. They found that they were the

bones of _____ _____ _____ and _____ _____.
_____ _____ _____ _____ people used Stonehenge as _____ _____ _____ for about 500 years.

Vocabulary Review

Answer Book p. 15

A. Choose the correct word for each meaning.

| advanced | monument | produce | suitable |

1 right or correct for someone or something: _____

2 difficult or a higher level of something: _____

3 a structure or a place that has historical value: _____

4 to create something or cause something to happen: _____

B. Fill in the blanks with the appropriate words or phrases from the box.

| prepare for | ideal | purpose | consist of | analyze |

5 Susan read her notes many times to _____ the history exam.

6 The _____ of the sink is to wash dishes.

7 A breakfast should _____ healthy foods like fruits and oatmeal.

8 Warm spring days have _____ weather for riding a bicycle.

9 Scientists will _____ why the experiment failed.

C. Choose the closest meaning for each highlighted word.

10 We will put the bookshelf in this small space.
   (A) temple   (B) room   (C) material   (D) construction

11 We will require a special tool to fix your smartphone.
   (A) weigh   (B) solve   (C) need   (D) place

12 The most famous characteristic of giraffes is their long neck.
   (A) feature   (B) direction   (C) account   (D) organ

13 Puppies are very active, so they love to play outside.
   (A) noisy   (B) rough   (C) distracting   (D) energetic

14 All the furniture will be transported by a truck tomorrow morning.
   (A) carried   (B) captured   (C) remained   (D) assumed

HACKERS APEX LISTENING
for the TOEFL iBT
Basic

CHAPTER 03

Function

Function

About the Question Type

Function questions ask you to determine the true meaning or intention behind a speaker's statement. This is usually different from what the speaker states directly.

These questions require you to listen again to part of a conversation or lecture. Some examples of the possible functions of a statement include: to explain a concept, to give an opinion, and to make a comparison.

Question Format

Listen again to part of the lecture. Then answer the question.
P: **********************
Why does the professor say this: 🎧

Key Strategies

- **Step 1** — Listen carefully to the replay, and then identify the intention behind what the speaker has said within the context.
- **Step 2** — Focus on the words that the speaker emphasizes and the tone of voice that they use. They often indicate the true intention behind statements.
- **Step 3** — Select the answer choice that best represents the true meaning or intention of the speaker.

Example

Answer Book p. 15

A. Listen to a conversation between a student and a professor.

C3_ExA

Note-taking

Professor's Request to Student
You've been working as a _____ teacher.
→ Share your _____ _____ in one of my courses

Student's Response
Would like to help

Listen again to part of the conversation. Then answer the question.
Why does the student say this: 🎧

(A) To express excitement about taking a course
(B) To show that she understands her responsibilities
(C) To imply that she is willing to help the professor
(D) To thank the professor for his time

Answer Book p. 15

B. Listen to part of a lecture in an astronomy class.

C3_ExB

Note-taking

How Polynesians Navigated with _____
1. _____ the sky into eight parts
2. _____ the positions of hundreds of stars
→ Found the _____ back to their islands this way

Listen again to part of the lecture. Then answer the question.
Why does the professor say this: 🎧

(A) To indicate that Polynesians had their own navigating method
(B) To suggest that Polynesians did not have to travel often
(C) To explain why Polynesians did not like modern technology
(D) To emphasize a problem with using advanced technology

Dictation

Answer Book p. 15

Listen again and fill in the blanks.

A.

S: Hi, Professor Daniels. Did you want to see me about something?

P: Hello, Ellen. Yes, thank you for coming... Um, so you've been _____ _____ _____ _____ _____. Is that right?

S: Yes. I've been _____ _____ at an elementary school every Friday. _____ _____ _____ _____ _____ now.

P: That is wonderful to hear.

S: Thank you, Professor. I've enjoyed it a lot.

P: Um, I'd like you to _____ _____ _____ _____ in one of my courses, Introduction to Education. You know, it would help the students understand _____ _____ _____ _____ _____.

S: I _____ _____ _____. I've learned so much from your classes, so I'd _____ _____ _____ _____.

P: Thank you, Ellen. I'll check the schedule and let you know.

B.

P: If you are on a boat in the middle of the Pacific Ocean, it will be very _____ _____ _____ where you are. Of course, you can use _____ _____ to help you. But, thousands of years ago, the Polynesian people didn't need it. Let's talk about how they were able to _____ _____ _____.

The Polynesians could travel thousands of miles across the Pacific Ocean and always _____ _____ _____ _____ _____. They noticed certain stars always appear in _____ _____ _____ in the sky at _____ _____ of the year. So, they _____ _____ _____ _____ eight parts. Each part had its own set of stars that _____ _____ _____. Then, they _____ _____ _____ of hundreds of stars. This helped them _____ _____ _____ back to their islands.

Listening Practice 1

Answer Book p. 16

Listen to a conversation between a student and a counselor at the University Counseling Center.

Note-taking

Student's Problem
Having trouble with _____ life

Counselor's Suggestion
Sign up for a _____ _____
→ A great _____ to meet new people

1. What are the speakers mainly discussing?
   (A) Advantages of college life
   (B) How to adapt to school life
   (C) Different types of school programs
   (D) How to cancel a class

2. What does the woman suggest to the man?
   (A) Find a new hobby
   (B) Meet people online
   (C) Join a school club
   (D) Attend a school event

Listen again to part of the conversation. Then answer the question.

3. Why does the woman say this: 🎧
   (A) To make the man feel better
   (B) To correct the man's mistake
   (C) To tell the man to hurry
   (D) To disagree with the man's idea

Dictation

Answer Book p. 16

Listen again and fill in the blanks.

M: Hi, my name is Mason Conner. I _____ _____ _____ today.

W: Of course. Welcome, Mason. How can I help you?

M: Well, I'm _____ _____ _____, um, college life.

W: It's your first year here, right? What are you _____ _____ _____?

M: Actually, I _____ _____ _____ _____ _____. There were only 180 people in my high school. And now, I'm in a place with _____ _____ _____!

W: Going from high school to university is _____ _____ _____ _____ _____. So, it can be a confusing experience for anyone.

M: _____ _____ _____. And also... Well... I guess I'm lonely, too. I'm shy, so it's hard to _____ _____ _____.

W: Don't worry. You're not _____ _____ _____. Let's see... What are some of your interests or hobbies?

M: Uh, I love to _____ _____.

W: Oh, did you know that the college has a photography club? How about _____ _____? It would be a great opportunity to _____ _____ _____. You can also do _____ _____ _____.

M: That sounds like a great idea!

Listening Practice 2

Answer Book p. 17

Listen to part of a lecture in an earth science class.

Note-taking

Factors of Firenadoes

Firenadoes: _____ made of gas, fire, and smoke
- A very hot _____, which needs a lot of _____
- _____

1. What is the main topic of the lecture?
   (A) The danger of forest fires
   (B) The formation of fire tornadoes
   (C) The efforts to control wildfires
   (D) The harmful effects of tornadoes

2. According to the professor, what is required for a very hot fire?
   (A) A very dry environment
   (B) Strong winds
   (C) Hot temperatures
   (D) A large amount of fuel

Listen again to part of the lecture. Then answer the question.

3. Why does the professor say this:
   (A) To ask the students to guess a number
   (B) To emphasize a point that she made
   (C) To show that fires are dangerous
   (D) To review a condition she introduced

Dictation

Answer Book p. 17

Listen again and fill in the blanks.

P: So... What are tornadoes? They are _____ _____ in the shape of a cone. But tornadoes can also _____ _____ _____ gas, fire, and smoke! These are called fire tornadoes, or "firenadoes," and today I'd like to discuss _____ _____ _____.

Well, fire tornadoes are very rare. You need _____ _____ _____. First of all, you must have a very hot fire. And for that, uh, you must have a lot of fuel. This can be dry wood, oil, hot gases in the air, or _____ _____ _____ _____ for a long time. Another factor is wind. If all of these conditions occur, _____ _____ _____ _____ a fire tornado.

Fire tornadoes often _____ _____ _____ _____. During a large fire, hot gases start to move the air around. This causes wind _____ _____ _____ _____ _____, and, uh, at different speeds. Occasionally, the fire will quickly _____ _____ _____ into the air and... create a fire tornado.

So, let me give you an example... In 1926, _____ _____ _____ _____ happened at a storage facility in California. Lightning _____ _____ _____ _____ that was full of oil. This started a fire. Because of the huge amount of oil, the fire had enough fuel _____ _____ for several days. It grew _____ _____ _____ hot gases moved the air around the fire and this created wind. So there was a lot of fuel, a very hot fire, and also a lot of wind. Because of this, many fire tornadoes formed. There were _____ _____ _____ _____. Some were very tall and, uh, _____ _____ _____ _____ _____ away from the original fire.

Listening Practice 3

Listen to a conversation between a student and a professor.

C3_P3

Note-taking

Student's Problem
Worried because her _____ is not working hard

Professor's Suggestion
May be worth changing the _____ of the project
→ _____ it with Justin

1. Why does the student go to see the professor?
   (A) To request a different assignment
   (B) To get information about a group contest
   (C) To express concern about a partner
   (D) To ask about changing a project grade

2. Why is the professor surprised by the student's comments?
   (A) Because he expected a better result on an assignment
   (B) Because he thought a student would work hard
   (C) Because he knew some students were close friends
   (D) Because he felt the team started their work late

Listen again to part of the conversation. Then answer the question.

3. Why does the professor mean when he says this: 🎧
   (A) He wants the group to work harder.
   (B) He thinks they should choose a different topic.
   (C) He agrees that the project is meaningful.
   (D) He suggests that the student find a new team.

Dictation

Answer Book p. 18

Listen again and fill in the blanks.

S: Umm... Professor Stone? May I _____ _____ _____ about something?

P: Sure, Sarah. How can I help?

S: It's about the group project. My partner is Justin, but, um... _____ _____ because he's not really _____ _____ _____.

P: Oh, really? That's surprising. He was _____ _____ _____ _____ _____ _____ last semester. It seems strange that he's _____ _____ _____.

S: That's what I thought, too. Um, I don't know what to do.

P: Maybe something about the project is bothering him. Hmm... Is _____ _____ _____ _____ too difficult?

S: No, but... Actually, Justin didn't _____ _____ _____ the topic that much. He even _____ _____ _____ _____ two days ago, but I thought it would be too late.

P: It _____ _____ _____ _____. You have two weeks left.

S: Do you think that's enough time?

P: If you _____ _____ _____ with a clear plan, well, yes. You'll be able to _____ _____ _____ _____. Why don't you _____ _____ _____ _____ _____ Justin?

S: I will. Thanks for the advice, Professor Stone.

Listening Practice 4

Answer Book p. 19

Listen to part of a lecture in an art history class.

Note-taking

Sculptures for Portraits
- Made of _____ _____ who died
- Made of the Roman _____

Sculptures for _____
Appeared in public and private _____ and baths

1. What is the lecture mainly about?
   (A) The functions of Roman sculpture
   (B) A comparison of Greek and Roman sculpture
   (C) The characteristics of Roman statues
   (D) The origins of Roman portraits

2. What does the professor say about portrait sculpture?
   (A) It was used to honor relatives and ancestors.
   (B) It was mainly for the lower class.
   (C) It was the most expensive type of sculpture.
   (D) It was less common in new territories.

Listen again to part of the lecture. Then answer the question.

3. What does the professor imply when he says this: 🎧
   (A) Private statues did not always bring good luck.
   (B) Statues for decoration were not the highest quality.
   (C) Garden statues were rarely displayed in public.
   (D) Museums often had their own sculptors.

Dictation

Answer Book p. 19

Listen again and fill in the blanks.

P: Let's get started. We discussed _____ _____ _____ _____ _____ in the last class. Now, we're going to move on to Roman sculpture. Roman sculpture had a few _____ _____ _____.

The most important one was for portraits, or uh, artworks of people. Portrait sculpture _____ _____ _____ the upper class. It was used to _____ _____ _____ _____ _____ _____. So, uh, upper class families hired artists to make sculptures of family members _____ _____. Then, the sculptures _____ _____ in the tombs of these dead family members.

But, uh, portraits were also made of _____ _____ _____.
As the Roman Empire spread, they put statues of the emperor in new territories. This way, people would _____ _____ _____ the appearance of the emperor. This had a couple of purposes. First, the people would _____ _____ _____ _____, which also appeared on Roman coins. Um, they would trade and pay taxes with these coins. Second, it would _____ _____ _____ _____. Typically, he would be wearing military armor, which _____ _____ _____ and authority.

Lastly... Sculptures were also _____ _____ _____. They appeared in both public and private gardens and baths. Often, the subjects were gods or goddesses. Romans believed these sculptures _____ _____ _____ _____ _____ to the home. Uh, and it did take some skill to produce these sculptures, but they weren't _____ _____ _____ the other types of statues. Let's just say they were _____ _____ _____ museums.

iBT Listening Test 1

Answer Book p. 20

TOEFL Listening

Note-taking

Student's Problem

Has not received her _____

Employee's Response

- School's computer server _____ _____ last week.
  → Some files were _____.
- Will call the school's IT _____ tomorrow

1. What are the speakers mainly discussing?
   - Ⓐ The student's broken computer
   - Ⓑ A job opening at the library
   - Ⓒ The student's missing pay
   - Ⓓ A school project the student is doing

2. According to the conversation, why were some files lost?
   - Ⓐ An employee made a mistake.
   - Ⓑ A computer server stopped working.
   - Ⓒ A department hired a new worker.
   - Ⓓ A new system was introduced.

3. What does the employee offer to do for the student?
   - Ⓐ Change some account information
   - Ⓑ Have a form signed by a professor
   - Ⓒ Call a bank on the phone
   - Ⓓ Contact a school department

Listen again to part of the conversation. Then answer the question.

4. What does the employee imply when he says this:
   - Ⓐ He checked the student's bank account.
   - Ⓑ He remembered the cause of a problem.
   - Ⓒ He was just told of an earlier request.
   - Ⓓ He did not finish an assigned task.

Dictation

Answer Book p. 20

Listen again and fill in the blanks.

W: Hi, I talked to you on the phone yesterday. My name is Erin Parsons...

M: Oh, yes! You had a question about _____ _____ _____?

W: Well, I work at the school library. I _____ _____ _____ _____ _____ _____ last Friday, but I still haven't received anything.

M: Hmm... That's strange. Are you a new worker? It _____ _____ _____ for the system to update new employee information.

W: I've been there _____ _____ _____. It's _____ _____ _____ this has happened. I checked with the bank, and there's _____ _____ with my account.

M: Oh, I almost forgot! Actually, we had _____ _____ _____ last week. Our computer server _____ _____ and some files _____ _____. They included a list of employees and their pay.

W: Then what can I do now? When can I _____ _____ _____?

M: Um, I'm sorry, but you'll _____ _____ _____ until the server is fixed. But I'll call the school's IT department tomorrow and let you know.

W: All right. I appreciate it.

iBT Listening Test 2

TOEFL Listening

Note-taking

The Pygmalion Effect

- Background: An _____ Greek story
  → _____ truly loved the statue, and the goddess made his wish _____ _____.

- Experiment: Robert Resenthal's experiment with students
  → Those who were _____ to do _____ performed the best.

1 What is the main topic of the lecture?
   Ⓐ The best way to teach students about psychology
   Ⓑ The influence of negative thoughts on students
   Ⓒ The power of believing in yourself
   Ⓓ The effects of a psychological phenomenon

2 According to the professor, what did the Greek goddess do for Pygmalion?
   Ⓐ She gave him a work of art.
   Ⓑ She turned him into a god.
   Ⓒ She made a statue alive.
   Ⓓ She made him a better sculptor.

3 According to the professor, what can happen as a result of expectations?
   Ⓐ Students obey their teachers more often.
   Ⓑ Students work harder to satisfy expectations.
   Ⓒ Students feel less pressure about taking tests.
   Ⓓ Students respect their teachers' decisions.

Listen again to part of the lecture. Then answer the question.

4 Why does the professor say this:
   Ⓐ To remind the students of an earlier lesson
   Ⓑ To imply that an experiment was successful
   Ⓒ To point out a problem with an experiment
   Ⓓ To show that a test was easy to pass

Dictation

Listen again and fill in the blanks.

P: Have you ever had a teacher who _____ _____ _____? Or what about one who thought that you weren't good enough? Think about which teacher _____ _____ _____ _____. Well, this _____ _____ _____ today's topic. It's _____ _____ _____ called the Pygmalion Effect.

Now, um, the name Pygmalion _____ _____ an ancient Greek story. It's a story about a sculptor named Pygmalion who _____ _____ _____ _____ a statue he made. He asked Aphrodite, the ancient Greek goddess of love, to _____ _____ _____ _____ ... Because Pygmalion truly loved the statue, the goddess made his wish come true. So the Pygmalion Effect describes a situation where wishing about something strongly can _____ _____ _____ _____. In other words, positive expectations can _____ _____ _____ _____ _____ _____ _____. Um, when someone expects you to do well, there is _____ _____ _____ that you will do well... This happens because people change their behavior _____ _____ _____ ... So if your teacher thinks you're smart, you might study harder _____ _____ _____ _____ _____.

Anyway, in 1968, the psychologist Robert Rosenthal _____ _____ _____ to test the Pygmalion Effect. He made some elementary school students _____ _____ _____ _____ at the beginning of the first semester. Then, he told the students' teachers _____ _____ _____ _____ _____ _____ to be good students. However, _____ _____ _____ _____ the teachers _____ _____. These _____ _____ _____

_____ the students' test scores... After eight months, he tested the students again. You can probably guess what he found. The students who were _____ _____ _____ _____ actually performed _____ _____. This shows _____ _____ _____ the Pygmalion Effect.

Vocabulary Review

Answer Book p. 22

A. Choose the correct word for each meaning.

conduct	random	authority	territory

1 the power to control other people: _____

2 to perform an activity, such as an experiment: _____

3 done without a rule or pattern: _____

4 land ruled by a country or government: _____

B. Fill in the blanks with the appropriate words from the box.

navigate	trade	appointment	worth	original

5 The student has a doctor's _____ at 2 p.m. this afternoon.

6 The large diamond is _____ almost $1 million.

7 Nowadays, sailors _____ with GPS instead of looking at the stars.

8 Ancient people used to _____ and buy things with seashells.

9 The _____ fire started in my town, and now it is spreading to other towns.

C. Choose the closest meaning for each highlighted word or phrase.

10 Your teacher will recognize you even after your graduation.
    (A) welcome   (B) remember   (C) grow   (D) perform

11 The sculpture in the park was made by a famous artist.
    (A) portrait   (B) armor   (C) effect   (D) statue

12 Green is a rare eye color since only two percent of people have it.
    (A) clear   (B) uncommon   (C) specific (D) unfortunate

13 Kate plans to sign up for a yoga class in her neighborhood.
    (A) register   (B) appear   (C) fix   (D) display

14 The party will be a good opportunity for you to make new friends.
    (A) experiment   (B) hobby   (C) interest (D) chance

HACKERS APEX LISTENING
for the TOEFL iBT
Basic

CHAPTER 04

Attitude

Attitude

About the Question Type

Attitude questions ask you to identify the speaker's attitude or opinion regarding ideas mentioned in a conversation or lecture.

These questions require you to recognize the speaker's feelings, likes and dislikes, or reasons for particular feelings. These questions sometimes require you to listen again to part of the listening passage.

Question Format

- What does the man/woman mean/imply when he/she says this: 🎧
- What is the professor's attitude toward ~?
- What is the professor's opinion of ~?

Key Strategies

- **Step 1** — Pay close attention to parts of the talk where the speaker expresses personal opinions, suggestions, or feelings.
- **Step 2** — Listen to the speaker's tone of voice and way of talking. This can make it easier to identify the speaker's attitude towards a topic.
- **Step 3** — Select the answer choice that best illustrates the speaker's attitude or opinion.

Example

Answer Book p. 22

A. Listen to a conversation between a student and a professor.

C4_ExA

Note-taking

Student's Problem

His essay grade is _____ than he expected.

Professor's Solution
- Ask _____ to read the essay
- Use a program that _____ the spelling and grammar

What is the professor's opinion of the student's friends?

(A) She was surprised by the quality of their essays.
(B) She believes it would be helpful to ask their opinion.
(C) She feels that they deserve better grades.
(D) She is confident that they will improve in class.

Answer Book p. 22

B. Listen to part of a lecture in a biology class.

C4_ExB

Note-taking

Why Emperor Penguins Are in Danger

_____ _____ → Less sea ice in Antarctica

How It Affects Chicks and Krill
- Sea ice is _____ _____ before the chicks learn swimming.
- Number of krill will _____.

Listen again to part of the lecture. Then answer the question.
What does the professor mean when she says this: 🎧

(A) She wants to start a campaign to protect animals.
(B) She is concerned about endangered animals.
(C) She thinks people do not care about climate change.
(D) She wants to hear ideas about climate change.

CHAPTER 04 | Attitude 75

Dictation

Answer Book p. 22

Listen again and fill in the blanks.

A.

S: Professor Evans, could I ask you about my essay? Um, my grade is _____ _____ _____ _____, so...

P: Oh, well, you chose a good topic. However, um, the essay had _____ _____ _____, and there were _____ _____ _____ and _____ _____ _____.

S: Oh, I'm sorry. I didn't check the essay carefully before I submitted it. Do you have any advice on how to avoid _____ _____ _____?

P: Well, you can ask your classmates to read your essay. Um, they can read it from _____ _____ _____ _____ _____ and tell you which parts of the essay are not clear... You should also use a program that checks the _____ _____ _____.

S: Ah! I see... Thank you, Professor Evans. That's good advice.

P: You're welcome. I'm sure you'll do better next time, Kevin.

B.

P: So... Because of _____ _____, Antarctica has less sea ice than normal. This can cause many problems. For instance, the emperor penguins in Antarctica can _____ _____.
You see, emperor penguins depend on sea ice to _____ _____ _____ _____. They also use it to _____ _____ _____. However, as the temperature rises, the ice is _____ _____ before the chicks learn _____ _____ _____. As a result, many of them drown... Another problem is that krill are decreasing. Um, krill are a type of small sea animal that emperor penguins eat. If there is less ice, the number of krill will also decrease. So emperor penguins are _____ _____ _____ by the loss of sea ice, but they are also unable to _____ _____ _____. I really hope we can _____ _____ _____.

Listening Practice 1

Answer Book p. 23

Listen to a conversation between a student and a university employee at the registrar's office.

Note-taking

Student's Question
A course has been _____.
→ What other courses can I take _____?

Employee's Answer
Take a _____ course
→ Speak to the professor about it

1. Why does the student visit the registrar's office?

   (A) To change her major
   (B) To make a formal complaint
   (C) To ask about a canceled course
   (D) To get information about graduation

Listen again to part of the conversation. Then answer the question.

2. What does the student mean when she says this: 🎧

   (A) She is concerned about a topic choice.
   (B) She is determined to take a course.
   (C) She is willing to accept a professor's offer.
   (D) She believes it will be difficult to join a class.

Listen again to part of the conversation. Then answer the question.

3. Why does the employee say this: 🎧

   (A) To encourage the student to speak to a professor
   (B) To inform the student that a professor is waiting
   (C) To correct wrong information about a professor
   (D) To tell the student that a professor is kind

Dictation

Answer Book p. 23

Listen again and fill in the blanks.

W: Good morning. Um, I _____ _____ one of the courses for psychology majors, but it's been _____. May I ask what happened?

M: I see... According to our records, the course was canceled this semester because not enough students _____ _____ _____ it. _____ _____ 10 students are needed for a course to continue.

W: _____ _____ _____... Um, could you tell me what other courses _____ _____ _____ _____? Um, I need _____ _____ _____ _____ _____...

M: Of course. If you're interested in _____ _____, I'd suggest Ethics in Psychology. There may be room for one more. But you'll _____ _____ _____ _____ Professor Nichols about it first.

W: I guess I _____ _____ _____. So where can I find Professor Nichols?

M: She's in Bryan Hall, next to the Science Building. You can also e-mail her at s.nichols@franklin.edu. The class _____ _____ _____, so I'm sure she will accept you. Still, _____ _____ _____.

W: Thank you so much. I appreciate all your help.

M: No problem. Good luck!

Listening Practice 2

Answer Book p. 24

Listen to part of a lecture in an environmental science class.

C4_P2

Note-taking

Formation of Fresh Water

Seawater turns into a _____ → _____ again

Causes of Decrease in Fresh Water
- _____ from factories
- _____ of water
- Climate change

1 What does the professor mainly talk about?

(A) The process of formation of fresh water
(B) The plants and animals that depend on fresh water
(C) The importance of the fresh water environment
(D) The many uses of fresh water resources

2 What is the professor's opinion of fresh water?

(A) It has more disadvantages than advantages.
(B) It is dangerous for some animals to drink.
(C) It should be used mostly to produce electricity.
(D) It is necessary for both humans and other living things.

Listen again to part of the lecture. Then answer the question.

3 Why does the professor say this:

(A) To indicate where water comes from
(B) To give a real example of a problem
(C) To describe the characteristics of a place
(D) To criticize policies about water use

Dictation

Answer Book p. 24

Listen again and fill in the blanks.

P: Let's continue our discussion of the natural environment. Our next topic is something plants and animals _____ _____ _____. But, we _____ _____ it, too... I'm talking about fresh water.
When seawater is heated by the sun, it turns into a gas and _____ _____ _____ _____. During the process, salt is _____ _____ because it's heavy. In the atmosphere, water cools and _____ _____ _____ again. Then, it _____ _____ _____ _____ as fresh water, _____ _____ _____ _____ rain or snow. From there, it enters rivers and lakes...
And fresh water has many uses. It _____ _____ _____, which means _____ _____ _____ plants and animals. Around 40 percent of all fish and 10 percent of all animals need fresh water. But it isn't just them... We use it to _____ _____, catch fish, and _____ _____. Of course, we also need it to drink, cook, and wash.
The problem is... fresh water supplies _____ _____ _____. Pollution from factories and other sources reduces the quality of fresh water and makes it _____ _____ _____. Another problem is, uh, overuse. Lots of water is _____ _____ farms and in homes. If we use too much, rivers and lakes _____ _____. Just think. The Colorado was once a powerful river... But, now, the amount of water there _____ _____... And, lastly, climate change can cause too much rain in some parts but _____ _____ _____ _____. These are serious problems that _____ _____ _____, our economies, and most life on the planet.

Listening Practice 3

Answer Book p. 25

Listen to a conversation between a student and a university employee.

Note-taking

Student's Request
Wants to take a _____ class for beginners at the school _____

Employee's Answer
Purchase a _____ to take a class
→ Can use it for a _____

1 What are the speakers mainly discussing?
   (A) A special discount for students
   (B) A schedule for a fitness program
   (C) A requirement to take a sports class
   (D) A change to a gym's website

2 Why does the university require the student to pay the fee?
   (A) To pay teachers for the gym classes
   (B) To cover the cost of a new building
   (C) To change some old equipment
   (D) To extend a gym's opening hours

3 How does the student seem to feel about the pass?
   (A) It does not last long enough.
   (B) It gives access to few facilities.
   (C) It has a reasonable price.
   (D) It offers many classes to take.

Dictation

Answer Book p. 25

Listen again and fill in the blanks.

W: Excuse me... I saw on the website that the school gym is _____ _____ _____ _____ for beginners.

M: That's right. Are you _____ _____ _____?

W: Yes! I'm really impressed by _____ _____ _____ _____ _____. I _____ _____ _____ _____ in it.

M: OK. Um, have you _____ _____ _____ yet? You will need one to _____ _____ _____.

W: Um, I thought I could _____ _____ _____ in the gym with my student ID card.

M: Well, that's true. But if you want to take classes _____ _____ _____ _____, you _____ _____ _____ a gym pass... You know, we have to _____ _____ _____.

W: Oh, I didn't know that. Uh, so how much is the pass?

M: It's $15 and you can _____ _____ _____ _____ _____. You can then take any class you want.

W: Hmm... That's _____ _____ _____ a regular fitness club membership. I'll _____ _____ for a semester and see how it goes.

M: OK. Here's the registration form.

Listening Practice 4

Listen to part of a lecture in an art class.

Note-taking

Girl with the Red Balloon
- Sent to auction → _____ itself
- Banksy's Intention
  : Art should not be an _____ for rich people
  → Ironically, he increased its _____.

1. What is the lecture mainly about?
   (A) What a famous artist did
   (B) The popularity of modern art
   (C) Why graffiti causes controversy
   (D) The value of modern art

Listen again to part of the lecture. Then answer the question.

2. Why does the professor say this:
   (A) To stress the message behind a drawing
   (B) To describe the atmosphere at an auction
   (C) To introduce a shocking event
   (D) To comment on the quality of some art

Listen again to part of the lecture. Then answer the question.

3. What does the professor mean when he says this:
   (A) He thinks that Banksy made an unfortunate mistake.
   (B) He feels that Banksy's action caused an unintended result.
   (C) He believes that Banksy's art should be worth more.
   (D) He is disappointed by rich people's response to Banksy's art.

Dictation

Answer Book p. 26

Listen again and fill in the blanks.

P: Modern Art is about creating something totally new or unique. Well, today, I'm going to introduce _____ _____ _____ called Banksy and _____ _____ _____ _____ _____ _____. His works _____ _____ because, um, they are often public graffiti, which is illegal. And, uh, they are usually about _____ _____. Now, _____ _____ _____ _____ is probably *Girl with the Red Balloon*. It shows a little girl, and she has lost her balloon. The red balloon is _____ _____, and the girl is trying to catch it. The painting _____ _____ _____, "There is always hope". The artwork is _____ _____ _____ _____. I personally like the simple drawing with its positive message, too. People even wanted to own it, so it was _____ _____ _____. And here comes the interesting part. When it _____ _____ _____ _____ _____, the painting started to go down and half of it was _____ _____ _____. The painting _____ _____! It turned out that Banksy had installed a paper-shredding device inside the frame of the painting.

S: Why would he do that? I mean, destroy his own art...

P: Well, Banksy thought art should not be _____ _____ _____ _____ _____. Also, he believed art should not be _____ _____ _____. And this is quite ironic, if you think about it... By shredding the art, he actually _____ _____ _____. Later, the shredded work was sold in another auction with a new name called *Love is in the Bin*. Its _____ _____ from $1.3 million to $24.5 million.

iBT Listening Test 1

TOEFL Listening

Note-taking

Professor's Suggestion to Student

You are a _____ for a _____ from the Zellman Foundation

Requirements

- _____ that prove how many hours you worked
- A _____ about your experience
- A letter of _____ from a professor

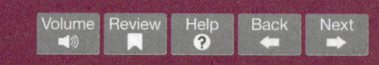

1. What is the conversation mainly about?
   - Ⓐ A student's performance on a recent test
   - Ⓑ The requirements for taking a course
   - Ⓒ A student's opportunity to receive a scholarship
   - Ⓓ The activities of a community organization

2. What does the professor say about the Zellman Foundation?
   - Ⓐ It gives financial support to volunteers.
   - Ⓑ It recently raised a large amount of money.
   - Ⓒ It is looking for students who want a job.
   - Ⓓ It operates several volunteer programs.

3. What is the student's attitude toward an offer?
   - Ⓐ She is excited about becoming a volunteer.
   - Ⓑ She is worried that she is not qualified.
   - Ⓒ She is happy about being considered.
   - Ⓓ She is sorry that she cannot provide an answer.

Listen again to part of the conversation. Then answer the question.

4. Why does the professor say this:
   - Ⓐ To tell the student that she has worked enough hours
   - Ⓑ To imply that he will provide a letter of recommendation
   - Ⓒ To indicate that some documents are not needed
   - Ⓓ To suggest that an application process has changed

Dictation

Answer Book p. 27

Listen again and fill in the blanks.

S: Hi, Professor Coleman. I'm here because I _____ _____ _____. You asked me to _____ _____ your office.

P: Hello, Katherine. Yes, I was _____ _____ _____ _____ you submitted about your volunteer work. And, um, I want to let you know that you are _____ _____ _____ _____ _____.

S: Thank you, Professor. Um, I am? What kind of scholarship?

P: Yes, it's a community service scholarship. Um, the Zellman Foundation offers it to students who have done _____ _____ _____ _____ of _____ _____ in the local community.

S: I don't know what to say. Um, of course, _____ _____ _____.

P: It's a wonderful opportunity. You will receive $3,000 _____ _____ _____ _____.

S: Wow! I can use that to pay for college. Is there anything that I have to do?

P: Well, you'll _____ _____ _____ _____ that prove _____ _____ _____ you worked. You should also _____ _____ _____ about your experience. The last thing is _____ _____ _____ _____ from a professor. But, obviously, you don't have to worry about this.

S: Thank you, Professor Coleman. I appreciate that.

iBT Listening Test 2

Answer Book p. 27

TOEFL Listening

ECONOMICS

Note-taking

How Cartel Affects the _____

_____: An organization formed by companies to control a _____
- Companies: Work together to remove _____
- Countries: Formed OPEC, the _____ of Petroleum Exporting Countries
  → Increase or decrease oil _____ to control oil _____

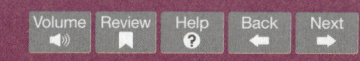

1. What is the lecture mainly about?
    - Ⓐ How criminal groups form
    - Ⓑ Why illegal businesses are harmful
    - Ⓒ How organizations control a market
    - Ⓓ Strategies that can increase profits

2. What is the professor's opinion of competition?
    - Ⓐ It benefits consumers.
    - Ⓑ It increases profits for other companies.
    - Ⓒ It leads to lower product quality.
    - Ⓓ It makes companies work together.

3. According to the professor, why do oil prices increase when oil production decreases?
    - Ⓐ Because OPEC countries prefer competition
    - Ⓑ Because OPEC refuses to trade with other countries
    - Ⓒ Because oil production needs a lot of money
    - Ⓓ Because the need for oil is larger than the production

Listen again to part of the lecture. Then answer the question.

4. Why does the professor say this:
    - Ⓐ To remind the students about an earlier lesson
    - Ⓑ To explain the process of oil production
    - Ⓒ To show how OPEC was formed
    - Ⓓ To point out why OPEC is so powerful

Dictation

Answer Book p. 28

Listen again and fill in the blanks.

P: When you hear the word cartel, you might think of a large group of criminals. Well, um, in economics, it _____ _____ _____ _____. In general, an economic cartel is an organization formed by companies _____ _____ _____ _____. Let's talk about how a cartel _____ _____ _____.

Companies in a cartel _____ _____ _____ _____ _____ so that they can _____ _____ more easily. Normally, competition _____ _____ _____ _____ like you and me. When companies compete, they have to _____ _____ to improve their products and to sell them _____ _____ _____. Sometimes, however, companies _____ _____ _____ _____. That way, they have _____ _____ _____ _____ _____.

They can also _____ _____ _____ for products that people need for living. These companies know that customers _____ _____ _____ _____ and eventually have to buy products from them.

But, companies _____ _____ _____ _____ that form cartels now. Countries do it, too. For example, OPEC, the Organization of Petroleum Exporting Countries, is a powerful cartel. It is _____ _____ _____ _____ _____ that _____ _____, including Iran, Iraq, and Saudi Arabia. And as you know, _____ _____ _____. So, in 1960, countries that _____ _____ formed OPEC, and they meet regularly to _____ _____ _____ _____ _____. When they increase oil production, oil prices _____ _____. But when they decrease oil production, oil prices _____ _____ as the production is _____ _____.

_____ _____. Um, 44 percent of the oil production in the world _____ _____ countries in OPEC, so the decision _____ _____ _____. In this way, OPEC controls _____ _____ _____ _____ for oil.

Vocabulary Review

Answer Book p. 29

A. Choose the correct word for each meaning.

| maintain | supply | consumer | decrease |

1. to reduce the number of something: _____
2. to keep something in the same condition: _____
3. someone who pays money for products or services: _____
4. an amount of something that can be used: _____

B. Fill in the blanks with the appropriate words or phrases from the box.

| waste | extinct | carefully | caused | left behind |

5. Frank worked very _____ so that he wouldn't make any mistakes.
6. The dinosaurs became _____ about 65 million years ago.
7. Our puppy was _____ at home because dogs cannot enter the museum.
8. An accident on the highway _____ the traffic jam yesterday.
9. If you leave the lights on when you're out, you will _____ electricity.

C. Choose the closest meaning for each highlighted word.

10. The regular cause of dry skin is drinking too little water.
    (A) positive   (B) weak   (C) normal   (D) ironic

11. The video contains a message about protecting jungle animals.
    (A) continues   (B) includes   (C) submits   (D) improves

12. After a few minutes in the hot car, the ice cream was totally melted.
    (A) completely   (B) personally   (C) obviously   (D) occasionally

13. The scientist will accept an award at the ceremony for her discovery.
    (A) describe   (B) bother   (C) receive   (D) translate

14. The store offers a 20 percent discount on all products.
    (A) owns   (B) provides   (C) records   (D) proves

HACKERS APEX LISTENING
for the TOEFL iBT
Basic

CHAPTER 05

Organization

Organization

■ About the Question Type

Organization questions ask you to identify how a speaker organizes a lecture or presents certain information. Alternatively, you may be asked the reason the speaker mentions a specific piece of information.

Sometimes, you may be asked to determine how specific information relates to the discussion as a whole. Common ways of organizing include: cause and effect, compare and contrast, and problem and solution.

■ Question Format

- How does the professor introduce/clarify/explain ~?
- How is the lecture organized?
- Why does the man/woman mention ~?
- Why does the man/woman talk about ~?

■ Key Strategies

- **Step 1** — While listening to the passage, identify the overall organization or structure of the discussion.

- **Step 2** — If the question asks about the organizational structure of the passage, identify how the main idea and its supporting details are organized. If the question asks about the reason why the speaker mentions a specific piece of information, identify how that information connects to the talk as a whole.

- **Step 3** — Select the answer choice that best describes the organizational structure of the passage or the purpose of a specific piece of information.

Example

Answer Book p. 29

A. Listen to a conversation between a student and a student center employee.

C5_ExA

Note-taking

Student's Request
Looking for a _____ on campus

Employee's Response
Computer lab is looking for a _____ _____.
→ Help other students using the _____

Why does the student mention his major?

(A) To describe some classes that he took
(B) To get job recommendations
(C) To imply that he has a busy schedule
(D) To explain why he cannot find a job

Answer Book p. 29

B. Listen to part of a lecture in an architecture class.

C5_ExB

Note-taking

Baroque Architecture in the Palace of Versailles
• Use of _____
  e.g. _____ in the Hall of Mirrors
• Decorations with a repeating _____
  e.g. Louis XIV, the _____ _____

How does the professor organize the lecture?

(A) By comparing two types of architectural structures
(B) By introducing different styles of architecture
(C) By illustrating an example of an architectural style
(D) By emphasizing the importance of a famous structure

Dictation

Answer Book p. 29

Listen again and fill in the blanks.

A.

M: Hi. I'm _____ _____ _____ _____ on campus. I need _____ _____ _____ for books and other costs.

W: OK, but, um, it's a little bit late in the semester. Most of the jobs on campus _____ _____ _____ already. _____ _____ _____ _____ are you interested in?

M: I'm not sure. Um, I'm a computer science major. Is there anything _____ _____ this?

W: Let me check... Oh, you're quite lucky. The computer lab is looking for _____ _____ _____. You'll be helping other students _____ _____ _____. Students sometimes _____ _____ _____ things like connecting to the Internet or to a printer.

M: All right. So _____ _____ _____ _____?

W: Give me a minute. I'll _____ _____ _____ for you.

B.

P: Today, we're going to look at _____ _____. The Baroque style was popular in Europe during the 17th and 18th centuries. The Palace of Versailles _____ _____ _____.

Now, Baroque architecture is famous for _____ _____ _____ _____. To create different shades, architects used paint and other materials. In the Palace of Versailles, they placed mirrors in a room called the Hall of Mirrors. This _____ _____ _____ _____ all around the room.

Another key element of Baroque architecture is decorations. These often have _____ _____ _____, such as a particular animal or, um, symbol. In the Palace of Versailles, the theme is Louis XIV, the French king who _____ _____ _____. His name and face can be seen _____ _____ _____, from the walls and ceilings to even the floors!

Listening Practice 1

Answer Book p. 30

Listen to a conversation between a student and a university housing office employee.

Note-taking

Student's Problem
Other students are really _____.
→ Wants to _____ into another building

Employee's Suggestion
- Waitlist
- Post a _____ on the board or wear earplugs

1. Why does the student go to the university housing office?
   (A) To complain about a university website
   (B) To get information on a new dormitory rule
   (C) To find out a university building's location
   (D) To ask about moving to another dormitory

2. Why does the employee mention a notice board?
   (A) To show the student where to find more information
   (B) To suggest a solution to the student's problem
   (C) To tell the student about an announcement
   (D) To confirm that a list has already been posted

3. What is the student's opinion of the waitlist?
   (A) He thinks it should be updated more often.
   (B) He believes it might not have a long wait time.
   (C) He wishes that he had heard about it earlier.
   (D) He hopes it is replaced with a better system.

Dictation

Answer Book p. 30

Listen again and fill in the blanks.

M: Good morning. Um, the other students in my dormitory are _____ _____. Could I _____ _____ _____ _____?

W: I'm sorry, but that isn't possible right now.

M: But why? I checked the university's website, and there's _____ _____ _____ changing rooms.

W: That's true. But all of the dorms are _____ _____. I can _____ _____ _____ _____ _____, though.

M: The waitlist? Is that going to _____ _____ _____? The midterm exams are next month. I won't be able to _____ _____ _____ for the exams with _____ _____ _____. Can't I get a new room sooner?

W: I'm afraid not. But there are some things you can do right away. Uh, _____ _____ _____ _____ on the notice board in your dormitory. You could _____ _____ _____ _____ _____. If that doesn't work, maybe wear earplugs when you study.

M: I guess so. Um, I forgot to ask... _____ _____ _____ _____ _____?

W: Let me check... You will be number seven once I update it.

M: Really? That's not too bad. This might not _____ _____ _____ after all.

Listening Practice 2

Answer Book p. 31

Listen to part of a lecture in a geology class.

Note-taking

Shapes of _____ _____

- Crescent Dune
  → Looks like a _____ that isn't full
  → Forms when wind blows in _____ direction
- _____ Dune
  → Forms when wind blows in _____ directions

1. What is the main topic of the lecture?

   (A) How beaches and deserts are similar
   (B) Which factors cause sand to form
   (C) How sand dunes become different shapes
   (D) Where to find the world's biggest sand dunes

2. How does the professor organize the lecture?

   (A) By encouraging the students to use their imagination
   (B) By showing the students pictures of sand dunes
   (C) By talking about the result of an experiment
   (D) By describing similarities and differences

3. What is the professor's attitude toward star dunes?

   (A) He believes the name is unclear.
   (B) He is impressed by their size.
   (C) He thinks more people should see them.
   (D) He wishes they were easier to find.

Dictation

Answer Book p. 31

Listen again and fill in the blanks.

P: So, I'm sure many of you have been to a beach. Or maybe you've seen _____ _____ _____ _____ like the Sahara Desert in Africa. If you have, then you know what a sand dune is... Now, let's talk about how _____ _____ _____ _____ _____ _____ are created. Basically, sand dunes are hills _____ _____ _____... They form when wind continuously _____ _____ _____ _____ or a desert. Sand is light, so wind can move it easily. But wind doesn't always _____ _____ _____ _____. Because wind blows in different directions, sand _____ _____ _____ _____ _____. Um, that's why you have many shapes of sand dunes.

The most common shape is the crescent. Um, try imagining what it looks like... _____ _____ _____ _____, it _____ _____ _____ _____ when it isn't full. This shape forms when wind blows in one direction. Anyway, crescent dunes can be very wide... _____ _____ _____ 100 meters long.

But what happens when the wind blows in different directions? Then, you get _____ _____ _____ called the star. _____ _____ _____ what this one looks like. As the name suggests, it _____ _____ _____ _____. But it's also very tall. They can be _____ _____. Some of you might not know this, but we have one here in Colorado. It's 225 meters high, and it is _____ _____ _____ in the country.

Now, let's look at images of some other sand dunes. _____ _____ _____ _____ _____ how their shapes were formed.

Listening Practice 3

Answer Book p. 31

Listen to a conversation between a student and a professor.

C5_P3

Note-taking

Student's Question
Should I write about how people _____ about the
_____ _____?

Professor's Suggestion
- Focus on each _____ campaign promises
- Make sure the _____ are true

1 What are the speakers mainly discussing?
   (A) A difficult lecture topic
   (B) An upcoming student election
   (C) A recent midterm exam
   (D) A new class assignment

2 How does the professor emphasize the importance of accurate opinions?
   (A) By showing how to prevent mistakes
   (B) By explaining how to do an interview
   (C) By giving several research sources
   (D) By describing another student's experience

3 What is the professor's attitude toward the idea of interviewing professors?
   (A) He thinks it would take a long time.
   (B) He believes it would be easy to do.
   (C) He is interested in participating.
   (D) He is sure that there are enough professors.

Dictation

Answer Book p. 32

Listen again and fill in the blanks.

S: Are you busy, Professor Wilkins?

P: Well, I'm grading exams for another class, but I have a few minutes. What do you need, Eva?

S: Um, at the end of yesterday's lecture, you told us to write an article about _____ _____ _____ _____. You said to include various _____ _____ _____... Does this mean I should write about how people _____ _____ _____ _____?

P: Well, that might be _____ _____. I suggest focusing on each _____ _____ _____... You know, what they _____ _____ _____ when they become president.

S: Oh, I see. Um, then maybe I could _____ _____ _____ and ask if they _____ _____ _____ _____ those promises. I could _____ _____ _____ _____.

P: Good idea. Just make sure the opinions are true. I had one student who _____ _____ what someone said to make his article better. I gave him an F.

S: I'll _____ _____ _____ _____. Oh, and I'm also _____ professors, too.

P: Hmm... That would _____ _____ _____ _____. Just doing student interviews would be enough.

S: OK, I'll do that. Thanks for your help.

Listening Practice 4

Answer Book p. 32

Listen to part of a lecture in a linguistics class.

Note-taking

English Words from _____
- Come from French directly
  → _____ in a French way
  e.g. Café, cuisine, brunette, critique, and chic
- Feel like _____ English words
  e.g. Surprise, effort, and police

1 What is the main topic of the lecture?

(A) The common features of European languages
(B) The differences between English and French
(C) The reasons that English became widespread
(D) The influence of French on the English language

2 What does the professor say about the French language?

(A) It shares over 1,000 words with English.
(B) It has words that sound like German.
(C) It has a vocabulary of about 15,000 words.
(D) It began to change a thousand years ago.

3 Why does the professor mention the Normans who ruled England?

(A) To show the origin of a popular English phrase
(B) To explain why some French words feel like natural English
(C) To suggest that the French people were very powerful
(D) To emphasize the long history of England

Dictation

Answer Book p. 32

Listen again and fill in the blanks.

P: As you know, English is a very old language. It, uh, started in around AD 550. In the beginning, it _____ _____ _____ _____ German and Latin. However, you may not realize that French also _____ _____ _____ _____ _____ English.
For instance, consider how many words _____ _____ _____ _____. Some words are even used and spelled in _____ _____ _____ _____. These include *café*, *cuisine*, *brunette*, *critique*, and *chic*, to name just a few examples. Phrases like *en route*, *Déjà vu*, and *film noir* are also equally common. However, these are often pronounced in a French way and _____ _____ unfamiliar accent marks. Nevertheless, none of _____ _____ _____ _____ _____ needs translation.
In total, there are 1,700 words that English and French use in almost the same way. But not all of these have a French sound. Many words like *surprise* or *effort* or *police* do not _____ _____ French words at all. They _____ _____ natural English words. And it feels that way because... well, they are. Many words like these _____ _____ _____ the English language over a thousand years ago. That was when the Normans, a powerful group of people from France, _____ _____ England. The Normans _____ _____ _____ _____. During this period, over 10,000 French words _____ _____ _____ _____.
To this day, English and French still have _____ _____ _____.
Um, I believe that the average English speaker can understand about 15,000 French words. That is true whether they can speak French or not.

iBT Listening Test 1

TOEFL Listening

Note-taking

Organization of the Paper

1. Start with Gregor Mendel
   → Mention his main _____ first
2. Discuss the _____ with flowers
   → Write about how and why Mendel's ideas were not _____ at first

1 What is the conversation mainly about?
- Ⓐ How to organize ideas for a paper
- Ⓑ Which topics to select for a group project
- Ⓒ Where to find good research material
- Ⓓ What to include in an experiment

2 Why does the professor talk about Mendel's Laws?
- Ⓐ To explain how Mendel became famous
- Ⓑ To suggest how to begin an assignment
- Ⓒ To emphasize the importance of Mendel
- Ⓓ To remind the student what to study for a test

3 According to the professor, what played an important role in Mendel's work?
- Ⓐ Help from other scientists
- Ⓑ Support from his family
- Ⓒ Past research on genetics
- Ⓓ Tests with flowers

Listen again to part of the conversation. Then answer the question.

4 What does the professor mean when he says this:
- Ⓐ He is impressed with the student's knowledge.
- Ⓑ He thinks the student should gather more information.
- Ⓒ He agrees that some information is not correct.
- Ⓓ He wants the student to review a past lecture.

Dictation

Answer Book p. 33

Listen again and fill in the blanks.

S: Hi, Professor Reed, I was, uh, wondering if you could _____ _____ _____ _____ about my assignment. I'm _____ _____ _____ about the development of modern genetics.

P: Hi, Andrea. I like the topic, but, uh, it's very broad. How do you plan to _____ _____ _____?

S: Well, I want to start with Gregor Mendel since he's _____ _____ _____ _____ of modern genetics.

P: In that case, I would suggest that you mention _____ _____ _____ first... So, uh, talk about Mendel's Laws.

S: I agree... And then I was going to discuss _____ _____ _____ _____.

P: They _____ _____ _____ _____... But, um, I think you should also include _____ _____ _____.

S: What do you mean by that?

P: It would be good to write about how and why Mendel's ideas _____ _____ _____ _____ other scientists at first... And then, uh, discuss how his work _____ _____ _____ again.

S: I'm not _____ _____ that. I'd _____ _____ _____ _____.

P: That would be wise. I can _____ _____ _____ if you like.

S: I'd appreciate that, Professor... Thank you!

iBT Listening Test 2

TOEFL Listening

Note-taking

1600s ~ 1700s
- Many Europeans decided to _____ to America.
- There were 13 British _____ in America.

Late 1700s

Colonies joined together and started the American _____ _____.

→ They signed the Declaration of _____.

1 What is the main topic of the lecture?
   Ⓐ The friendship between America and Great Britain
   Ⓑ The reason Americans became wealthy
   Ⓒ The beginning of the United States
   Ⓓ The discovery of American land

2 According to the professor, why did many Europeans move to America?
   Ⓐ To fight in wars
   Ⓑ To become rich
   Ⓒ To sell European products
   Ⓓ To spread their religion

3 How does the professor explain the issue with taxes?
   Ⓐ By comparing America and Great Britain's tax systems
   Ⓑ By asking the students for their opinion
   Ⓒ By explaining where the British used taxes
   Ⓓ By showing the students how to pay taxes

Listen again to part of the lecture. Then answer the question.

4 What does the professor imply when he says this:
   Ⓐ The colonies had good reasons to feel confident.
   Ⓑ The British were very successful traders.
   Ⓒ The colonies made a wise decision to buy land.
   Ⓓ The British made a mistake in starting a war.

Dictation

Answer Book p. 34

Listen again and fill in the blanks.

C5_T2_D

P: Today, America and Great Britain _____ _____ _____ _____. However, 250 years ago, they _____ _____ _____... The Americans _____ _____. This is how the United States became a country.

After the land of America was discovered, many Europeans like the Spanish, French, and British _____ _____ there. Um, most of them wanted to _____ _____ _____ _____. In 1607, the British _____ _____ _____ in Virginia. They grew tobacco there and sold it in Europe. This _____ _____ _____, so they formed more colonies. By the 1700s, there were 13 British colonies in America.

But, soon after, problems began. First, Britain was very far from America. At the time, it took about four months to get to America by boat. This made it hard for the British to _____ _____ _____... Another issue was taxes. You know, we pay taxes to the government _____ _____ _____ _____ _____. The people who lived in American colonies also paid taxes since these colonies _____ _____, _____ _____ _____ _____. However, they _____ _____ _____ _____ _____ because of the long distance. Now, _____ _____ _____ _____ if you did not get what you _____ _____?

S: I would feel angry...

P: Exactly. And the colonies _____ _____ that they could _____ _____ _____ without the British. Uh, this makes sense, right? They were rich, after all. They owned _____ _____ _____ _____. So, in 1775, the 13 colonies _____ _____ and

_____ _____ _____ _____ _____. This lasted until 1783. But in 1776, which was uh, before the war ended, the Americans _____ _____ _____ _____ _____. This was the document that created the United States of America, and the 13 colonies became _____ _____ _____ _____.

Vocabulary Review

Answer Book p. 35

A. Choose the correct word for each meaning.

| grade | chic | distance | opinion |

1. the length of the space between two objects: _____
2. personal thoughts about someone or something: _____
3. trendy and stylish in terms of fashion: _____
4. to give a score to students' work: _____

B. Fill in the blanks with the appropriate words from the box.

| quality | contribution | rule | connect | represent |

5. My teammate made an important _____ to the win by scoring 30 points.
6. The city's new tall buildings _____ its growing wealth and power.
7. Claire's kindness was her best _____ and helped her make friends.
8. The Internet can _____ people who live on different sides of the world.
9. The new queen will _____ a nation of 70 million people.

C. Choose the closest meaning for each highlighted word or phrase.

10. The repair person fixed the issue with Fred's phone.
    (A) cost (B) decoration (C) symbol (D) problem

11. He says that he will only buy a particular brand of headphones.
    (A) possible (B) certain (C) impressive (D) general

12. Amy should concentrate on her studies more than her hobbies.
    (A) make sense (B) fill in (C) focus on (D) take over

13. Can you recommend something fun for us to do this afternoon?
    (A) suggest (B) guess (C) realize (D) work

14. Everyone knew Nina's family was wealthy because they had a big house.
    (A) lonely (B) various (C) broad (D) rich

HACKERS APEX LISTENING
for the TOEFL iBT
Basic

CHAPTER 06

Connecting Contents

Connecting Contents

About the Question Type

Connecting Contents questions ask you to complete a table or chart that shows how the ideas directly mentioned in a conversation or lecture relate to one another.

List questions require you to identify whether the statements listed in a table are true or false. Matching questions ask you to classify the statements or identify which category they belong to, while Ordering questions require you to put the steps of a process or series of events in the correct order.

Question Format

List
- Indicate whether each of the following is mentioned/included/suggested/etc.
  Click in the correct box for each phrase.

	Yes/Included/Suggested	No/Not Included/Not Suggested
Statement A		
Statement B		
Statement C		

Matching
- Indicate for each example what type of ~.

Ordering
- The professor explains the steps ~. Put the steps listed below in the correct order.

Key Strategies

- **Step 1** — Pay attention to the important details and overall flow of the talk.
- **Step 2** — Identify the number of ideas being discussed, and predict which type of question will be asked. Types of questions include List, Matching, and Ordering.
- **Step 3** — Select the answer choices in the table or chart that best represent the information in the passage for each item.

Example

Answer Book p. 35

A. Listen to a conversation between a student and a professor.

C6_ExA

Note-taking

Student's Question
How can I _____ _____ a midterm exam?

Professor's Suggestion
• Can _____ the final test score
• Write a _____ instead of a test

Indicate whether each of the following is mentioned as something the student can do to make up the midterm exam. *Click in the correct box for each phrase.*

	Yes	No
(A) Take another midterm test		
(B) Take the final exam only		
(C) Write a paper about a subject		
(D) Give a speech about a topic		

Answer Book p. 35

B. Listen to part of a lecture in a history class.

C6_ExB

Note-taking

Process of Ancient Chinese _____

1. _____ bark, and clean it in water
2. _____ or _____ bark to release pulp
3. Beat bark with a _____ to get fibers, and mix them with _____ and water
4. Place the mixture on the _____, and let it dry

The professor explains the process of ancient Chinese papermaking. Put the steps listed below in the correct order. *Drag each answer choice to the space where it belongs.*

Step 1	
Step 2	
Step 3	
Step 4	

(A) Fibers and pulp were mixed with water.
(B) A screen was dried in the sun.
(C) Bark was boiled or steamed.
(D) Bark was collected and washed in water.

Dictation

Listen again and fill in the blanks.

A.

S: Hello, Professor Hamilton. I'm here to ask how I can _____ _____ _____ _____ _____. As I told you before, I missed the exam because I _____ _____ _____ _____ _____ that day.

P: Hi, Rachel. Well, I can _____ your final test score to cover your midterm score. This way, you don't have to _____ _____ _____.

S: Um, I'm not sure I'll _____ _____ _____ _____ on the final... Can I take a test with different questions on another day?

P: Well, that would _____ _____ _____ the other students... Hmm... How about _____ _____ _____ instead?

S: Could you _____ _____ _____ _____?

P: You can _____ _____ _____ related to our class. It will be _____ _____ _____ to review what you've learned.

S: Sounds interesting. I'd like to write a paper, then.

B.

P: The process for _____ _____ was invented around AD 150. Before then, people _____ _____ _____ _____ _____, but these were, uh, not convenient. Then, a Chinese man named Cai Lun made paper with the bark of trees.

To make paper, the first step was to cut bark from a tree and _____ _____ _____ a bundle. This bundle was cleaned in water. Next, the bark was boiled or steamed. This caused the bark _____ _____ and _____ _____ a sticky liquid known as pulp. Then, the softened bark was beaten with a wooden hammer to _____ _____ _____ _____ fibers. The fibers and pulp were _____ _____ _____. Finally, a thin layer of the mixture was _____ _____ a screen and _____ _____ _____ _____ to dry. When the screen was removed, the paper was made.

Listening Practice 1

Answer Book p. 37

Listen to a conversation between a student and a university employee.

Note-taking

Student's Problem
Will be in a different country on the _____ day

What's Provided in the Orientation
- A _____ of the campus
- Information about how to _____ _____ for courses

1 What is the main topic of the conversation?

(A) An upcoming school event
(B) A change to a travel schedule
(C) An issue with an official form
(D) A tour of several schools

2 What did the student plan to do next month?

(A) Talk to a professor
(B) Study abroad
(C) Look for a part-time job
(D) Take a family vacation

3 Indicate in the table below whether each of the following is an advantage of attending the orientation. *Click in the correct box for each phrase.*

	Advantage	Not an Advantage
(A) See where everything is on campus		
(B) Learn how to sign up for courses		
(C) Meet other students		
(D) Participate in organized social activities		

Dictation

Answer Book p. 37

Listen again and fill in the blanks.

M: Hi. I heard that the orientation _____ _____ _____ next month.

W: That's right. Do you _____ _____ _____ about it?

M: Um, I have a problem... My family will be _____ _____ in a different country _____ _____ _____ _____. We've already _____ _____ _____, so I'm not sure if we can _____ _____ _____.

W: I see... Well, students _____ _____ _____ _____ _____ to the orientation, but I _____ _____ _____ _____.

M: Um... May I ask why? I don't know why it's so important.

W: Sure. First, there will be a _____ _____ _____ _____ _____. It would _____ _____ _____ _____ where everything is.

M: Well, I guess I agree with that.

W: Right. It will also provide information about how to _____ _____ _____ _____. Many students are attending it _____ _____ _____.

M: I don't want to miss that, either. Um, and it _____ _____ _____ to meet other students as well.

W: Good point. There aren't any social activities, but you'd probably _____ _____ _____ _____ anyway.

M: OK. I'll talk to my parents about this tonight.

Listening Practice 2

Listen to part of a lecture in a literature class.

Note-taking

Legends
- Based on _____ events
- Have a _____ as the main character

Folktales
- Passed down by word of _____
- Changed because of the _____ of listeners

1. What is the lecture mainly about?
   (A) Stories shared by different countries
   (B) The cultural value of traditional stories
   (C) The connection between folklore and culture
   (D) Characteristics of two kinds of folklore

2. Why does the professor mention Little Red Riding Hood?
   (A) To compare past and present folktales
   (B) To explain how folktales are passed down
   (C) To give the oldest example of a folktale
   (D) To show how the story of a folktale changed

3. Indicate whether each of the following describes legends or folktales. *Click in the correct box for each phrase.*

	Legends	Folktales
(A) They are rarely written down.		
(B) They are based on real events.		
(C) The stories depend on what listeners like.		
(D) The stories have a hero.		

Dictation

Answer Book p. 38

Listen again and fill in the blanks.

P: As I mentioned earlier, folklore is a broad concept. It includes the stories and cultural traditions that _____ _____ a particular group of people. Now, I'd like to talk about two important parts of folklore... legends and folktales.
OK... All legends have _____ _____ _____. First, they _____ _____ _____ actual events, although they sometimes include magical creatures like monsters or dragons. Another characteristic of a legend is that it _____ _____ _____. The main character is always someone who can do what normal people cannot do. Um, an example with _____ _____ _____ _____ is the Greek legend about the Minotaur... Does anyone know the story?

S: Um, it's about a monster that was half-man and half-bull.

P: That's right. _____ _____ _____ _____, the Minotaur _____ _____ _____ the hero Theseus, who would later become the king of Athens. Researchers believe that Theseus was a king in the 8th or 9th century BC. And they assume that monsters in legends were used to explain things that were _____ _____ _____ at that time, such as _____ _____.
So, what about folktales? Well, to begin with, folktales are generally _____ _____ from person to person by _____ _____ _____. They are rarely _____ _____. Next, they change as time passes. This is because people change the stories to _____ _____ _____ of listeners. Think about Little Red Riding Hood. In the earliest version of this story, Little Red Riding Hood was actually eaten by the wolf. However, in later ones, she _____ _____ _____ the woodcutter.

Listening Practice 3

Answer Book p. 38

Listen to a conversation between a student and a professor.

Note-taking

Student's Question
Could I get information about a field _____?

Activities at the Museum
- A dinosaur _____
- A session about the process of digging up _____
- A _____ by a researcher in archaeology

1 Why does the student go to see the professor?

(A) To ask for a change in his grade
(B) To get information about a school trip
(C) To explain why he was late for a class
(D) To request permission to join a trip

2 Why does the professor mention the midterm exam?

(A) To indicate that missing a class affects grades
(B) To explain why a field trip will be delayed
(C) To suggest that the student should study harder
(D) To emphasize the importance of a field trip

3 What activities will be included in the field trip? Indicate whether each of the following will be included or not. *Click in the correct box for each phrase.*

	Included	Not Included
(A) Viewing some exhibits		
(B) Taking a guided tour with a curator		
(C) Learning how to dig up fossils		
(D) Listening to a talk		

Dictation

Answer Book p. 39

Listen again and fill in the blanks.

S: Hi, Professor Lewis. I'm sorry I _____ _____ _____ _____. Um, as I said in my e-mail, I _____ _____ _____ because I was ill.

P: That's fine, Greg. I understand your situation and it won't _____ _____ _____.

S: Thanks. Um, and I heard that there will be _____ _____ _____ to the Museum of Natural History next week. Could I _____ _____ _____ about it?

P: Right. There is a new _____ _____ that I want everyone to see. As our midterm will be about dinosaurs and their fossils, things from the exhibition will _____ _____ _____ _____.

S: OK. Um, then I guess there will be a curator's tour of the exhibition...

P: No, that _____ _____ _____. But there will be a session on learning _____ _____ _____ _____ _____.

S: Wow. I've always wanted to _____ _____ _____.

P: It should be interesting. Uh, the field trip will _____ _____ _____ _____ by Dr. Malcolm, _____ _____ _____ _____ _____ _____ in archaeology.

S: I see... Thanks for organizing this. I'm really _____ _____ _____ _____.

Listening Practice 4

Answer Book p. 39

Listen to part of a lecture in a film class.

C6_P4

Note-taking

The Silent Film Era
- Different types of songs were played _____.
- Movies with large budgets had a _____.

End of the Silent Film Era
Sound-recording _____ allowed the _____ of actors' voices, sound effects, and music.

---

1 What is the main topic of the lecture?

(A) The change in music in the silent film era
(B) The various types of silent films
(C) Famous actors of the silent film era
(D) Popular songs in early film history

2 Why does the professor mention *The Birth of a Nation*?

(A) To give an example of a film with a soundtrack
(B) To introduce the first silent film in America
(C) To highlight a film director's most famous work
(D) To emphasize that silent films were expensive

3 Indicate whether each of the following is related to the characteristics of music in silent film. *Click in the correct box for each phrase.*

	Yes	No
(A) Music was played as a live performance.		
(B) Most of the music was written by the film director.		
(C) Silent films eventually included bands and orchestras.		
(D) Recording technology made silent films more popular.		

Dictation

Listen again and fill in the blanks.

P: Has anyone seen a silent film? If you have, raise your hand. Just a few of you... Well, silent films actually were not totally silent. At the theater, there was music during silent films. And, uh, there were some changes in _____ _____ _____ _____ during the silent film era.

Um, in this era, the music was _____ _____ during silent films. In the beginning, it was usually played by _____ _____ _____. Pianists had to play _____ _____ _____ _____ for different films and audiences. They would play classical songs or songs that were popular at that time, such as folk or jazz.

Gradually, silent films included bands and even entire orchestras. As this trend developed, the music changed too. People _____ _____ musical scores just for films. Uh, a musical score is _____ _____ _____ _____ _____. Then, around 1908, films with soundtracks appeared. Now, does anyone know what a soundtrack is?

S: Uh, it's _____ _____ _____ songs and sounds in a film.

P: Exactly! So, by 1915, movies with _____ _____ usually had soundtracks. The American film *The Birth of a Nation*, for example, included three music types. It used classical music, melodies from popular songs, and original music. By original music, I mean, music that was created just for this film.

But, soon, the silent film era ended when sound-recording technology was introduced. This technology _____ _____ _____ _____ _____ the sounds of actors' voices, sound effects, and music. Then, in a studio, these sound recordings _____ _____ _____ the film. Audiences thought this combination gave a more realistic movie experience. Therefore, the silent film _____ _____.

iBT Listening Test 1

Answer Book p. 40

TOEFL Listening

Note-taking

Student's Problem

Trying to _____ a report, but keeps getting an _____ _____

Librarian's Solution

- Apply for a _____ _____ to use the printers
- Pay for the printing _____ at the end of each _____
- Put the card on the _____, and enter your student ID number

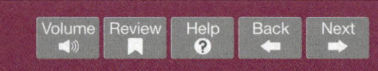

1 What is the student's problem?

   Ⓐ He cannot access the Internet from his laptop.
   Ⓑ He was not able to log in to a library website.
   Ⓒ He cannot find a book for a school assignment.
   Ⓓ He was not able to print a document.

2 According to the librarian, why was a policy changed?

   Ⓐ To improve the security of a building
   Ⓑ To save some money
   Ⓒ To upgrade a computer system
   Ⓓ To answer students' complaints

3 How does the student emphasize his point about the school's unfair decision?

   Ⓐ By giving the opinions of his friends
   Ⓑ By comparing with other universities
   Ⓒ By asking for an explanation of the school's policy
   Ⓓ By mentioning the importance of a document

4 In the conversation, the librarian gives several instructions for using a printer in the library. Indicate whether each of the following is one of those instructions or not.

   Click in the correct box for each phrase.

	Yes	No
Ⓐ Fill out an application form		
Ⓑ Pay for a card in advance		
Ⓒ Use a card scanner		
Ⓓ Enter a student ID number		

Dictation

Answer Book p. 40

Listen again and fill in the blanks.

M: Excuse me. I'm trying to _____ _____ _____, but I keep getting an error message on the computer.

W: Um, did you make a printer card? From last week, students _____ _____ _____ _____ _____ _____, and you have to apply for a printer card to use the printers. The school wants us to _____ _____, so we _____ _____ _____.

M: Really? That doesn't seem like _____ _____ _____. I mean, all of my friends' universities don't make students _____ _____ _____.

W: I understand, but there's nothing I can do. Uh, if you want to _____ _____ _____ _____, I have the form right here.

M: I guess I don't _____ _____ _____... Um, do I need to _____ _____ _____ _____ _____?

W: No. You should _____ _____ _____ _____ _____ at the end of each month. We'll send a text message about it.

M: Got it. Uh, so how do I _____ _____ _____?

W: Just _____ _____ _____ _____ the scanner next to the computer and enter your student ID number on its screen. After that, you'll be able to _____ _____ _____.

M: I see... Thanks for explaining everything.

iBT Listening Test 2

TOEFL Listening

Note-taking

Five Stages of Grief

1. You _____ reality.
2. The _____ comes out and you feel _____.
3. You feel helpless and try to _____ with yourself or with _____.
4. You realize reality and experience _____.
5. You _____ reality.

1. What is the lecture mainly about?
   - Ⓐ The different ways of expressing feelings
   - Ⓑ The process of feeling grief
   - Ⓒ What factors affect emotions
   - Ⓓ How to avoid depression

2. How does the professor organize the lecture?
   - Ⓐ By reading his research paper
   - Ⓑ By telling a personal experience
   - Ⓒ By asking the students to imagine a situation
   - Ⓓ By describing the results of an experiment

3. According to the professor, what can a therapist help people to do?
   - Ⓐ Overcome feelings of depression
   - Ⓑ Understand the meaning of life
   - Ⓒ Listen to other people
   - Ⓓ Express anger properly

4. In the lecture, the professor describes some steps that people go through when they feel deep sadness. Put the steps listed below in the correct order.

   Drag each answer choice to the space where it belongs.

Step 1	
Step 2	
Step 3	
Step 4	
Step 5	

   - Ⓐ People accept the reality of a situation.
   - Ⓑ People try to bargain with themselves or God.
   - Ⓒ People deny sad news.
   - Ⓓ People get angry because of deep pain.
   - Ⓔ People experience depression.

Dictation

Answer Book p. 41

Listen again and fill in the blanks.

P: Have you ever _____ _____ _____? You probably felt very sad. But did you have some other feelings _____ _____ _____ _____? Today, I'd like to talk about the five stages of grief. The five stages of grief are _____ _____ _____ _____ _____ when they experience _____ _____. In 1969, psychiatrist Elisabeth Kübler-Ross _____ _____ _____ in her book, *On Death and Dying*. Um, let's _____ _____ _____ through an example...

So let's say that you've learned that you are dying. Of course, the news will _____ _____. In response, you may _____ _____ _____ that it's true. This gives you time to _____ _____ _____ _____ _____ you're feeling. That's the first stage.

When you can _____ _____ _____ the possibility of death, the pain you've been hiding _____ _____. And this causes you to feel angry. Like the first stage, anger is another way to _____ _____ _____ _____ directly.

Once you've _____ _____ _____, you start to _____ _____. This is when bargaining begins. When you bargain, you try to _____ _____ _____ _____ _____ with yourself or with God. You may say things like, "If I _____ _____ _____ _____, then maybe God will _____ _____ _____." Of course, that's impossible.

Then, you will _____ _____ when you realize that you _____ _____ _____. You will, um, _____ _____ _____ _____ _____ clearly and _____ _____ _____ _____ _____. It may be useful to _____ _____ _____

_____ at this stage.

Finally, the last stage is _____ _____. Uh, this doesn't mean you are happy... It just means that you _____ _____ _____ and _____ _____ _____ _____ to continue living.

Vocabulary Review

Answer Book p. 42

A. Choose the correct word for each meaning.

| deny | folklore | defeat | distinct |

1 to refuse to accept that something is real or true: _____

2 clearly different from others: _____

3 to cause someone or something to lose, especially in a fight or a war: _____

4 traditional cultures and stories of a certain community: _____

B. Fill in the blanks with the appropriate words or phrases from the box.

| necessary | audience | attend | deal with | policy |

5 The library announced a new _____ about borrowing rare books.

6 More than eight students _____ a drawing class on Thursdays.

7 It is _____ to study every day to get good grades.

8 The school hired a plumber to _____ a problem with the pipes.

9 The _____ was excited to watch the new movie.

C. Choose the closest meaning for each highlighted word or phrase.

10 The color purple is a combination of red and blue.
   (A) mixture   (B) bundle   (C) layer   (D) concept

11 The school organized a special lecture about how to become a reporter.
   (A) overcame   (B) bargained   (C) prepared   (D) released

12 He went through a difficult time after he moved to a new city.
   (A) matched   (B) affected   (C) raised   (D) experienced

13 The sun gradually set during our late afternoon soccer game.
   (A) strongly   (B) slowly   (C) rarely   (D) currently

14 The music festival will be held on May 25th in Thompson Square.
   (A) covered   (B) entered   (C) reviewed   (D) opened

HACKERS APEX LISTENING
for the TOEFL iBT
Basic

CHAPTER 07

Inference

Inference

About the Question Type

Inference questions ask you to infer the correct answer by using information that is implied, or not stated directly, in the conversation or lecture.

These questions require you to draw a conclusion based on a comprehensive understanding of the overall context and by connecting information mentioned in the conversation or lecture. Sometimes, questions may be about a speaker, an idea, or what a speaker will do next.

Question Format

- What can be inferred about ~?
- What does the professor imply about ~?
- What will the man/woman probably do next?

Key Strategies

- **Step 1** — Understand the overall context of the talk, and determine whether the question is about a speaker, an idea, or what a speaker will do next.
- **Step 2** — If the question is about a speaker or an idea, find information that is connected to the speaker or idea. If the question is about what a speaker will do next, listen to the statements that a speaker makes near the end of the conversation or lecture.
- **Step 3** — Select the answer choice that is best supported by information in the conversation or lecture.

Example

Answer Book p. 42

A. Listen to a conversation between a student and a faculty advisor for the university newspaper.

C7_ExA

Note-taking

Student's Request

Noticed a small _____ in an article in the school _____

Advisor's Response

• Will write an _____ notice and publish it
• A _____ will be in next month's _____.

What will the man probably do next?

(A) Review next month's article
(B) Write a letter to the editor
(C) Change an appointment date
(D) Prepare a note of apology

Answer Book p. 42

B. Listen to part of a lecture in a linguistics class.

C7_ExB

Note-taking

Spanish in Spain and _____

• The same _____ is pronounced with a _____ sound.
  e.g. Barcelona
• Different words are used to refer to the same _____.
  e.g. Potato, computer

What can be inferred about Spanish?

(A) Spanish has changed over time because of global influences.
(B) Spanish in Mexico has the most variation.
(C) Spanish is spoken differently in Spain and in Mexico.
(D) Spanish is difficult because of its different sounds.

Dictation

Answer Book p. 43

Listen again and fill in the blanks.

A.

W: Hello, I'd like to talk to you about an article. It was in this month's issue of _____ _____ _____.

M: All right... Which article did you _____ _____ _____?

W: Well, it's the one on page six. It's about the school's history. I _____ _____ _____ _____ in one of the facts.

M: Really? Let me see that...

W: It's _____ _____ in paragraph three. It says that the school building was built on June 10, 1971, but, um, _____ _____ _____ is June 20, 1971.

M: Oh, you're right! Thank you for _____ _____ _____.

W: Um, I just thought _____ _____ _____.

M: Absolutely. I'll _____ _____ _____ _____ _____ and make sure it gets published. There will also be a correction in next month's issue. I'll let you know when it _____ _____.

B.

P: So _____ _____ _____ _____ is variation. This, um, means that the same language can be spoken differently. It depends on where it is used... Let me give you some examples with Spanish. In Spain, words _____ _____ a c before an i or an e, like *Barcelona*, _____ _____ _____ a th sound, as in *Bar-thelona*. However, in Mexico, the same letter is pronounced with an s sound, as in *Bar-selona*. Um, you'll also notice that different words may be used to _____ _____ _____ _____. For instance, a potato is *patata* in Spain, but *papa* in Mexico. Or, a computer is *ordenador* in Spain, but *computadora* in Mexico. Um, you might think this _____ _____. However, Spanish speakers _____ _____ _____ just fine.

Listening Practice 1

Answer Book p. 44

Listen to a conversation between a student and a librarian.

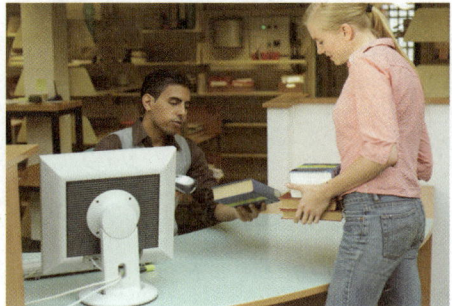

Note-taking

Student's Request
Would like to _____ the books again

Librarian's Response
- Can't borrow a book another student has _____
- Use the copy that the library _____

1 What are the speakers mainly discussing?

(A) Using a library's computer system
(B) Paying a fee for late books
(C) Borrowing books for a longer time
(D) Replacing a student library card

2 Why does the librarian tell the student about a staff meeting?

(A) To explain why a policy was changed
(B) To mention that the library is closing
(C) To ask the student to return later
(D) To tell the student that the staff is busy

3 What will the student probably do next?

(A) Ask a professor to move a deadline
(B) Fill out a request form
(C) Visit another school's library
(D) Find a copy of a book

Dictation

Answer Book p. 44

Listen again and fill in the blanks.

W: Hi. I, uh, borrowed these books for a school project. _____ _____ _____ is today, but I'd like to _____ _____ _____ for two weeks.

M: You can borrow these two, but you'll _____ _____ _____ the other one.

W: Oh? That's strange. I've done this before. Why can't I _____ _____ _____ for all of them?

M: The library staff had a meeting, and we, uh, decided to _____ _____ _____. It _____ _____ _____ _____ to extend the due dates for all books. Now, you can't borrow a book that _____ _____ _____ _____.

W: I see... But I really need all three books to _____ _____ _____. Don't you have other copies _____ _____ _____ _____? My project is _____ _____ _____ _____.

M: Well, according to my computer, all of the copies are not here right now... You can use the copy that _____ _____ _____, but you'll have to use it here.

W: OK... I'll _____ _____ _____ _____ now.

Listening Practice 2

Listen to part of a lecture in a biology class.

Note-taking

Pupils of _____

- Vertical pupils: Help measure the _____ to prey
- _____ pupils e.g. Tigers, eagles

Pupils of Prey

_____ pupils: Give a very _____ view

---

1 What does the professor mainly discuss?

(A) Factors that help predators catch prey
(B) The reasons some animals can see at night
(C) Differences in the pupils of predators and prey
(D) The development of eye pupils in animals

2 What type of pupils do these animals have? Indicate the pupil type for each animal. *Click in the correct box for each phrase.*

	Vertical pupils	Round pupils	Horizontal pupils
(A) Crocodile			
(B) Tiger			
(C) Eagle			
(D) Sheep			

3 What does the professor imply about prey animals that are eating grass?

(A) They are easily killed by predators.
(B) They can eat and find predators at the same time.
(C) They eat more during the day than at night.
(D) They can avoid predators by looking down.

Dictation

Listen again and fill in the blanks.

P: All right. So we know that meat-eaters like lions, bears, and sharks are predators. And we know that deer, rabbits, and other grass-eaters are prey. But _____ _____ _____ isn't the only thing that determines this. Eye pupils, uh, you know, the round, black holes _____ _____ _____ of your eyes... are also related to whether an animal is _____ _____ _____ _____.

Let's consider the eyes of certain predators, like crocodiles or cats. They have vertical pupils. Their pupils are long and narrow. This is because it helps them accurately _____ _____ _____ to their prey. If they know _____ _____ _____ their prey is, they'll know the distance to jump. One interesting thing about vertical pupils, though, is that they _____ _____ _____ _____ _____ that, um, hunt very close to the ground. Other types of predators that are quite large, like tigers, or predators that _____ _____ _____, like eagles, typically have round pupils just like people.

Now, for grass-eaters... Think about what is important for them to survive. They must be able to _____ _____, right? So, they need to see around themselves _____ _____ _____ _____. A horizontal-shaped pupil _____ _____ _____ _____ from many directions. This gives those animals a very wide view. Then, they can see predators that _____ _____ from many different angles. Also, they can roll their eyes to _____ _____ _____ _____.

So a sheep, for example, has to lower its head when it eats. But it can roll its eyes to get a full view of _____ _____. This way, it knows that it's safe while it eats.

Listening Practice 3

Answer Book p. 45

Listen to a conversation between a student and a university employee at the registrar's office.

Note-taking

Student's Question
How can I get a new _____ _____ ?

Employee's Answer
• Fill out the _____ _____ and pay the $20 _____
• Make a _____ card

1. Why does the student visit the registrar's office?
   (A) To return another student's ID card
   (B) To replace a lost ID card
   (C) To make a payment for a class
   (D) To ask about late fees for a course

2. Indicate whether each of the following is mentioned about student ID cards. *Click in the correct box for each phrase.*

	Yes	No
(A) New cards cost $20 to make.		
(B) Temporary cards are free.		
(C) New cards take four weeks to make.		
(D) Temporary ones can be used for three months.		

3. What can be inferred about the student?
   (A) She is willing to pay for a charge.
   (B) She remembered where a missing item is.
   (C) She threw away an important document.
   (D) She has to request another card.

Dictation

Answer Book p. 45

Listen again and fill in the blanks.

W: Excuse me, I have a question... I _____ _____ _____ _____ _____. Could you tell me how to _____ _____ _____ _____?

M: Yes, of course. Just _____ _____ _____ _____ _____, and pay the $20 fee.

W: Oh, uh, I _____ _____ _____ _____ right now... But I could bring some later this week.

M: That's OK. Then, I can make a _____ _____ for you. It's free. It _____ _____ _____ to _____ _____ _____, so you'll need it anyway.

W: All right. So, um, _____ _____ _____ the temporary card?

M: You can use it _____ _____ _____. If you still don't have a new ID card by then, _____ _____ _____ _____ another temporary one.

W: OK... But, uh, what happens if I find my old ID card?

M: Well, you can use your old ID card if you don't have a new one yet. Otherwise, you'll have to _____ _____ _____.

W: I see. Thanks for your help... _____ _____ _____ with the $20.

Listening Practice 4

Answer Book p. 46

Listen to part of a lecture in a history class.

Note-taking

Propylaea and Its Three Parts

Propylaea: Entrance to the _____
- Central Room: Provided the main _____ to the Acropolis
- Eastern Room: Had beautiful _____
- Western Room: Contained _____ of Greek battles

1. What is the main topic of the lecture?
   (A) The religions of Ancient Greece
   (B) A historical site in Greece
   (C) The history of the Acropolis
   (D) An ancient construction method

2. Why does the professor mention Pausanias?
   (A) To identify the designer of a famous room
   (B) To emphasize the beauty of a room
   (C) To show that artworks had religious meanings
   (D) To introduce one of Greece's great military leaders

3. What does the professor imply about the original construction of the Propylaea?
   (A) It was designed by the military.
   (B) It was built very quickly.
   (C) It was finished after the war.
   (D) It was never completed.

Dictation

Answer Book p. 46

Listen again and fill in the blanks.

P: All right. So we've been learning about ancient Greece, and last time we discussed the Acropolis. Uh, if you remember, the Acropolis is _____ _____ _____ _____ _____ _____ above the city of Athens. It has _____ _____ _____, and Propylaea is one of them. This sounds difficult, but in Greek, it means "before the gates." So, the Propylaea is basically _____ _____ _____ the Acropolis. Construction of the Propylaea began in 435 BC. The structure was built to honor the goddess Athena. It was composed of three parts. First, it had a central room. This provided _____ _____ _____ _____ the Acropolis. Here, the room _____ _____ _____ _____ marble. Interestingly, however, the ground was not paved. It was just natural ground. This probably had some religious reason...

There were also eastern and western rooms. The eastern room _____ _____ _____ _____ its ceiling. It was painted blue with gold stars, so it must have been very beautiful... like the night sky! A Greek writer called Pausanias once said nothing _____ _____ _____ _____ _____ _____. And this was 600 years after the construction of the room. The western room was also impressive. It contained paintings of _____ _____ _____. This showed Greece's military strength. So, uh, the Propylaea had _____ _____ _____ _____ _____.

Anyway, before its construction was completed, _____ _____ _____ Athens and Sparta began. Afterward, people tried to _____ _____ _____. However, to this day, no one is sure what it was supposed to _____ _____. We'll talk about this war next time...

iBT Listening Test 1

Answer Book p. 47

TOEFL Listening

Note-taking

Student's Problem

Having some _____ with the lessons

Professor's Response

- Find _____ _____ on biology or read the _____ mentioned in class
- Don't worry too much about your _____

CHAPTER 07 | Inference 145

1 What are the speakers mainly discussing?
- Ⓐ Requirements for a class project
- Ⓑ Moving to an easier class
- Ⓒ Ways to understand a class better
- Ⓓ Why the student received a bad grade

2 How does the professor help the student?
- Ⓐ By recommending sources of information
- Ⓑ By introducing a tutoring program
- Ⓒ By providing a detailed lesson plan
- Ⓓ By reviewing a concept discussed in class

3 Why does the professor mention articles?
- Ⓐ To show her knowledge of a subject
- Ⓑ To remind the student of an assignment
- Ⓒ To suggest some materials for reading
- Ⓓ To correct a statement the student made

4 What can be inferred about the professor?
- Ⓐ She is currently teaching another course.
- Ⓑ She has written some research articles.
- Ⓒ She posted some online lecture videos.
- Ⓓ She is opening more courses next semester.

Dictation

Answer Book p. 47

Listen again and fill in the blanks.

S: Excuse me, Professor Bennett? _____ _____ _____ a biology class before, so, uh, I'm _____ _____ _____ _____ your lessons. Everyone else seems to be doing fine _____ _____. So I'm, uh, _____ _____ _____ _____...

P: Hi, Lawrence. I'm sorry to hear that you're _____ _____...

S: Thank you, but the thing is... I don't want to _____ _____ _____ _____. So I was wondering if you had any advice.

P: Hmm... You could _____ _____ _____ on biology or _____ _____ _____ I mentioned in class.

S: I'll _____ _____ _____ some videos. Are there _____ _____ _____ you'd recommend?

P: Sure. I can _____ _____ _____ to some videos. They _____ _____ _____ we discuss in class.

S: That would be great, Professor Bennett.

P: Of course. And _____ _____ _____ _____ about your grade. I have another student like you in my other course. She's _____ _____, so I'm sure you'll also do well.

S: _____ _____ _____ _____, Professor.

iBT Listening Test 2

TOEFL Listening

Note-taking

Bolshoi
- Tries to make a big _____
- _____ movements on the stage

Mariinsky
- _____ and artistic
- Known as _____ ballets
- Performed in front of the _____ _____

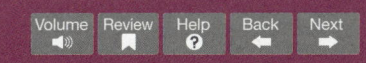

1. What is the main topic of the lecture?
   - Ⓐ The early history of Russian ballet
   - Ⓑ The development of Russian dance styles
   - Ⓒ The differences between two ballet companies
   - Ⓓ The importance of the ballet *Swan Lake* in Russia

2. According to the professor, what made Mariinsky more upper class than Bolshoi?
   - Ⓐ It was started by a rich person.
   - Ⓑ It is much older than Bolshoi.
   - Ⓒ It spent a lot of money to produce ballets.
   - Ⓓ It originally gave performances for royalty.

3. Indicate whether each of the following is related to Bolshoi dancers or Mariinsky dancers.

   Click in the correct box for each phrase.

	Bolshoi dancers	Mariinsky dancers
Ⓐ They have elegant and graceful movements.		
Ⓑ They use strong and bold movements.		
Ⓒ They show a lot of emotion.		
Ⓓ They usually wear traditional ballet costumes.		

4. What can be inferred about Mariinsky's version of *Swan Lake*?
   - Ⓐ It has a happy ending.
   - Ⓑ It includes a good magician.
   - Ⓒ It was based on Russian history.
   - Ⓓ It changed over time.

Dictation

Answer Book p. 48

Listen again and fill in the blanks.

P: Has anyone heard of Bolshoi or Mariinksy? They are famous Russian ballet companies. Both have _____ _____ _____ and _____ _____ _____ _____. In fact, they are often _____ _____ _____ _____ because they have contrasting styles. So what are _____ _____ _____ _____?
Well, in Russian, Bolshoi means "big." And Bolshoi tries to _____ _____ _____ _____. The dancers are strong and athletic, so they _____ _____ _____ on the stage. The performances are also very _____ _____ _____. So the audience can easily _____ _____ _____ of the characters.
In contrast, Mariinsky is _____ _____ _____. Its ballets are known as classical ballet. The dancers _____ _____ _____ _____. And, um, their movements are graceful and beautiful. Also, Mariinsky _____ _____ _____ _____ the Imperial Russian Ballet. This is because its ballets were performed _____ _____ _____ _____ _____ _____. So, Mariinsky is more "upper class" than Bolshoi in that way.
Now, the two companies don't just have different styles. They also perform the same ballet _____ _____ _____. Let's use *Swan Lake* _____ _____ _____. As you all know, *Swan Lake* is a story about a princess and a prince. Princess Odette _____ _____ _____ _____ _____ _____ an evil magician. She _____ _____ _____ _____ _____ the love of the prince, Siegfried. Well, in the Bolshoi version, _____ _____ _____ _____. The evil magician creates a bad storm. The storm keeps Odette and Siegfried _____ _____ _____ _____.

They _____ _____, and Odette dies. But in the Mariinsky performance, Siegfried _____ _____ _____ the evil magician. Then, he and Odette _____ _____ _____.

Vocabulary Review

Answer Book p. 49

A. Choose the correct word for each meaning.

temporary	entrance	approach	compare

1 to come closer to someone or something: _____
2 a door or a gate used to go inside a place: _____
3 used for a short period of time: _____
4 to check how things are different and similar: _____

B. Fill in the blanks with the appropriate words or phrases from the box.

requests	encouragement	refers to	surroundings	extends

5 The book's title _____ a popular song from the 1980s.
6 Tom _____ help with his homework when he is confused.
7 Jessica is from the city, so the country _____ feel strange to her.
8 Mr. Kim usually _____ the due date for class projects if students ask.
9 _____ from family and friends can make you feel better about a test.

C. Choose the closest meaning for each highlighted word or phrase.

10 I'm trying to determine where I should put the poster in my room.
   (A) borrow   (B) decide   (C) chase   (D) spell

11 The actress wore an elegant dress to the awards show.
   (A) emotional   (B) vertical   (C) political   (D) graceful

12 The fee for renting a snowboard is higher than I expected.
   (A) fact   (B) variation   (C) angle   (D) price

13 The scientists were able to detect a planet in another solar system.
   (A) measure   (B) discover   (C) honor   (D) send

14 The librarian will search for the old books in the university library.
   (A) look for   (B) come out   (C) apply for   (D) throw away

HACKERS APEX LISTENING
for the TOEFL iBT
Basic

Actual Test

Actual Test 1

Actual Test 2

Actual Test 1

TOEFL Listening
PART 1. Passage 1

Answer Book p. 49

Note-taking

Student's Request

Not sure I can interview all _____ people
→ Can I interview _____ people instead?

Professor's Answer

Will change the _____ to interviewing only two people
→ Will _____ the change to the class

Questions 1-5 of 11

1. What problem does the student have?
   - Ⓐ He has no time to finish an assignment.
   - Ⓑ He has difficulty with a homework requirement.
   - Ⓒ He cannot understand some class material.
   - Ⓓ He does not like the report topic he chose.

2. Why is the student unable to do an interview?
   - Ⓐ A company did not allow it to happen.
   - Ⓑ He is too busy with other assignments.
   - Ⓒ He cannot meet a person who is overseas.
   - Ⓓ An interview date has to be moved.

3. Why does the student mention people's jobs?
   - Ⓐ To explain why he cannot find people to interview
   - Ⓑ To show his interest in a specific career
   - Ⓒ To ask for permission to interview another person
   - Ⓓ To suggest that he has done his research

4. What can be inferred about the professor?
   - Ⓐ She will give the student more time.
   - Ⓑ She wants the student to send an e-mail.
   - Ⓒ She teaches in the Business Department.
   - Ⓓ She will announce a change through e-mail.

Listen again to part of the conversation. Then answer the question.

5. Why does the professor say this:
   - Ⓐ To emphasize that a requirement will stay the same
   - Ⓑ To encourage the student to study harder
   - Ⓒ To explain the reason for the length of a report
   - Ⓓ To agree with the student's request for a change

TOEFL Listening
PART 1. Passage 2

Note-taking

Emily Brontë
- Poet and _____ in England in the 19th century
- Wrote with the _____ Ellis Bell
- Wrote *Wuthering Heights*, which expressed _____ that were not popular at the time

J. K. Rowling
- Her _____ _____ is Joanne Rowling.
- Became incredibly _____

Questions 6-11 of 11

6. What is the lecture mainly about?
   - Ⓐ Traditional roles of women in history
   - Ⓑ How female characters appear in novels
   - Ⓒ Modern books written by women
   - Ⓓ Why female writers used fake names

7. According to the professor, what were women expected to do in 19th-century England?
   - Ⓐ Write poems
   - Ⓑ Stay at home
   - Ⓒ Teach at schools
   - Ⓓ Have many children

8. According to the professor, why did Brontë use the name Ellis Bell?
   - Ⓐ To hide her gender
   - Ⓑ To copy another author
   - Ⓒ To get more attention
   - Ⓓ To criticize male writers

9. What is the professor's opinion of *Wuthering Heights*?
   - Ⓐ It was very modern for its time.
   - Ⓑ It has characters that are very realistic.
   - Ⓒ It has themes that are still shocking today.
   - Ⓓ It is the best novel written by a woman.

10. Why does the professor use J. K. Rowling as an example?
    - Ⓐ To compare modern writing with traditional writing
    - Ⓑ To explain how women writers have improved
    - Ⓒ To tell the students about one of her favorite writers
    - Ⓓ To show how long gender has been an issue for writers

Listen again to part of the lecture. Then answer the question.

11. Why does the professor say this:
    - Ⓐ To encourage the students to do research on J. K. Rowling
    - Ⓑ To emphasize J. K. Rowling's accomplishment
    - Ⓒ To recommend a book by J. K. Rowling
    - Ⓓ To indicate she knows a lot about J. K. Rowling

TOEFL Listening
PART 2. Passage 1

Note-taking

Student's Question
What are the results of _____ _____ _____ for the student reporter position?

Editor's Answer
- Decided to _____ you as a reporter
- Details about the _____:
  - Starts on Monday with an _____ at 4 p.m.
  - Will meet the team and Allison, the _____ of the team

Questions 1-5 of 17

1. Why does the man go to see the woman?
   - Ⓐ To discuss errors in an article
   - Ⓑ To learn about a position
   - Ⓒ To ask about a meeting
   - Ⓓ To interview an employee

2. What impressed the woman about the man?
   - Ⓐ His friendly attitude
   - Ⓑ His previous experience
   - Ⓒ His work examples
   - Ⓓ His knowledge of school

3. How does the woman explain some job details?
   - Ⓐ By providing a document
   - Ⓑ By preparing a list of assignments
   - Ⓒ By describing the first day of work
   - Ⓓ By explaining how to write an article

4. What will the man probably do next?
   - Ⓐ Buy a camera
   - Ⓑ Write another article
   - Ⓒ Take a photograph
   - Ⓓ Look at a website

Listen again to part of the conversation. Then answer the question.

5. Why does the woman say this:
   - Ⓐ To thank the man for a suggestion
   - Ⓑ To say that an article was enjoyable
   - Ⓒ To agree with the man's ideas
   - Ⓓ To explain why the man was chosen

TOEFL Listening
PART 2. Passage 2

ANTHROPOLOGY

Note-taking

Mesopotamia
- Civilization that first began
- Developed the first _____ _____ called pictographs

Egypt
Used copper for making _____ and _____
→ Big _____ compared to the stone tools

Indus
- _____ than the two other civilizations
- First civilization to make an accurate _____ _____

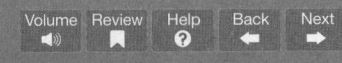

6. What is the main topic of the lecture?
   - Ⓐ The invention of ancient transportation
   - Ⓑ Development of the earliest civilizations
   - Ⓒ Agriculture of the ancient civilizations
   - Ⓓ The origin of a written language

7. According to the professor, what do the earliest civilizations have in common?
   - Ⓐ They had small populations.
   - Ⓑ They grew the same crops.
   - Ⓒ They started close to rivers.
   - Ⓓ They lasted only a short time.

8. What does the professor indicate about pictographs in Mesopotamia?
   - Ⓐ They were taught only to royalty.
   - Ⓑ They were only useful for simple sentences.
   - Ⓒ They were not used after 100 BC.
   - Ⓓ They were adopted by other cultures.

9. How does the professor explain the Indus civilization?
   - Ⓐ By comparing it to a later civilization
   - Ⓑ By describing how it originated
   - Ⓒ By introducing its two major features
   - Ⓓ By discussing its relationship to other societies

Listen again to part of the lecture. Then answer the question.

10. Why does the professor say this:
    - Ⓐ To point out that the Great Pyramid was never finished
    - Ⓑ To highlight that building the pyramids was hard work
    - Ⓒ To suggest that he wants to end the lecture soon
    - Ⓓ To show that ancient stone workers were highly skilled

11. In the lecture, the professor mentions features of three ancient civilizations. Indicate whether each of the following is a characteristic of Mesopotamia, Egypt, or Indus.

    Click in the correct box for each phrase.

	Mesopotamia	Egypt	Indus
Ⓐ Was ruled by a religious king			
Ⓑ Developed an accurate measuring system			
Ⓒ Used advanced tools and weapons			
Ⓓ Invented the first written language			

TOEFL Listening
PART 2. Passage 3

PHYSIOLOGY

Note-taking

Types and Causes of _____

- Types
  - _____ _____ : Blind to all colors
  - Red-and-green colorblindness: Cannot easily see the colors _____ and _____

- Causes
  - _____
  - Diseases or injuries that _____ eyes or brain e.g. Diabetes

Questions 12-17 of 17

12. What is the main topic of the lecture?
    - Ⓐ Difficulties of living with colorblindness
    - Ⓑ Diseases that cause colorblindness
    - Ⓒ Types and causes of colorblindness
    - Ⓓ Ways to overcome colorblindness

13. What does the professor say about complete colorblindness?
    - Ⓐ It results from disease.
    - Ⓑ It is extremely rare.
    - Ⓒ It is caused by one missing cone.
    - Ⓓ It occurs in older people.

14. How does the professor explain red-and-green colorblindness?
    - Ⓐ By emphasizing how unique it is
    - Ⓑ By comparing it with another condition
    - Ⓒ By giving a familiar example
    - Ⓓ By showing pictures of various colors

15. What can be inferred about colorblindness?
    - Ⓐ It affects men more than women.
    - Ⓑ It can occur at birth or later in life.
    - Ⓒ It can become worse over time.
    - Ⓓ It may lead to complete blindness.

16. Why does the professor mention diabetes?
    - Ⓐ To give a possible cause of colorblindness
    - Ⓑ To provide an example of a genetic disease
    - Ⓒ To explain how many people have colorblindness
    - Ⓓ To indicate how serious the disease can be

Listen again to part of the lecture. Then answer the question.

17. What does the professor mean when he says this:
    - Ⓐ None of the students in the class are colorblind.
    - Ⓑ Most people are unaware that they know colorblind people.
    - Ⓒ Colorblindness is rarer than most people think.
    - Ⓓ Even people with normal vision do not see colors the same way.

Actual Test 2

TOEFL Listening
PART 1. Passage 1

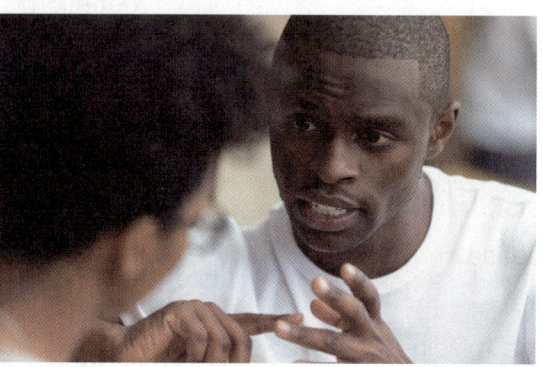

Note-taking

Student's Question

Is the student lounge going to be open during the _____ _____?

→ Could we _____ _____ it to stay open?

Employee's Suggestion

- Use the library
  → Too _____ to keep the lounge open
- Study in the _____ common areas

Questions 1-5 of 11

1. What is the conversation mainly about?
   - Ⓐ Opening hours of the student lounge
   - Ⓑ Available school facilities during a vacation
   - Ⓒ Where to find the entrance to a school building
   - Ⓓ How to reserve a room during the winter break

2. According to the employee, why are there fewer students during winter?
   - Ⓐ There are not enough dorm rooms.
   - Ⓑ The winter programs are not interesting.
   - Ⓒ The students go home to be with family.
   - Ⓓ There are fewer professors on campus.

3. What can be inferred about the dormitory common areas?
   - Ⓐ They have places to eat.
   - Ⓑ They must be used quietly.
   - Ⓒ They are for students who live in the dorms.
   - Ⓓ They must be reserved in advance.

4. In the conversation, several options for the student are discussed. Indicate whether each of the following is an option the student will consider.

   Click in the correct box for each phrase.

	Yes	No
Ⓐ Using the library		
Ⓑ Studying in a dorm room		
Ⓒ Using a classroom		
Ⓓ Trying the cafeteria		

   Listen again to part of the conversation. Then answer the question.

5. What does the employee mean when she says this: 🎧
   - Ⓐ The student has to pay a fee.
   - Ⓑ The university refused a request.
   - Ⓒ The lounge will be closed.
   - Ⓓ The library will be repaired.

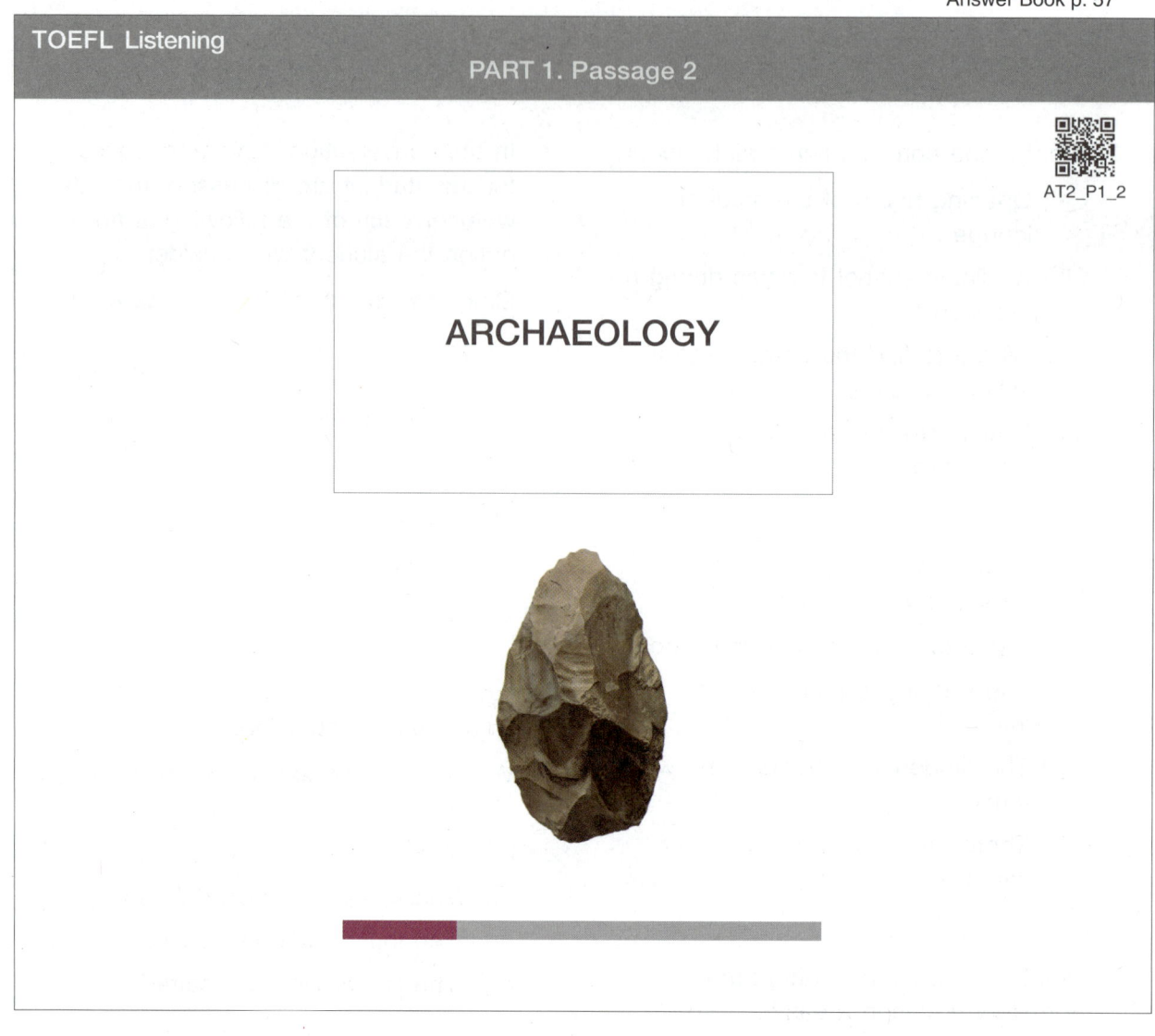

Note-taking

Old Stone Age

- Lasted for _____ of years
- _____ _____ : Most significant invention

_____ **Stone Age**

- Made _____ of tools smoother to cut through _____ _____ easily
- _____ and spearheads → Could kill animals from far away

New Stone Age

- A wider variety of _____
- Improved tools such as a _____ hand axe and _____ farming tools
  → Led to the development of permanent _____ _____

Questions 6-11 of 11

6. What is the main topic of the lecture?
   - (A) The origin of agricultural societies
   - (B) The use of weapons by early humans
   - (C) The development of ancient tools
   - (D) The first human settlements

7. What does the professor say about the first stone tools?
   - (A) Some of them were quite complicated.
   - (B) The exact date of their invention is unknown.
   - (C) They were not developed until around 10,000 BC.
   - (D) Most of them were used for protection.

8. Why does the professor mention the hand axe?
   - (A) To explain the first tool used by ancient humans
   - (B) To introduce an important invention of the Old Stone Age
   - (C) To demonstrate a common tool made from bones
   - (D) To highlight the lack of skill in the Old Stone Age

9. What was a result of the smoother surfaces of tools in the Middle Stone Age?
   - (A) Making smaller tools became possible.
   - (B) The tools became easier to hold.
   - (C) Cutting through animal skin became easier.
   - (D) The stone hammers were no longer useful.

10. What does the professor imply about arrows and spearheads?
    - (A) They were not effective to hunt large animals.
    - (B) They allowed one person to hunt alone.
    - (C) They made hunting less dangerous.
    - (D) They were easily broken.

11. What is the professor's attitude toward tools in the New Stone Age?
    - (A) She is sure they led to permanent farming communities.
    - (B) She thinks they were similar to tools of the Old Stone Age.
    - (C) She is confident they were made less than 2,000 years ago.
    - (D) She believes they were not useful for cutting trees.

TOEFL Listening

PART 2. Passage 1

Note-taking

Things to Include in the Application
- A copy of the _____ _____
- A letter of _____
- A statement of purpose: An essay that describes _____ and _____ in school
- An _____ _____ about an internship

Questions 1-5 of 17

1. What is the main topic of the conversation?
   - (A) Internship programs for the summer
   - (B) How to apply for graduate school
   - (C) Study tips for getting a better grade
   - (D) How to get official documents from a school

2. What does the student need to write about?
   - (A) Her work experiences
   - (B) Her career plans after graduation
   - (C) Her career goals
   - (D) Her passions and achievements

3. Why does the student mention a government facility?
   - (A) To tell the professor where she is going
   - (B) To indicate where she worked in the past
   - (C) To ask about the location of an office
   - (D) To show her job interests

4. Indicate whether each of the following is mentioned as something the student should do.

   Click in the correct box for each phrase.

	Yes	No
(A) Get an academic record		
(B) Request a letter of recommendation		
(C) Write a statement of purpose		
(D) Include an official document from an internship		

   Listen again to part of the conversation. Then answer the question.

5. What does the professor mean when he says this:
   - (A) He thinks the student can be organized.
   - (B) He is sure the student will find a good friend.
   - (C) He believes the student will become a good professor.
   - (D) He is confident that the student will pass a test.

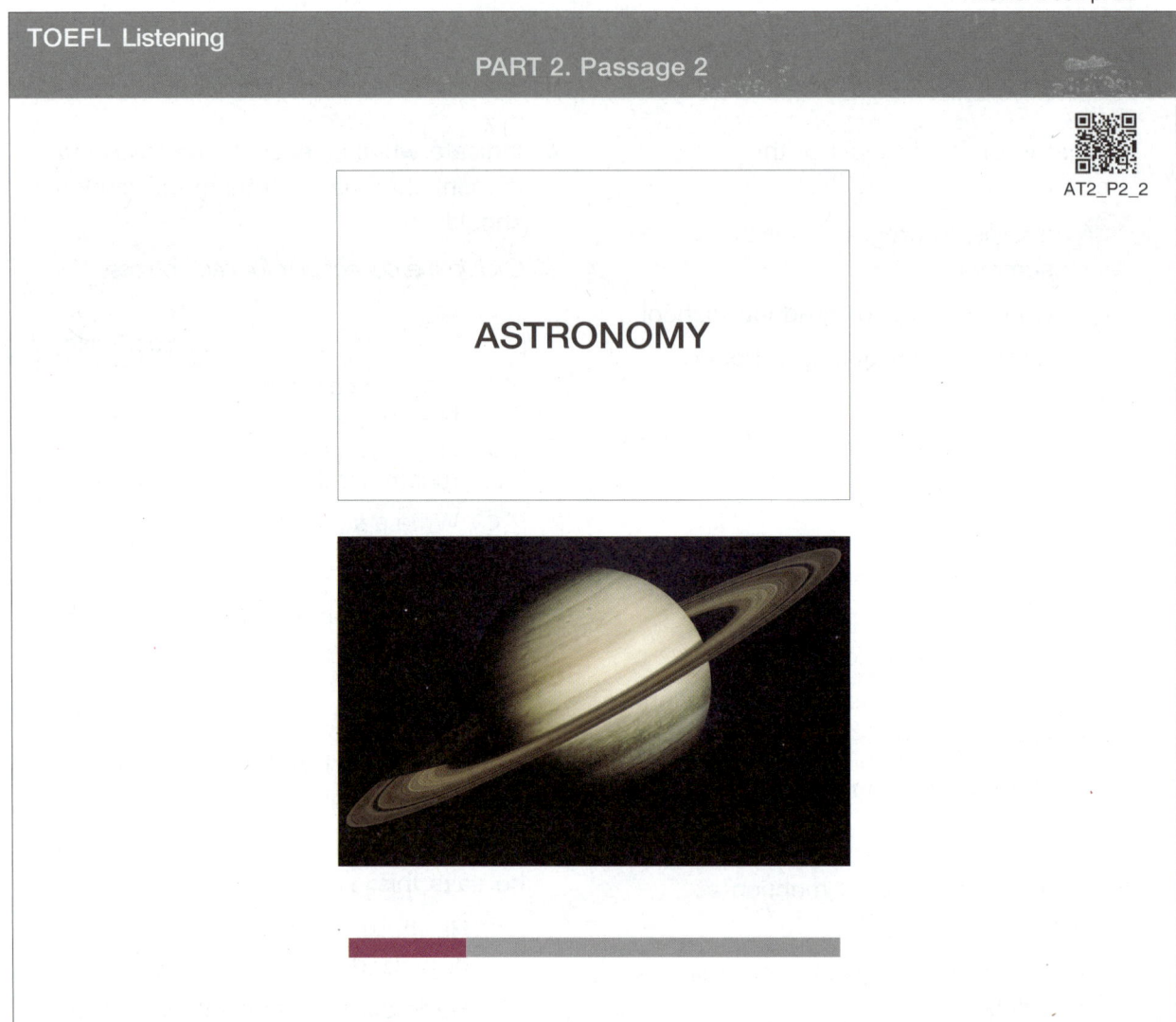

Note-taking

Terrestrial _____

- Four planets that are _____ to the Sun: Mercury, Venus, Earth, and Mars
- Hard _____, made of rocks and metals
- Small in size and have _____ atmospheres

Gas _____

- Jupiter, Saturn, Uranus, and Neptune
- Surfaces made up of _____
- Much _____ than terrestrial planets
- Have _____ atmospheres

Questions 6-11 of 17

6. What is the main topic of the lecture?
   - Ⓐ The various kinds of atmospheres
   - Ⓑ The formation of the solar system
   - Ⓒ Two types of planets in the solar system
   - Ⓓ Two recent scientific studies about planets

7. What does the professor say about the terrestrial planets?
   - Ⓐ They have a lot of water.
   - Ⓑ They have hard surfaces.
   - Ⓒ They have different shapes.
   - Ⓓ They have few rocks and metals.

8. Why does the professor mention volcanoes in the lecture?
   - Ⓐ To give an example of a mystery in the solar system
   - Ⓑ To show how terrestrial planets formed
   - Ⓒ To highlight some natural disasters on Earth
   - Ⓓ To explain how secondary atmospheres were created

9. What does the professor say about the surfaces of gas giants?
   - Ⓐ They become hot during the day.
   - Ⓑ They are surrounded by dust and ice.
   - Ⓒ They mainly contain helium and hydrogen.
   - Ⓓ They usually consist of hot liquids.

10. What does the professor imply about Saturn's rings?
    - Ⓐ They are smaller than Jupiter's rings.
    - Ⓑ They are older than the planet itself.
    - Ⓒ They are hard to see without a telescope.
    - Ⓓ They are clearer than those of other gas giants.

11. In the lecture, the professor explains the characteristics of terrestrial planets and gas giants. Indicate whether each of the following is mentioned as a characteristic of each type.

    Click in the correct box for each phrase.

	Terrestrial planets	Gas giants
Ⓐ They are closer to the Sun.		
Ⓑ They don't have solid surfaces.		
Ⓒ They are larger than the other type.		
Ⓓ Their atmosphere formed after their creation.		

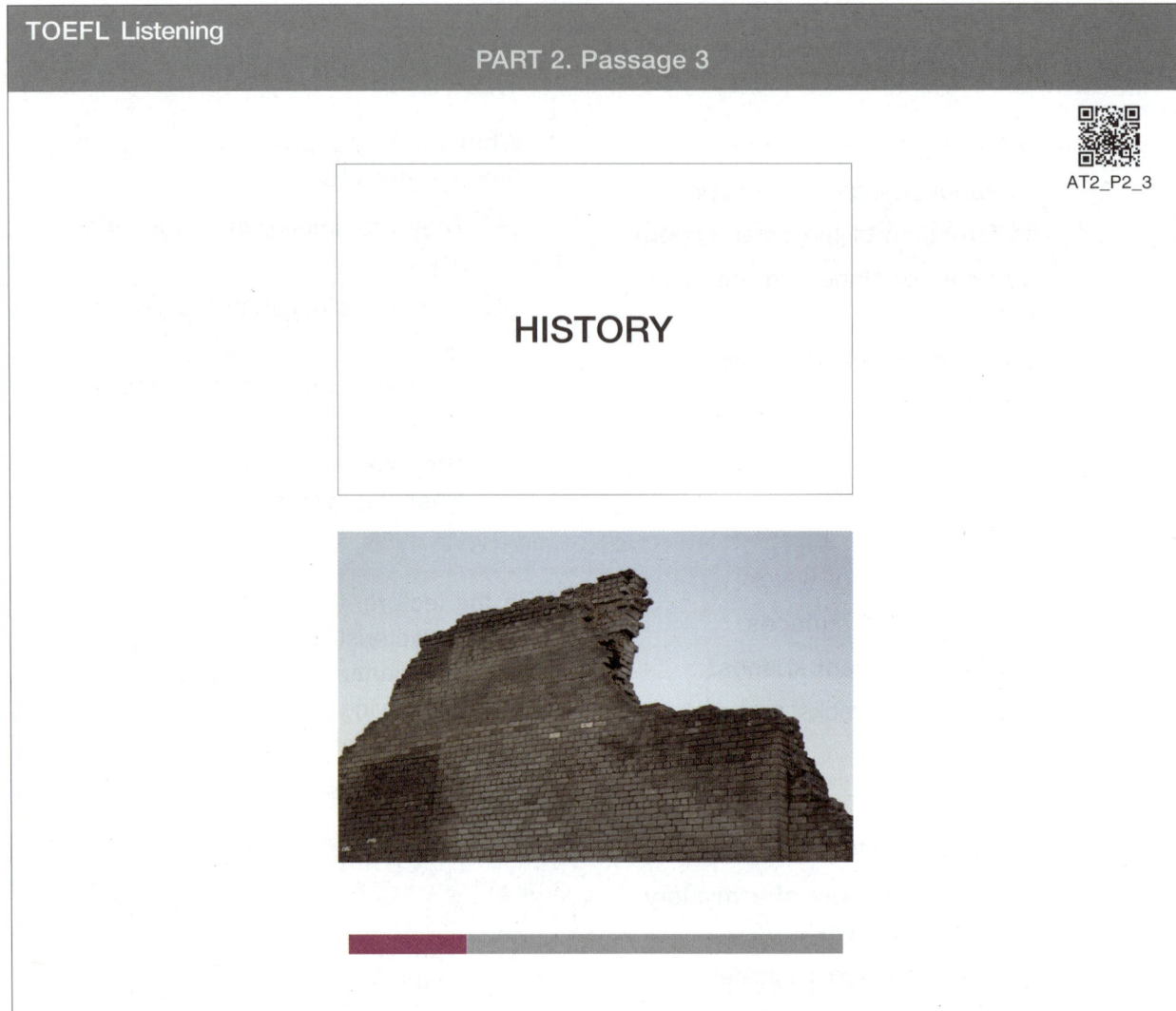

Note-taking

Mid-1950s

Thousands of _____ Germans had moved to West Germany.
→ A law in 1956 _____ all travel to the West.

1961 ~ 1970s

Construction of the _____ _____ began.
→ Secured the _____ with wire fences, concrete blocks, mines, etc.

1980s

People started the _____ _____.
→ East and West Germany united, and the wall was _____.

12 What is the lecture mainly about?
- Ⓐ The cause of the Cold War
- Ⓑ An agreement that ended World War II
- Ⓒ The formation of East Germany
- Ⓓ The separation of a city

13 According to the professor, why did East Germany build the wall?
- Ⓐ To guarantee that people followed a new law
- Ⓑ To punish East Germans in West Germany
- Ⓒ To allow West Germans to live in East Germany
- Ⓓ To protect the city against the Soviet Union

14 According to the professor, what are two methods used to secure the East German border?

Choose 2 answers.
- Ⓐ Explosive bombs
- Ⓑ Guard dogs
- Ⓒ Deep tunnels
- Ⓓ Watch towers

15 According to the professor, what caused the East German government to weaken in the 1980s?
- Ⓐ Attacks from West Germany
- Ⓑ Economic issues
- Ⓒ Natural disasters
- Ⓓ New trade rules

16 What does the professor imply about the opening of the border?
- Ⓐ It was opposed by all East Germans.
- Ⓑ It was decided by vote.
- Ⓒ It was caused by peaceful protests.
- Ⓓ It lasted only a few months.

Listen again to part of the lecture. Then answer the question.

17 Why does the professor say this:
- Ⓐ To show that many people gained freedom
- Ⓑ To emphasize the danger of trying to escape
- Ⓒ To express a negative opinion of the revolution
- Ⓓ To give an example of a personal problem

Photo Credits

www.shutterstock.com

p. 59   "Loyalton, California Fire Tornado-2020-08-16" by Katelynn & Jordan Hewlett, AP / CC BY-SA 4.0

MEMO

HACKERS
APEX
LISTENING
for the
TOEFL iBT® Basic

COPYRIGHT © 2022, by Hackers Language Research Institute

July 21, 2022

All rights reserved. No part of this publication may be reproduced, stored in a retrieval system, or transmitted, in any form or by any means, electronic, mechanical, photocopying, recording, or otherwise, without the prior written permission of the author and the publisher.

Hackers Language Research Institute
23, Gangnam-daero 61-gil, Seocho-gu, Seoul, Korea
Inquiries publishing@hackers.com

ISBN 978-89-6542-067-5 (53740)

Printed in South Korea

3 4 5 6 7 8 9 10   29 28 27 26 25

The Most Preferred Education Brand in Korea,
HACKERS BOOK(www.HackersBook.com)
• Free supplementary study materials

No. 1 in Hankyung Business' Most Preferred Brand Rankings 2019, Education Group category

HACKERS
APEX LISTENING for the TOEFL iBT® Basic

Answer Book

HACKERS
APEX
LISTENING
for the
TOEFL iBT® Basic

Answer Book

* Underlined words in the script are the answers to the Dictation exercise.

CHAPTER 01
Main Purpose/Topic

Example
본문 p.15

A. (D)   B. (C)

A.

Note-taking

Student's Problem
Needs help choosing the topic of the paper

Professor's Suggestion
Decide what you are going to focus on
e.g. Development of the air force and the aircraft

Listen to a conversation between a student and a professor.

S: Professor Adams, I need your help choosing the topic of my paper. I would like to write about World War II, but there is too much information. Do you have any advice for me?

P: Um, it's a good topic, but I think you have to decide what you are going to focus on. For instance, what do you find most interesting about World War II?

S: Well, my grandfather was a pilot at that time, so I often hear stories about the air force during World War II.

P: That's interesting. Hmm... You could write about how the air force evolved during the war and the development of the aircraft. You can interview your grandfather about that, too.

S: That's great! I really appreciate your help.

P: No problem. It's my pleasure.

학생과 교수 사이의 대화를 들으시오.

S: Adams 교수님, 제 보고서 주제를 고르는 데 교수님의 도움이 필요해요. 제2차 세계 대전에 관해 쓰고 싶은데, 정보가 너무 많아서요. 제게 조언해주실 것이 있으신가요?

P: 음, 좋은 주제이긴 한데, 네가 어떤 것에 중점을 둘지 정해야 할 것 같구나. 예를 들어, 제2차 세계 대전의 어떤 점이 가장 흥미롭니?

S: 음, 제 할아버지가 그 당시 조종사이셨기 때문에, 종종 제2차 세계 대전 동안의 공군에 대한 이야기를 듣곤 해요.

P: 그거 흥미롭구나. 흠... 전쟁 동안 공군이 어떻게 발전했는지와 항공기의 발달에 관해 쓸 수도 있겠구나. 그것에 대해 네 할아버지를 인터뷰할 수도 있고.

S: 좋아요! 도움에 정말 감사드립니다.

P: 천만에. 도움이 되어 기쁘단다.

paper 명 보고서   World War II 제2차 세계 대전
focus on ~에 중점을 두다   pilot 명 조종사   air force 공군
evolve 동 발전하다   development 명 발달, 발전
aircraft 명 항공기   appreciate 동 고마워하다; 진가를 알아보다
pleasure 명 기쁨, 즐거움

학생은 왜 교수를 찾아가는가?
(A) 시험에 대한 정보를 얻기 위해
(B) 그의 발표 주제를 바꾸기 위해
(C) 전문가와의 인터뷰를 마련하기 위해
(D) 그의 보고서 주제에 대한 조언을 요청하기 위해

B.

Note-taking

Raccoons' Paws
• Extremely sensitive paws
• Used to tell whether something is safe[good] to eat
• Moisture on the food makes them wet.
  → Improves the sense of touch

Listen to part of a lecture in a biology class.

P: All of us, whether human or animal, depend on our senses every day. We use our eyes to see, our tongues to taste, and so on... In animals, some senses are stronger than others. Um, for example... Dogs have powerful noses, and bats have sensitive ears. But what about raccoons? Raccoons like to wet their food, and this has something to do with their sense of touch.

Raccoons have extremely sensitive paws. So, the raccoon uses its paws to gather information about different objects. In this way, it can tell whether something is good or safe to eat. Now, when a raccoon washes its food, the moisture on the food makes the paws wet. For raccoons, moisture improves their sense of touch.

생물학 강의의 일부를 들으시오.

P: 사람이든 동물이든, 우리 모두는 매일 우리의 감각에 의존합니다. 우리는 눈을 이용해서 보고, 혀를 이용해서 맛을 보는 등 하죠... 동물들의 경우, 어떤 감각들은 다른 누구보다 더 강력해요. 음, 예를 들어... 개는 강력한 코를 가지고 있고, 박쥐는 민감한 귀를 가지고 있죠. 그런데 너구리는 어떨까요? 너구리는 그것들의 음식을 적시는 것을 좋아하는데, 이것은 그것들의 촉각과 관련이 있습니다.

너구리는 매우 민감한 발을 가지고 있습니다. 그래서, 너구리는 그것의 발을 이용해서 다양한 물체에 대한 정보를 수집해요. 이러한 방식으로, 그것은 어떤 것이 먹기에 좋거나 안전한지 알 수 있습니다. 자, 너구리가 그것의 먹이를 씻을 때, 먹이에 있는 수분은 발을 젖게 만드는데요. 너구리의 경우, 수분은 그것들의 촉각을 향상시킵니다.

depend on ~에 의존하다   sense 명 감각
taste 동 맛을 보다; 명 맛   sensitive 형 민감한

wet 동 적시다; 형 젖은   have something to do with ~과 관련이 있다
sense of touch 촉각   extremely 부 매우, 극도로
paw 명 (동물의) 발   gather 동 수집하다, 모으다
information 명 정보   object 명 물체, 사물   moisture 명 수분
improve 동 향상시키다

강의의 주된 주제는 무엇인가?
(A) 동물들이 어떻게 먹이를 사냥하는지
(B) 동물들이 어떻게 그들의 감각에 의존하는지
(C) 너구리가 왜 먹이를 적시는지
(D) 너구리가 왜 발로 물체를 쥐는지

Listening Practice 1   본문 p.17

1 (C)   **2** (D)   **3** (D)

Note-taking
Student's Question
How do I enter the campus <u>music</u> competition[contest]?

Application Procedure
1. Choose the <u>group</u> application on the website
2. Fill in the form and <u>submit</u> it
3. Upload a scan of a <u>student</u> ID

Listen to a conversation between a student and a student activities office employee.

M: Hello. Are you busy?
W: <u>Not at all</u>. How can I help you?
M: I have some questions about the, uh, music contest. ¹I heard there will be <u>a competition</u> on campus, but I'm not sure <u>how</u> to <u>enter</u>.
W: Actually, you <u>have to do it online</u>. I can give you the link. Are you <u>interested in</u> the solo or group competition?
M: Group. ²I'm in a band, and, um, we <u>have played together</u> for around three years now.
W: OK. Then, on the website, just choose the group application. <u>Fill in the form</u>, and submit it. ³Oh, and you must also <u>confirm</u> that you are a student here.
M: How can I do that?
W: <u>The easiest way</u> is to scan your student ID. Then, just upload it with the application.
M: Oh, I understand. Is there anything else I should know?
W: Well, I <u>suggest you arrive</u> an hour or two before the contest. It's always <u>good</u> to <u>be prepared</u>.
M: OK. I'll do that. Thanks for the advice!

학생과 학생활동과 사무실 직원 사이의 대화를 들으시오.

M: 안녕하세요. 바쁘신가요?
W: 전혀요. 어떻게 도와드릴까요?
M: 저는, 어, 음악 대회에 대해 몇 가지 질문들이 있어요. 캠퍼스에 대회가 있을 거라고 들었는데, 어떻게 신청해야 할지 잘 모르겠어요.
W: 사실은, 온라인으로 신청하셔야 해요. 제가 링크를 보내드릴 수 있어요. 개인 또는 단체 대회 중 어떤 것에 관심 있으신가요?
M: 단체 대회요. 저는 밴드에 있어요, 그리고, 음, 저희는 이제 3년 정도 함께 연주했어요.
W: 알겠습니다. 그럼, 홈페이지에서, 단체 신청을 고르시기만 하면 돼요. 양식을 작성하시고, 제출하세요. 아, 그리고 당신이 이곳의 학생이라는 것도 인증하셔야 해요.
M: 그건 어떻게 하면 되나요?
W: 가장 쉬운 방법은 학생증을 스캔하는 거예요. 그러고 나서, 그것을 신청서와 같이 올리시기만 하면 돼요.
M: 아, 알겠습니다. 또 제가 알아야 하는 다른 게 있을까요?
W: 음, 대회 한두 시간 전에는 도착하는 걸 추천해요. 준비가 되어 있는 것은 항상 좋죠.
M: 알겠습니다. 그렇게 할게요. 조언 감사합니다!

contest 명 대회, 경연   competition 명 대회, 경쟁
enter 동 신청하다; 들어가다   solo 명 개인
application 명 신청(서)   fill in ~을 작성하다
form 명 양식, 형식; 동 형성하다   submit 동 제출하다
confirm 동 인증하다, 확인하다   student ID 학생증
suggest 동 추천하다, 제안하다   prepared 형 준비가 되어 있는

1 학생은 왜 학생활동과 사무실을 찾아가는가?
(A) 그는 웹사이트에 대한 새 비밀번호가 필요하다.
(B) 그는 콘서트 티켓을 구하고 싶어 한다.
(C) 그는 대회에 신청하는 방법을 모른다.
(D) 그는 어떤 콘서트에 참석해야 하는지 결정할 수 없다.

2 학생은 그의 밴드에 관해 무엇이라고 말하는가?
(A) 그것은 많은 대회에 참가했다.
(B) 그것은 이전에 대중 앞에서 공연한 적이 전혀 없다.
(C) 그것은 캠퍼스에서 인기가 많다.
(D) 그것은 몇 년 동안 함께 연주해 왔다.

3 직원에 따르면, 학생은 무엇을 제공해야 하는가?
(A) 공연 시간 일정표
(B) 추천서
(C) 그의 음악 녹음본
(D) 그의 학생증 스캔본

Listening Practice 2   본문 p.19

1 (B)   **2** (A)   **3** (B)

Note-taking
Early 1500s ~ 1700s
• 1500s: Violins with three strings → <u>four</u> strings

- 1600s ~ 1700s: Stradivari created the perfect[ideal] design.

19th Century
Modern bow, chin and shoulder rest

Listen to part of a lecture in a music history class.

P: As we've discussed, the Renaissance was a period of great creativity in Italy. The country's arts culture was thriving as many wealthy people supported the arts, including music... Soon, um, Italy became famous for its musical instruments. ¹In particular, it became known as the place where the violin was invented and developed.

The violin was not the first stringed instrument in Italy... but it became the most popular. We can see pictures of violins in paintings from around 1530. At this time, violins were made with just three strings. Then, after around 1550, a fourth string was added. This is how violins look today.

Now, making violins was a family business, so many famous brands were named after families. The most famous of all was Stradivari. ²Antonio Stradivari created the perfect violin design in the late 1600s and early 1700s. Uh, he discovered the ideal size and shape for the best sound, and his violins became the standard. He crafted around one thousand violins and hundreds of them still exist.

S: I've heard about them. Aren't they expensive?

P: Oh, yes. Stradivari violins are still considered one of the best violins in the world, so they are worth millions of dollars.

Anyway... some helpful changes were made in the 19th century. ³For example, the modern bow was invented. Its length, weight, and balance allowed musicians to play longer without becoming tired. Also, a chin rest and a shoulder rest were added to make the violin easier to hold. With these new features, the modern violin was born.

음악사학 강의의 일부를 들으시오.

P: 우리가 논의했듯이, 이탈리아에서 르네상스는 뛰어난 창의성의 시기였습니다. 많은 부유한 사람들이 음악을 포함해 예술을 지원하면서 나라의 예술 문화가 번성하게 되었죠... 곧, 음, 이탈리아는 악기로 유명해졌어요. 특히, 그곳은 바이올린이 발명되어 발전된 곳으로 알려지게 되었죠.

바이올린은 이탈리아에서 첫 번째 현악기는 아니었지만... 가장 인기가 많게 되었어요. 우리는 1530년경의 그림들에서 바이올린의 그림을 볼 수 있는데요. 이때, 바이올린은 단 세 개의 현으로만 만들어졌어요. 그리고 1550년 이후쯤에, 네 번째 줄이 추가되었어요. 이것이 오늘날 바이올린의 모습이죠.

자, 바이올린을 만드는 것은 가업이었기 때문에, 많은 유명한 브랜드들이 가족의 이름을 따서 이름 지어졌습니다. 그 중 가장 유명한 것은 스트라디바리였어요. 안토니오 스트라디바리는 1600년대 후반과 1700년대 초에 완벽한 바이올린 디자인을 만들어 냈습니다. 어, 그는 최고의 소리를 위한 이상적인 크기와 모양을 알아냈고, 그의 바이올린은 표준이 되었어요. 그는 약 1,000개의 바이올린을 만들었고 그 중 수백 개가 여전히 존재합니다.

S: 그것들에 대해 들어본 적이 있어요. 그것들은 비싸지 않나요?

P: 아, 맞아요. 스트라디바리 바이올린은 여전히 세계 최고의 바이올린 중 하나로 여겨져서, 수백만 달러의 가치가 있어요.

어쨌든... 19세기에 몇몇 유용한 변화들이 이뤄졌는데요. 예를 들어, 현대의 활이 발명되었죠. 그것의 길이, 무게, 그리고 균형은 음악가들이 지치지 않고 더 오래 연주할 수 있게 해주었습니다. 또한, 바이올린을 잡기 쉽게 하기 위해 턱받침과 어깨 받침이 추가되었어요. 이러한 새로운 요소들로, 현대 바이올린이 탄생했습니다.

Renaissance 명 르네상스(14~16세기에 이탈리아에서 시작된 인간성 해방을 위한 문화 혁신 운동) period 명 시기, 기간
creativity 명 창의성 thrive 동 번성하다
support 동 지원하다, 지지하다 musical instrument 악기
in particular 특히 stringed instrument 현악기
family business 가업 be named after ~의 이름을 따서 이름 지어지다
ideal 형 이상적인 standard 명 표준, 수준
craft 동 (특히 손으로) 만들다 exist 동 존재하다
worth 형 ~의 가치가 있는 modern 형 현대의 bow 명 활
length 명 길이 weight 명 무게 balance 명 균형
rest 명 받침(대); 나머지; 휴식 feature 명 요소, 특징

1 강의의 주된 목적은 무엇인가?
(A) 르네상스 예술 문화를 이야기하기 위해
(B) 바이올린의 역사를 설명하기 위해
(C) 이탈리아에서의 음악의 중요성을 설명하기 위해
(D) 유명한 바이올리니스트의 삶을 탐구하기 위해

2 교수는 안토니오 스트라디바리에 관해 무엇이라고 말하는가?
(A) 그는 바이올린에 대한 완벽한 디자인을 고안해냈다.
(B) 그는 최초의 성공적인 바이올린 사업을 시작했다.
(C) 그는 바이올린에 턱받침과 어깨 받침을 추가했다.
(D) 그는 일생 동안 수백만 달러를 벌었다.

3 교수에 따르면, 현대 활 발명의 결과는 무엇이었는가?
(A) 바이올린이 더 큰 소리를 냈다.
(B) 공연자들이 더 오랫동안 연주할 수 있었다.
(C) 음악가들이 바이올린을 더 쉽게 잡을 수 있었다.
(D) 공연이 관람하기에 더 재미있어졌다.

Listening Practice 3 본문 p.21

1 (B) **2** (C) **3** (B)

Note-taking
Student's Problem
Visiting a museum on the 26th
→ Cannot take next week's exam

Professor's Solution
- Go to the exhibits by yourself before then
- Write a research paper instead

Listen to a conversation between a student and a professor.

P: Hi, Ashley. Um, what brings you here today?
S: ¹I have a problem that I'd like to ask you about.
P: Oh? What is it?
S: You see, my art class is visiting a museum on the 26th, and, uh, that's the same day as your exam.
P: I see... Does this mean you cannot take next week's exam?
S: Well, uh, I'd like to take it. ²I've read all the books and done all the exercises, so I'm prepared for the exam. ³But, uh, I also have to give a speech on one of the exhibits at the museum.
P: Well, can't you go to the exhibits by yourself before then?
S: I could, but our professor has arranged a special tour for us. Some artists are going to talk about their work. I would hate to miss that.
P: I understand. Maybe there's something we can do. Hmm... How about writing a research paper instead of taking the exam? I can pick a topic for you.
S: That would be great! Thank you, Professor.

학생과 교수 사이의 대화를 들으시오.

P: 안녕, Ashley. 음, 오늘 무슨 일로 이곳에 왔니?
S: 제가 교수님께 여쭤보고 싶은 문제가 있어서요.
P: 오? 무슨 일이니?
S: 그러니까, 제 미술 수업에서 26일에 박물관을 방문하는데, 어, 그게 교수님 시험이 있는 날과 같은 날이에요.
P: 그렇구나... 다음 주 시험을 볼 수 없다는 뜻이니?
S: 음, 어, 저는 그것을 보고 싶어요. 책들도 다 읽었고 연습문제도 다 풀어서, 시험에 대한 준비가 다 되어 있거든요. 하지만, 어, 저는 박물관의 전시품들 중 하나에 대해 연설도 해야 해요.
P: 음, 그 전에 혼자서 전시회를 갈 수는 없는 거니?
S: 갈 수는 있는데, 교수님께서 저희를 위해 특별 투어를 마련하셨어요. 몇몇 예술가들이 그들의 작품에 관해 이야기할 거예요. 저는 그것을 놓치고 싶지 않아요.
P: 알겠다. 어쩌면 우리가 할 수 있는 일이 있을지도 모르겠구나. 흠... 시험을 보는 것 대신에 연구 보고서를 쓰는 건 어떠니? 내가 네게 주제를 정해줄 수 있어.
S: 그거 정말 좋겠어요! 감사합니다, 교수님.

visit 〖동〗 방문하다   take an exam 시험을 보다
exercise 〖명〗 연습문제; 운동   give a speech 연설하다
exhibit 〖명〗 전시품, 전시   arrange a tour 투어를 마련하다
research paper 연구 보고서, 연구 논문

1 학생의 문제는 무엇인가?
 (A) 그녀는 시험 공부를 하기 위한 시간이 더 필요하다.
 (B) 그녀는 시험일과 같은 날에 현장 학습이 있다.
 (C) 그녀는 좋은 에세이 주제를 생각해낼 수 없다.
 (D) 그녀는 글쓰기 대회 마감일을 놓쳤다.

2 학생은 다음 주 시험에 관해 무엇이라고 말하는가?
 (A) 그녀는 그것이 어려울 것이라고 생각한다.
 (B) 그녀는 그것에 대해 준비가 되어 있지 않다.
 (C) 그녀는 그것을 위해 공부를 많이 했다.
 (D) 그녀는 그것이 취소되기를 바란다.

3 학생은 박물관을 방문한 후에 무엇을 해야 하는가?
 (A) 퀴즈 보기
 (B) 연설하기
 (C) 책 읽기
 (D) 몇몇 예술가들을 인터뷰하기

Listening Practice 4   본문 p.23

1 (C)   **2** (D)   **3** (B)

Note-taking
Goosebumps
: Small, raised areas on our skin

How They Happen
1. Nervous system sends signals to tiny muscles under the skin.
2. Some parts of the skin stick out.

Listen to part of a lecture in a physiology class.

P: Imagine this... You're watching a scary movie in a dark room. Suddenly, you hear a strange sound. You become afraid. Your body becomes tense, and the hair on your skin stands up... ¹What you're feeling are goosebumps. But, what exactly are they, and how do they occur?

To begin with, goosebumps are small, raised areas on our skin. They, uh, look like the skin of a bird after its feathers have been removed. That's why we call them "goose" bumps... Anyway, they tend to happen when we are cold, afraid, or even when we feel strong emotions.

Um, but goosebumps happen without our control. ²They're a natural response by the body to danger. What happens is that our nervous system sends signals to tiny muscles under the skin. This causes the skin to tighten. Then, this makes other parts of the skin stick out.

This happens in animals, too. Um, think of how animals react when they're threatened... Cats are a good example. When cats sense danger, their fur puffs up. So, um, this makes them appear bigger than they actually are. Therefore, they are less likely to be attacked... ³Also, in animals with lots of fur or hair, goosebumps create an extra layer of air around the body. This helps them stay warm.

Goosebumps in humans, however, don't have these functions. Well, um, they did before, when our bodies had thick hair. But we lost the hair as we evolved over time. Still, we get goosebumps just like our ancestors did.

생리학 강의의 일부를 들으시오.

P: 상상해보세요... 여러분이 어두운 방에서 무서운 영화를 보고 있어요. 갑자기, 여러분은 이상한 소리를 듣습니다. 여러분은 겁이 나죠. 몸이 긴장하게 되고, 피부에 있는 털이 섭니다. 여러분이 느끼는 것은 닭살입니다. 그런데, 그것들은 정확히 무엇이며, 어떻게 일어나는 것일까요?

우선, 닭살은 우리 피부에 작게 올라온 부위입니다. 그것들은, 어, 깃털이 제거되고 난 후의 새의 피부처럼 보입니다. 그래서 우리가 '거위' 돌기('닭살')라고 부르는 것이죠. 어쨌든, 그것들은 우리가 춥거나, 두렵거나, 또는 심지어 우리가 강한 감정을 느낄 때도 일어나는 경향이 있습니다.

음, 하지만 닭살은 우리의 통제 없이 발생해요. 그것들은 위험에 대한 신체의 자연스러운 반응이거든요. 무슨 일이 일어나냐면 우리의 신경계가 피부 밑에 있는 작은 근육들에 신호를 보내는데요. 이것이 피부를 팽팽하게 만들어요. 그리고, 이것은 피부의 다른 부분들이 튀어나오게 만듭니다.

이것은 동물에게도 발생합니다. 음, 동물들이 위협을 받았을 때 어떻게 반응하는지 생각해 보세요... 고양이가 좋은 예입니다. 고양이들은 위험을 감지하면, 털이 부풀어 올라요. 그래서, 음, 이것은 그것들이 실제보다 더 크게 보이게 해요. 따라서, 공격받을 가능성이 낮아지죠... 또한, 많은 털을 가진 동물들의 경우, 닭살은 몸 주변에 여분의 공기층을 만드는데요. 이것이 그것들이 따뜻함을 유지할 수 있도록 도와줘요.

하지만, 사람에게 있는 닭살의 경우, 이러한 기능들이 없습니다. 글쎄, 음, 예전에는 그랬죠, 우리 몸에 굵은 털이 많았을 때요. 하지만 시간이 지나 우리가 진화함에 따라 우리는 그 털을 잃었어요. 그래도, 우리의 조상들처럼 닭살이 돋고는 합니다.

tense 〖형〗 긴장한, 신경이 날카로운   goosebumps 〖명〗 닭살, 소름
raised 〖형〗 올라온; 올라와 있는   remove 〖동〗 제거하다
tend to ~하는 경향이 있다   emotion 〖명〗 감정
natural response 자연스러운 반응   nervous system 신경계
signal 〖명〗 신호   tighten 〖동〗 팽팽해지다; 팽팽하게 하다
stick out 튀어나오다; 튀어나오게 하다   threaten 〖동〗 위협하다
sense 〖동〗 감지하다   fur 〖명〗 (동물의) 털   puff up 부풀어 오르다
layer 〖명〗 층, 막   function 〖명〗 기능   ancestor 〖명〗 조상, 선조

1 강의의 주된 주제는 무엇인가?

(A) 사람 피부의 특징
(B) 사람들이 어둠을 두려워하는 이유
(C) 닭살이 어떻게 그리고 왜 발생하는지
(D) 동물들이 어떻게 위험에 반응하는지

2 교수에 따르면, 위험을 감지하면 몸에서 무슨 일이 일어나는가?

(A) 몸에서 땀이 나기 시작한다.
(B) 뇌가 기능을 더 빨리 한다.
(C) 일부 근육들이 이완된다.
(D) 피부의 일부분이 튀어나온다.

3 교수에 따르면, 닭살이 어떻게 동물들이 따뜻함을 유지하는 데 도움을 주는가?

(A) 체온을 변화시킴으로써
(B) 공기층을 형성함으로써
(C) 털을 더 많이 만들어냄으로써
(D) 찬 바람을 막아줌으로써

iBT Listening Test 1   본문 p.25

1 (A)   2 (A)   3 (B)   4 (D)

Note-taking

Suggestion to Student

Work as an assistant on the professor's research project

Research Assistant's Work

- Translate some documents from German into English
- Work around two months over the summer vacation
- A paid position
  → Can pay for tuition without a problem

Listen to a conversation between a student and a professor.

S: Hi, Professor Brown. I heard you wanted to see me.

P: Oh, yes. ¹I asked you to stop by because... I would like you to consider working as an assistant on my research project. ²Normally, I get applications from students for this, but I'd like to make an exception for you.

S: ³I appreciate that... Um, what would I have to do, exactly?

P: Mostly, you'd be translating some documents from German into English. I know that your German is strong, so I think the work would suit you well.

S: Thanks. If I took the position, how long would I have to work for the project?

P: The project will take around two months over the summer vacation.

S: ⁴Oh, in that case, I'm not sure if I can... I need to work to earn money for tuition fees during the summer break.

P: Well, this is a paid position. You would be able to pay for tuition without a problem. Does that make a difference?

S: That's great to hear! I'll definitely think about it.

P: Okay, then. I really hope you can join the team.

학생과 교수 사이의 대화를 들으시오.

S: 안녕하세요, Brown 교수님. 저를 보자고 하셨다고 들었어요.
P: 아, 그래. 네게 잠깐 들르라고 했단다. 왜냐하면... 네가 내 연구 프로젝트의 조교로 일하는 것을 고려해 보면 좋을 것 같아서야. 보통, 나는 학생들로부터 지원서를 받지만, 너는 예외로 하고자 한단다.
S: 감사합니다... 음, 정확히 제가 무엇을 해야 하나요?
P: 주로, 너는 독일어로 된 문서들을 영어로 번역하게 될 거야. 네가 독일어를 잘하는 것을 알고 있어서, 그 일이 네게 잘 맞을 것 같구나.
S: 감사합니다. 만약 제가 그 자리를 얻게 된다면, 그 프로젝트를 위해 얼마나 오래 일해야 하나요?
P: 프로젝트는 여름 방학 동안 두 달 정도 걸릴 거야.
S: 아, 그렇다면, 제가 할 수 있을지 잘 모르겠어요... 여름 방학 동안 등록금을 벌기 위해 일해야 하거든요.
P: 음, 이건 유급직이란다. 문제없이 등록금을 낼 수 있을 거야. 이게 도움이 될까?
S: 잘됐군요! 그것에 대해 꼭 생각해 보겠습니다.
P: 좋아, 그럼. 네가 정말 팀에 합류할 수 있기를 바란다.

stop by ~에 잠깐 들르다 assistant 명 조교, 조수
make an exception 예외로 하다 translate 동 번역하다
document 명 문서 strong 형 잘하는, 실력 있는; 강한
suit 동 ~에게 잘 맞다; 명 정장 position 명 (일)자리, ~직; 위치
vacation 명 방학 tuition fees 등록금
break 명 방학, 휴가; 파괴 paid 형 유급의
make a difference 도움이 되다, 영향을 주다
definitely 부 꼭, 반드시 join 동 합류하다, 참가하다

1 교수는 왜 학생을 보자고 했는가?
   (A) 프로젝트에 대한 일자리를 제안하기 위해
   (B) 여름 수업을 듣는 것을 추천하기 위해
   (C) 최근 강의에 대한 의견을 묻기 위해
   (D) 연구 보고서에 대해 조언을 주기 위해

2 교수는 보통 어떻게 자신의 프로젝트에 대한 조교를 선택하는가?
   (A) 지원자를 받음으로써
   (B) 다른 교수들에게 물어봄으로써
   (C) 온라인에 게시물을 올림으로써
   (D) 명단을 만듦으로써

3 교수에 따르면, 프로젝트는 어떤 것을 포함하는가?
   (A) 도서관에서 정보를 검색하는 것
   (B) 몇몇 문서를 번역하는 것
   (C) 독일 학생들에게 영어를 가르치는 것
   (D) 몇몇 읽기 자료를 정리하는 것

4 학생은 원래 여름 방학 동안 무엇을 할 계획이었는가?
   (A) 그녀는 취미에 시간을 보내고 싶어 했다.
   (B) 그녀는 도서관에서 일하려고 했다.
   (C) 그녀는 해외 유학을 가려고 했다.
   (D) 그녀는 등록금을 위해 돈을 벌려고 했다.

iBT Listening Test 2

1 (D) 2 (D) 3 (C) 4 (B)

Note-taking
Koala's Physical Characteristics
- A long digestive organ; caecum
  → Breaks down leaf fibers
- Unique genes in the liver
  → Remove toxins in the leaves
- A digestive system that works very slowly
  → Keeps food in the body for a long time

Listen to part of a lecture in a biology class.

P: So, I'm sure you all know what a koala is, right? ¹But, um, did you know it spends most of its life in eucalyptus trees and eats the leaves of this tree? Today, I'm going to talk about the koala and its main food source.

Both the koala and the eucalyptus tree are native to Australia... In fact, they evolved together over millions of years. Now, eucalyptus trees hold a lot of moisture... When the koala eats the leaves, it absorbs some of that moisture. ²This allows the koala to survive for several days without coming down from the tree for water. Actually, the name koala comes from a local word that means "no water."

But still, eucalyptus leaves are low in nutrition... They are tough and contain toxic substances. This makes them difficult to digest, a poor source of energy, and even dangerous to health. So, many animals avoid eucalyptus leaves. ³For the koala, however, they are the main food source. This is possible because of the special functions of its digestive system. For instance, it has a long digestive organ called the caecum that breaks down the tough leaves. Also, its liver has unique genes that can remove toxins in the leaves, which makes them safe to consume. Lastly, the koala's digestive system works very slowly, so it keeps food in its body for a long time. This allows it to gain as much energy as possible.

⁴Even though the koala has these abilities, it still gets little energy from eucalyptus leaves... As a result, koalas sleep for most of the day, often from 18 to 22 hours.

생물학 강의의 일부를 들으시오.

P: 자, 여러분 모두 코알라가 무엇인지 알고 있을 거예요, 그렇죠? 하지만, 음, 그것이 삶의 대부분을 유칼립투스 나무에서 보내고 이 나무의 잎을 먹는다는 것을 알고 있었나요? 오늘, 저는 코알라와 그것의 주요 먹이 공급원에 관해 이야기하려고 합니다.

코알라와 유칼립투스 나무 둘 다 호주가 원산지죠... 실제로, 그것들은 수백만 년에 걸쳐 함께 진화해왔습니다. 자, 유칼립투스 나무는 많은 수분을 머금고 있어요... 코알라가 그 잎을 먹으면, 그것은 그 수분의 일부를 흡수하죠. 이것은 코알라가 며칠 동안 물을 위해 나무에서 내려오지 않아도 생존할 수 있게 해줍니다. 사

실, 코알라라는 이름은 "물이 없다"를 의미하는 현지 단어에서 비롯되었어요.

하지만 여전히, 유칼립투스 잎은 영양가가 낮습니다... 그것들은 질기고 독성 물질을 포함하고 있어요. 이것은 그것들이 소화하기 어렵고, 부족한 에너지원이자, 건강에 위험하게까지 합니다. 그래서, 많은 동물들이 유칼립투스 잎을 피하죠. 그러나, 코알라에게는, 그것들이 주요 먹이 공급원입니다. 이것은 그것의 소화계 내 특별한 기능들 때문에 가능한 건데요. 예를 들어, 그것은 질긴 잎을 분해하는 맹장이라는 긴 소화 기관을 가지고 있어요. 또한, 그것의 간에 있는 독소를 제거할 수 있는 특별한 유전자를 가지고 있는데, 이것은 그것들을 안전하게 먹을 수 있도록 하죠. 마지막으로, 코알라의 소화계는 매우 느리게 작용해서, 그것은 몸 안에 음식을 오랫동안 가지고 있습니다. 이것은 그것이 가능한 한 많은 에너지를 얻을 수 있게 해주죠.

코알라가 이러한 능력들을 가지고 있음에도 불구하고, 그것은 여전히 유칼립투스 잎에서 에너지를 거의 얻지 못해요... 결과적으로, 코알라들은 하루의 대부분을, 대개 18시간에서 22시간 동안 잠듭니다.

eucalyptus 명 유칼립투스(오스트레일리아산 나무)
source 명 공급원, 근원   native 형 ~ 원산의, 토착의; 명 원주민
absorb 동 흡수하다   survive 동 생존하다
come from ~에서 비롯되다   nutrition 명 영양가   tough 형 질긴
toxic 형 독성의, 독이 있는   substance 명 물질   digest 동 소화하다
avoid 동 피하다   digestive system 소화계   caecum 명 맹장
break down ~을 분해하다   liver 명 간   unique 형 특별한
gene 명 유전자   toxin 명 독소   consume 동 먹다, 섭취하다
ability 명 능력

1 강의는 주로 무엇에 관한 것인가?
  (A) 코알라의 서식지가 왜 위협을 받고 있는지
  (B) 코알라가 어떻게 환경과 상호작용하는지
  (C) 코알라가 왜 호주에 유입되었는지
  (D) 코알라가 어떻게 영양분을 얻는지

2 교수에 따르면, 코알라의 이름은 어디에서 비롯되었는가?
  (A) 유칼립투스 잎을 뜻하는 현지어
  (B) 나무에 매달리는 그것의 습성
  (C) 먹을 때 그것이 내는 소리
  (D) 물 없이 생존할 수 있는 그것의 능력

3 교수에 따르면, 코알라의 어느 부분이 특별한 기능을 가졌는가?
  (A) 그것의 몸 크기
  (B) 그것의 날카로운 발톱
  (C) 그것의 소화계
  (D) 그것의 후각

4 교수에 따르면, 코알라는 왜 하루의 대부분을 잠든 상태로 보내는가?
  (A) 그것은 밤에 먹이를 찾아 다닌다.
  (B) 그것은 먹이에서 에너지를 거의 흡수하지 못한다.
  (C) 그것은 밝은 햇빛에서는 잘 볼 수 없다.
  (D) 그것은 독이 있는 잎을 먹은 것으로부터 회복해야 한다.

Vocabulary Review 본문 p.32

1 tough   2 confirm   3 gather
4 pleasure   5 emotion   6 function
7 depend on   8 remove   9 support
10 (C)   11 (B)   12 (A)
13 (D)   14 (B)

CHAPTER 02
Detail

Example 본문 p.35

A. (B)   **B.** (B), (D)

A.

Note-taking
Student's Problem
Looking for Jefferson Hall
→ Didn't get a text message

Employee's Suggestion
Change your phone number on the website to get important announcements through texts

---

Listen to a conversation between a student and a physics department employee.

W: Excuse me. I'm hoping you can help. I think I'm lost. I'm looking for Jefferson Hall because, um, I'm supposed to attend an orientation there at 10 a.m.

M: Oh, Jefferson Hall is across from the library. Uh, didn't you get a text message from us? We sent directions to every student.

W: Uh, I never received it...

M: That's strange... Um, let me check your information on the school website... Is your phone number 555-9028?

W: That's not correct, actually. My phone number is 555-9628.

M: I see. I suggest you log in to your account and change it, then. We send many important announcements through texts.

W: All right, thank you. I'll do that right after the gathering.

M: OK. And, uh, you should hurry if you want to get there on time.

학생과 물리학과 직원 사이의 대화를 들으시오.

W: 실례합니다. 절 좀 도와주셨으면 좋겠어요. 제가 길을 잃은 것 같아요. Jefferson Hall을 찾고 있는데요, 왜냐하면, 음, 오전 10시에

거기서 열리는 오리엔테이션에 참석하기로 되어 있거든요.

M: 오, Jefferson Hall은 도서관의 맞은편에 있어요. 어, 저희한테서 문자 메시지를 못 받으셨나요? 저희가 모든 학생들에게 길 안내를 보냈거든요.

W: 어, 저는 그것을 받은 적이 없는데요...

M: 이상하네요... 음, 학교 웹사이트에서 학생의 정보를 확인해 볼게요... 전화번호가 555-9028인가요?

W: 사실, 그건 맞지 않네요. 제 전화번호는 555-9628이에요.

M: 그렇군요. 그럼, 계정에 로그인해서 변경하는 걸 추천해요. 저희가 많은 중요한 공지사항을 문자로 보내거든요.

W: 알겠어요, 감사합니다. 모임이 끝나면 바로 할게요.

M: 네. 그리고, 어, 제시간에 도착하려면 서두르세요.

look for ~을 찾다 be supposed to ~하기로 되어 있다
attend 〔동〕 참석하다 orientation 〔명〕 오리엔테이션, 신입생 설명회
across from ~의 맞은편에 text message 문자 메시지
directions 〔명〕 길 안내, 지시(사항) account 〔명〕 계정; 계좌
announcement 〔명〕 공지사항, 발표 gathering 〔명〕 모임; 수집
hurry 〔동〕 서두르다 on time 제시간에

학생은 왜 자신의 전화번호를 업데이트해야 하는가?

(A) 그녀는 이벤트에 신청하고 싶어한다.
(B) 그녀는 중요한 메시지들을 받아야 한다.
(C) 그녀는 수업 과제를 제출해야 한다.
(D) 그녀는 도움을 청하기 위해 직원에게 전화해야 한다.

B.

Note-taking
Egyptian Boats
- Light boats: Good for <u>hunting</u> and <u>fishing</u> in shallow waters e.g. Skiff
- Large ships: Transported <u>heavy</u> <u>goods</u> and animals in deeper waters
- Others: Used for <u>religious</u> ceremonies

Listen to part of a lecture in a history class.

P: In the ancient world, many people <u>lived near large rivers</u>... In ancient Egypt, people lived near the Nile, a long and wide river. The Egyptians <u>depended on</u> the Nile, so they created many boats for <u>different purposes</u>.

One of them was called a skiff. It was a light boat made of thin pieces of wood that <u>were tied together</u>. [B]The skiff's light weight <u>was good for hunting and fishing in shallow waters</u>. The other kind of boat was a large ship. It could <u>transport heavy goods</u> and animals. So it was <u>more suitable for traveling</u> in deeper waters.

[D]Now, the Egyptians also used boats for <u>religious ceremonies</u>. Uh, they used the boats to carry images of their gods between temples, or to transport the dead bodies of important leaders.

역사학 강의의 일부를 들으시오.

P: 고대에는, 많은 사람들이 큰 강 근처에 살았습니다... 고대 이집트에서는, 사람들이 길고 넓은 강인 나일강 근처에 살았어요. 이집트인들은 나일강에 의존했기 때문에, 다양한 용도의 많은 배를 만들었습니다.

그것들 중 하나는 스키프라고 불렸습니다. 그것은 얇은 나무 조각들을 함께 묶어서 만든 가벼운 배였어요. 스키프의 가벼운 무게는 얕은 물에서 사냥과 낚시를 하기에 좋았습니다. 다른 종류의 배는 큰 선박이었습니다. 그것은 무거운 물건과 동물들도 운반할 수 있었어요. 그래서 그것은 더 깊은 물에서 이동하기에 더 적합했죠.

자, 이집트인들은 종교의식을 위해서도 배들을 이용했습니다. 어, 그들은 신전들 간에 신들의 그림을 운반하거나, 중요한 지도자들의 사체를 운반하는 데 배들을 이용했어요.

ancient 〔형〕 고대의 depend on ~에 의존하다
purpose 〔명〕 용도; 목적 skiff 〔명〕 스키프(보통 한 사람이 타는 소형 보트)
tie 〔동〕 (끈 등으로) 묶다 shallow 〔형〕 얕은 ship 〔명〕 선박, 배
transport 〔동〕 운반하다; 〔명〕 수송 suitable 〔형〕 적합한, 적절한
travel 〔동〕 이동하다; 여행하다 religious ceremony 종교의식
carry 〔동〕 운반하다 temple 〔명〕 신전

교수에 따르면, 고대 이집트 배의 두 가지 기능은 무엇인가?
2개의 답을 고르시오.

(A) 적을 공격하기
(B) 사냥과 낚시하기
(C) 다른 나라로 이동하기
(D) 종교의식

Listening Practice 1 본문 p.37

1 (A) 2 (D) 3 (C)

Note-taking
Student's Problem
Doesn't <u>understand</u> the <u>material</u> very well

Professor's Solution
- Read some <u>related</u> <u>books</u>
- Join a <u>study</u> <u>group</u> for the class

Listen to a conversation between a student and a professor.

S: Hello, Professor Carter. I think you <u>asked</u> <u>me</u> <u>to visit</u> your office in the last class.

P: Hi, Emily. I wanted to see how you are doing. Are you <u>prepared for</u> the midterm exam?

S: [1]Well, I'm studying every day, but this class has been... um... difficult for me. Even though I study a lot, I <u>don't</u> <u>understand</u> <u>the</u> <u>material</u> very well.

P: I thought so... Well, your quiz score in the last class was low, but don't worry. [2]The class is <u>quite advanced</u>, so it can be tough. Hmm... Do you want me to <u>suggest</u> <u>some</u> <u>tips</u> for you?

S: Yes, that would be great! I really need some help.

P: ³There are some related books you can read. Let me give you a list of them... Here. I think you can find them in the library. Um, another option is joining a study group. Many students are looking for members, so I'm sure you can find one for this class.

S: That's a great idea! Thanks for all your help, Professor.

학생과 교수 사이의 대화를 들으시오.

S: 안녕하세요, Carter 교수님. 지난 수업 시간에 사무실로 찾아오라고 하셨던 것 같아서요.

P: 안녕, Emily. 네가 어떻게 하고 있는지 알고 싶었단다. 중간고사 준비는 다 되었니?

S: 음, 저는 매일 공부하고 있지만, 이 수업은... 음... 저에게 어려워요. 공부를 많이 하는데도, 자료를 잘 이해하지 못하겠어요.

P: 그럴 것 같았단다... 음, 저번 수업에서 네 퀴즈 점수가 낮았지만, 걱정하지 마라. 수업이 꽤 상급이라서, 어려울 수 있어. 흠... 내가 몇 가지 조언을 제시해줄까?

S: 네, 그러면 정말 좋겠어요! 저는 도움이 정말 필요해요.

P: 네가 읽을 수 있는 관련 책들이 좀 있어. 그것들의 목록을 줄게... 여기있다. 도서관에서 그것들을 찾을 수 있을 거야. 음, 또 다른 방법은 스터디 그룹에 가입하는 거야. 많은 학생들이 조원을 찾고 있으니, 이 수업에 관한 것도 찾을 수 있을 거라고 확신한다.

S: 그거 좋은 생각이네요! 많은 도움에 감사드려요, 교수님.

---

midterm exam 중간고사　prepare for ~을 준비하다
material 명 자료; 재료　advanced 형 상급의, 고등의
tough 형 어려운, 힘든　suggest 동 제시하다, 제안하다
tip 명 조언　related 형 관련된　list 명 목록, 명단
option 명 방법, 방안; 선택사항　join 동 가입하다

1 학생의 문제는 무엇인가?

　(A) 그녀는 수업을 이해하는 데 어려움이 있다.
　(B) 그녀는 중간고사에서 낙제했다.
　(C) 그녀는 어떤 책을 읽어야 할지 모른다.
　(D) 그녀는 보고서를 쓰는 데 시간이 더 필요하다.

2 교수는 그의 수업에 관해 무엇이라고 말하는가?

　(A) 그것은 많은 읽기 자료를 준다.
　(B) 그것에는 토론 시간이 포함된다.
　(C) 그것은 다르게 가르쳐질 것이다.
　(D) 그것은 내용이 어렵다.

3 교수는 학생에게 무엇을 제공하는가?

　(A) 도서관 카드
　(B) 보충 퀴즈
　(C) 도서 목록
　(D) 조별 과제

Listening Practice 2　　본문 p.39

1 (C)　**2** (D)　**3** (A)

Note-taking
Factors of Habitats
- Space[Room] to move around
  e.g. Snow leopards need lots of space.
- Shelter　e.g. Rabbits
- Food and water
  e.g. A jungle for tigers

Listen to part of a lecture in an environmental science class.

P: Imagine your ideal home... It is probably warm, safe, and close to everything that you need... ¹Well, um, even animals need homes like these. They're called habitats, and today I'd like to tell you what they should consist of.

A habitat is a place where an organism such as a plant or an animal lives. But now, a good habitat doesn't just provide a place to live. It also provides everything needed to survive. So it has to have four parts: space, shelter, food, and water.

Um, by space, I mean room to move around... ²Some animals, like, uh, snow leopards need lots of space. That way, they can find food, water, and other resources without having to fight with other snow leopards... For smaller animals, less space might be needed. So, squirrels don't need as much space as a snow leopard.

Let's move on to shelter now. Shelters provide animals a place to eat, sleep, and raise a family. ³A good shelter should also provide protection from bad weather or dangerous animals. So, uh, rabbits... They build their shelters underground. That way, they can be safe and hide from their predators.

Every habitat should also have enough food and water. For example, tigers will survive better in a jungle, where they can hunt for large animals and drink from a river... On the other hand, a city park might be a good home for squirrels. They can gather seeds and nuts there, or drink water that collects on the ground.

환경 과학 강의의 일부를 들으시오.

P: 여러분의 이상적인 집을 상상해보세요... 그것은 아마 따뜻하고, 안전하고, 여러분이 필요로 하는 모든 것과 가까이에 있을 것입니다... 자, 음, 동물들도 이와 같은 집이 필요하죠. 그것들은 서식지라고 불리는데, 오늘 저는 그것들이 무엇으로 구성되어야 하는지 이야기하고자 합니다.

서식지는 식물 혹은 동물과 같은 유기체가 사는 곳입니다. 하지만 이제, 좋은 서식지는 단지 살 곳만 제공하는 것이 아닙니다. 그것은 생존에 필요한 모든 것도 제공하죠. 그래서 그것에는 네 가지 요소들, 즉 공간, 은신처, 먹이, 그리고 물이 있어야 합니다.

음, 공간이란, 움직일 수 있는 공간을 말하는 거예요... 눈표범과 같은, 어, 어떤 동물들은 많은 공간을 필요로 합니다. 그렇게 해서, 그것들은 다른 눈표범들과 싸우지 않고 음식, 물, 그리고 다른 자원들을 찾을 수 있죠. 더 작은 동물들의 경우, 더 적은 공간을 필요로 할 수도 있습니다. 그래서, 다람쥐는 눈표범만큼 많은 공간을 필요로 하지 않죠.

이제 은신처로 넘어가겠습니다. 은신처는 동물들에게 먹고, 자고, 가족을 부양하는 장소를 제공합니다. 좋은 은신처는 나쁜 날씨나 위험한 동물들로부터도 보호를 해줘야겠죠. 그래서, 어, 토끼들... 그것들은 지하에 은신처를 짓습니다. 그렇게 해서, 그것들은 안전할 수 있고 그것들의 포식자로부터 숨을 수 있어요.

모든 서식지에는 충분한 먹이와 물도 있어야 합니다. 예를 들어, 호랑이들은 큰 동물들을 사냥하고 강에서 물을 마실 수 있는 정글에서 더 잘 살아남을 것입니다... 반면에, 다람쥐들에게는 도시공원이 좋은 집일 수 있어요. 그것들은 그곳에서 씨앗과 견과류를 모을 수 있고, 혹은 땅에 고인 물을 마실 수 있죠.

ideal (형) 이상적인 habitat (명) 서식지
consist of ~으로 구성되다 organism (명) 유기체, 생물
provide (동) 제공하다 survive (동) 생존하다, 살아남다
space (명) 공간 shelter (명) 은신처 room (명) 공간
snow leopard 눈표범 resource (명) 자원 move on 넘어가다
raise a family 가족을 부양하다 protection (명) 보호
underground (부) 지하에 predator (명) 포식자 seed (명) 씨앗
collect (동) 모이다; 모으다

1 강의의 주된 주제는 무엇인가?
(A) 야생동물을 보호하는 방법
(B) 동물들이 무엇을 먹기 좋아하는지
(C) 무엇이 좋은 서식지를 만드는지
(D) 동물들이 집을 짓는 방법

2 교수에 따르면, 눈표범에 대한 설명으로 옳은 것은?
(A) 그것들은 대가족으로 산다.
(B) 그것들은 자주 집을 바꾼다.
(C) 그것들은 많은 양의 음식을 보관한다.
(D) 그것들은 많은 공간을 필요로 한다.

3 교수는 은신처에 관해 무엇이라고 말하는가?
(A) 그것들은 외부의 위험으로부터 보호를 해준다.
(B) 그것들은 동물들에게 움직일 수 있는 작은 공간을 준다.
(C) 그것들은 보통 지하에서 발견된다.
(D) 그것들은 동물들이 떠나기 전까지 1년 정도 유지된다.

Listening Practice 3

본문 p.41

1 (A) 2 (C) 3 (C)

Note-taking

Student's Problem

Needs a new place because the <u>construction</u> work is too noisy

Student's Needs
- 40 members → Has to be <u>big</u>
- A <u>piano</u> and a stage

Listen to a conversation between a student and a facilities manager at the university.

W: Hi, Mr. Bowman. Could I <u>speak</u> <u>with</u> <u>you</u>?
M: Sure. What would you like to talk about?
W: Well... As you know, our choir group is <u>participating</u> <u>in</u> <u>a</u> <u>contest</u> next month. ¹It's <u>an</u> <u>important</u> <u>event</u> for us, but I don't think we can practice in Gemma Hall anymore. We <u>need</u> <u>a</u> <u>new</u> <u>place</u>.
M: Oh? What's the problem?
W: ²The construction work in the science department office is <u>too noisy</u>. It's so distracting since we're in the next building. We can't <u>even</u> <u>hear</u> <u>ourselves</u>!
M: OK, OK... Let me find you another place. Is there <u>anything</u> <u>you</u> <u>need</u>?
W: ³We have 40 members, so it <u>has to be big</u>. We also need a piano and a stage.
M: All right. Is that it?
W: Oh, one more thing. We <u>practice</u> <u>daily</u> from 9 a.m. to noon. Everyone in the choir <u>has</u> <u>already</u> <u>agreed</u> <u>to</u> this schedule.
M: OK. <u>Stop</u> <u>by</u> <u>my</u> <u>office</u> before your practice tomorrow. I'll let you know what's available.

대학에서 학생과 시설 관리자 사이의 대화를 들으시오.

W: 안녕하세요, Bowman씨. 얘기 좀 할 수 있을까요?
M: 물론이죠. 무엇에 대해 얘기를 하고 싶으신가요?
W: 음... 아시다시피, 저희 합창단이 다음 달에 대회에 참가해요. 그것은 저희한테 중요한 행사인데, Gemma Hall에서는 더 이상 연습할 수 없을 것 같아요. 저희는 새로운 장소가 필요해요.
M: 오? 무엇이 문제인가요?
W: 과학학과 사무실에서 하는 공사 작업이 너무 시끄러워요. 저희가 옆 건물에 있어서 정말 집중을 할 수가 없어요. 심지어 저희 소리도 스스로 들을 수가 없어요!
M: 네, 네... 다른 곳을 찾아드릴게요. 필요하신 것이 있나요?
W: 저희가 구성원이 40명이어서, 커야 해요. 저희는 피아노와 무대도 필요해요.
M: 좋아요. 그게 전부인가요?
W: 아, 한 가지 더요. 저희는 매일 오전 9시부터 정오까지 연습해요. 합창단의 모든 사람들이 이미 이 일정에 대해 합의했어요.
M: 알겠어요. 내일 연습 전에 제 사무실에 들르세요. 제가 이용 가능한 곳을 알려 드릴게요.

choir group 합창단 construction (명) 공사, 건설
noisy (형) 시끄러운 distracting (형) 집중을 방해하는 daily (부) 매일
agree to ~에 대해 합의하다 schedule (명) 일정
stop by ~에 들르다 available (형) 이용 가능한, 이용할 수 있는

1 학생은 왜 관리자와 이야기하는가?

   (A) 연습할 장소를 요청하기 위해
   (B) 시끄러운 학생들에 대해 불평하기 위해
   (C) 음악 장비를 빌리기 위해
   (D) 학교 대회에 관해 물어보기 위해

2 학생에 따르면, Gemma Hall의 단점은 무엇인가?

   (A) 그곳에는 피아노 무대가 없다.
   (B) 그곳은 과학학과 건물을 공유한다.
   (C) 그곳은 공사 현장과 너무 가깝다.
   (D) 그곳은 수업이 끝난 후에 가기 어렵다.

3 학생에 따르면, 합창단이 필요로 하는 것은 무엇인가?

   (A) 더 나은 악기
   (B) 추가 연습 시간
   (C) 넓은 공간
   (D) 스케줄 변경

Listening Practice 4
본문 p. 43

1 (D)   2 (B)   3 (B)

Note-taking
How Sperm Whales Make Sounds
The spermaceti, a special organ, makes various sounds.

Why Sperm Whales Make Sounds
- To hunt → Don't have good eyesight
- To communicate with each other

Listen to part of a lecture in a biology class.

P: How many of you know the book *Moby Dick*? It's a classic, and its main character is a sperm whale. ¹Sperm whales have many unique characteristics. Today, we will learn about how they use sounds.

But first, let's talk about several other characteristics of sperm whales. These whales have the biggest brains of any animal. They also dive deeper than any other marine mammal, and they use their sharp teeth to capture and hold squid, their favorite food...

Now, let's see how they make sounds. The huge head of a sperm whale contains a special organ called the spermaceti. That's where the whale got its name. The spermaceti is full of thick, waxy oil. It can make various sounds for specific purposes. ²One is a series of clicking noises, which the whale produces for hunting. You see, the sperm whale does not have good eyesight, so it uses sound to find prey. When the clicking sound hits something, like squid in the water, the noise sounds a little different. This way, the whale can know that something is there.

But scientists think the main use of sound is for communication with other sperm whales. They do not know exactly what the whales are saying yet. They believe, uh, sperm whales can send general messages to each other. When they communicate, they use a language with regular patterns. They repeat these patterns to create different messages. ³But, uh, researchers are still trying to understand the sperm whale's messages. If they do, maybe one day we could talk to sperm whales with underwater speakers and microphones!

생물학 강의의 일부를 들으시오.

P: 여러분 중 몇 명이나 '모비 딕'이라는 책을 알고 있나요? 그것은 고전인데, 주인공이 향유고래입니다. 향유고래는 많은 독특한 특징을 가지고 있어요. 오늘, 우리는 그것들이 어떻게 소리를 이용하는지에 대해 배울 것입니다.

하지만 먼저, 향유고래의 몇 가지 다른 특징들에 관해 이야기해 보겠습니다. 이 고래들은 모든 동물 중에서 가장 큰 뇌를 가지고 있어요. 그것들은 또한 다른 해양 포유동물보다 더 깊이 잠수하고, 날카로운 이빨을 사용해서 그것들이 가장 좋아하는 먹이인 오징어를 포획하고 잡죠...

이제, 그것들이 어떻게 소리를 내는지 알아봅시다. 향유고래의 거대한 머리에는 경뇌라고 불리는 특별한 장기가 포함되어 있어요. 여기서 그 고래가 그 이름을 갖게 되었죠. 경뇌는 걸쭉하고 왁스 같은 기름으로 가득 차 있습니다. 그것은 특정한 목적을 위해 다양한 소리를 낼 수 있어요. 하나는 고래가 사냥을 위해 내는 일련의 딸각거리는 소리입니다. 알다시피, 향유고래는 시력이 좋지 않기 때문에, 먹이를 찾기 위해 소리를 이용해요. 딸각거리는 소리가 물속에서 오징어와 같은 무언가에 부딪히면, 그 소리는 조금 다르게 들립니다. 이런 식으로, 고래는 그곳에 무언가가 있다는 것을 알 수 있답니다.

하지만 과학자들은 소리의 주된 용도가 다른 향유고래들과의 의사소통을 위한 것이라고 생각합니다. 그들은 아직 고래들이 정확히 무엇을 말하고 있는지 알지 못해요. 그들은, 어, 향유고래가 서로에게 일반적인 메시지를 전달할 수 있다고 생각해요. 그것들이 의사소통을 할 때, 규칙적인 패턴들을 가진 언어를 사용합니다. 그것들은 이러한 패턴들을 반복해서 다른 메시지를 만들어내죠. 하지만, 어, 연구원들은 여전히 향유고래의 메시지를 이해하기 위해 노력하고 있어요. 만약 그들이 해낸다면, 어쩌면 언젠가 우리는 수중 스피커와 마이크를 가지고 향유고래와 대화할 수도 있을 거예요!

classic 명 고전, 명작   main character 주인공
sperm whale 향유고래   unique 형 독특한, 특별한
characteristic 명 특징   marine mammal 해양 포유동물
capture 동 포획하다   organ 명 장기   spermaceti 명 경뇌
thick 형 걸쭉한; 두꺼운   waxy 형 왁스 같은   a series of 일련의
clicking 형 딸각거리는   produce 동 만들어내다, 생산하다
eyesight 명 시력   prey 명 먹이   communication 명 의사소통
general 형 일반적인   regular 형 규칙적인
microphone 명 마이크

1 강의의 주된 주제는 무엇인가?

   (A) 향유고래의 사냥
   (B) 가장 큰 고래 종의 특징

(C) 해양 포유동물의 의사소통 방법
(D) 향유고래가 소리를 이용하는 방법

2 향유고래는 왜 먹이를 사냥할 때 딸각거리는 소리를 이용하는가?
(A) 그것은 주로 매우 깊은 물에서 먹이를 찾는다.
(B) 그것의 시력이 별로 좋지 않다.
(C) 그것의 딸각거리는 소리는 먼 거리를 이동하지 않는다.
(D) 그것은 그것의 먹이보다 느리게 헤엄친다.

3 교수는 향유고래의 언어에 대해 무엇이라고 말하는가?
(A) 그것에는 주로 무작위의 패턴들이 포함되어 있다.
(B) 과학자들은 여전히 그것을 이해하려고 노력하고 있다.
(C) 그것은 각 고래 집단에 따라 다르다.
(D) 연구원들은 그것을 이용해서 고래와 대화한다.

iBT Listening Test 1   본문 p. 45

1 (C)   **2** (B)   **3** (B)   **4** (C)

Note-taking
Differences between Frogs and Toads
• Physically
- Frogs: More <u>active</u>, thinner and have stronger and longer <u>back</u> <u>legs</u>
- Toads: A short and <u>wide</u> body, short and <u>thick</u> legs
• Skin
- Frogs: Smooth and <u>wet</u>
- Toads: Dry skin that feels thick and <u>rough</u>

Listen to a conversation between a student and a professor.

S: Professor, do you have time to talk? I have some questions about yesterday's lecture...
P: Oh... It was the class on frogs and toads, right?
S: Yes. ¹I'm still not sure about the differences between frogs and toads.
P: ²Well, they are quite similar in many ways, like how they behave or what they eat. Let's see... OK, the best way is to look at some physical differences. In general, frogs are more active. They are thinner and have stronger and longer back legs, so they can jump far.
S: So then, toads are the opposite?
P: Pretty much. They've got a short and wide body, so they look fatter and rounder. Their legs are also short and thick. ³And they like to walk around instead of jumping.
S: I've got it. Anything else?
P: Another big difference is skin. If you look at a frog, its skin is smooth and wet. ⁴Frogs typically stay near the water. This is because they lose moisture quickly. Meanwhile, toads have dry skin that feels thick and rough.

S: I think I understand it better now. Thank you, Professor.

학생과 교수 사이의 대화를 들으시오.

S: 교수님, 얘기할 시간이 있으신가요? 어제 강의에 대해 몇 가지 질문이 있는데요...
P: 아... 개구리와 두꺼비에 관한 수업이었지, 그렇지?
S: 네. 저는 아직도 개구리와 두꺼비의 차이점을 잘 모르겠어요.
P: 음, 그것들은 행동하는 방식이나 먹는 것과 같이 여러 면에서 꽤 비슷하지. 한번 보자... 그래, 가장 좋은 방법은 신체적인 차이를 보는 거야. 일반적으로, 개구리는 더 활동적이야. 그것들은 더 날씬하고 더 강하면서 긴 뒷다리를 가지고 있어서, 멀리 뛸 수 있단다.
S: 그럼, 두꺼비는 그 반대인가요?
P: 거의 그렇지. 그것들은 짧고 넓은 몸통을 가지고 있어서, 더 뚱뚱하고 둥글게 보이지. 그것들의 다리 또한 짧고 굵어. 그리고 그것들은 뛰는 것 대신 걸어다니는 것을 좋아한단다.
S: 알겠습니다. 또 다른 건 없나요?
P: 또 다른 큰 차이점은 피부란다. 만약 네가 개구리를 본다면, 그것의 피부는 매끄럽고 축축할 거야. 개구리는 보통 물 근처에 머무르지. 이것은 그것들이 수분을 빨리 잃기 때문이란다. 한편, 두꺼비는 두껍고 거칠게 느껴지는 건조한 피부를 가지고 있어.
S: 이제 더 잘 이해하게 된 것 같아요. 감사합니다, 교수님.

toad 명 두꺼비   behave 동 행동하다   physical 형 신체적인   active 형 활동적인   back leg 뒷다리   opposite 형 반대의   smooth 형 매끈한   wet 형 축축한, 젖은   typically 부 보통, 일반적으로   dry 형 건조한   rough 형 거친

1 학생의 문제는 무엇인가?
(A) 그녀는 에세이 주제를 생각해낼 수 없다.
(B) 그녀는 여러 수업을 빠졌다.
(C) 그녀는 강의를 이해하지 못했다.
(D) 그녀는 과제에 대해 낮은 점수를 받았다.

2 교수에 따르면, 개구리와 두꺼비를 구별하는 가장 좋은 방법은 무엇인가?
(A) 그것들이 무엇을 먹는지 보는 것
(B) 신체적 특징을 비교하는 것
(C) 생활 환경을 살펴보는 것
(D) 행동 패턴을 분석하는 것

3 교수에 따르면, 두꺼비의 특징은 무엇인가?
(A) 그것들은 긴 뒷다리를 가지고 있다.
(B) 그것들은 걸어다니는 것을 선호한다.
(C) 그것들은 부드러운 피부를 가지고 있다.
(D) 그것들은 얇은 몸통을 가지고 있다.

4 대화에 따르면, 개구리가 물 가까이에 머무는 이유는 무엇인가?
(A) 그것들은 알을 지켜봐야 한다.
(B) 그것들은 두꺼비보다 물을 더 자주 마신다.
(C) 그것들의 피부는 수분을 매우 빨리 잃을 수 있다.
(D) 그것들의 주 먹이가 물속에서 산다.

iBT Listening Test 2

본문 p.48

1 (C)　　2 (C)　　3 (D)　　4 (B)

Note-taking
Mysteries of Stonehenge
Stonehenge: A stone circle in England, made up of 83 giant stones
- How It Was Built: Stones come from far away and are very heavy.
  → Would have required hundreds of people to move them
- Why It Was Built: Bones of many ancient leaders and royal families around Stonehenge
  → Was probably used as a burial site for about 500 years

Listen to part of a lecture in an archaeology class.

P: Does anyone like archaeology or mysteries? ¹Then, you will be interested in learning about today's topic, an important monument called Stonehenge.

Stonehenge is basically a stone circle which is located in Salisbury, England. ²There are 83 giant stones. Um, most of them are standing, while some are lying on top of the standing stones. Together, the stones form a circle. Many of the stones are broken, and only some of them remain.

Scientists believe Stonehenge was built between 5,000 and 3,000 BC. Because of its age, people wonder how it was built. The stones come from far away, and they're very heavy. Um, each stone weighs 25 tons on average. That's about the same weight as a large bus filled with people. It is hard to imagine how people could have moved them or placed them on top of other stones. You know, at the time, the wheel wasn't invented yet, and people only had simple tools made of wood and stone. ⁴It would have required hundreds of people to move the stones. But, um, we can only imagine what happened. There are no documents about the construction.

The purpose of Stonehenge is another mystery that we aren't sure about. ³But still, scientists have been able to gather some clues. Researchers discovered human bones around Stonehenge and analyzed them. They found that they were the bones of many ancient leaders and royal families. It is assumed that people used Stonehenge as a burial site for about 500 years.

고고학 강의의 일부를 들으시오.

P: 고고학이나 수수께끼를 좋아하는 분 있나요? 그렇다면, 여러분은 오늘의 주제인 스톤헨지라고 불리는 중요한 유적에 대해 배우는 것에 흥미를 느낄 겁니다.

스톤헨지는 기본적으로 영국 솔즈베리에 위치한 환상 열석입니다. 83개의 거대한 돌들이 있죠. 음, 그것들의 대부분은 서 있는 반면, 일부는 그 서 있는 돌들 위에 놓여 있습니다. 다 함께, 그 돌들은 원을 형성하죠. 그 돌들 중 많은 것들이 부서졌고, 몇 개만이 남아 있습니다.

과학자들은 스톤헨지가 기원전 5,000년에서 3,000년 사이에 지어졌다고 믿습니다. 그것의 연대 때문에, 사람들은 그것이 어떻게 지어졌는지 궁금해하죠. 그 돌들은 먼 곳에서 왔고, 매우 무겁습니다. 음, 각 돌의 무게는 평균적으로 25톤이에요. 그것은 사람들로 가득 찬 대형 버스와 거의 똑같은 무게죠. 사람들이 어떻게 그것을 옮겼는지 또는 어떻게 다른 돌들 위에 놓을 수 있었는지는 상상하기 어려워요. 그러니까, 그 당시에는 바퀴가 아직 발명되지 않았고, 사람들은 나무와 돌로 만들어진 간단한 도구들만 가지고 있었으니까요. 돌을 옮기려면 수백 명의 사람들을 필요로 했을 것입니다. 하지만, 음, 우리는 무슨 일이 있었는지 오직 상상만 할 수 있겠죠. 건설에 관한 문서가 없거든요.

스톤헨지의 목적은 우리가 잘 알지 못하는 또 다른 수수께끼입니다. 하지만 그래도, 과학자들은 몇 가지 단서들을 모을 수 있었어요. 연구원들이 스톤헨지 주변에서 인간의 뼈들을 발견해서 그것들을 분석했는데요. 그들은 그것들이 많은 고대 지도자들과 왕족의 뼈라는 것을 알아냈습니다. 사람들이 약 500년 동안 스톤헨지를 매장지로 사용했을 것이라고 추정되는 것이죠.

monument ⑲ 유적; 기념물　basically ⑼ 기본적으로
stone circle 환상 열석(거대한 돌이 둥글게 줄지어 놓은 고대 유적)
be located in ~에 위치해 있다
Salisbury ⑲ 솔즈베리(영국 윌트셔주의 도시)
lie ⑧ 놓여 있다; 눕다　form ⑧ 형성하다; ⑲ 종류
remain ⑧ 남아 있다　weigh ⑧ 무게가 ~이다
on average 평균적으로　place ⑧ 놓다, 두다
require ⑧ 필요하다, 요구하다　construction ⑲ 건설
clue ⑲ 단서　discover ⑧ 발견하다　analyze ⑧ 분석하다
assume ⑧ 추정하다　burial site 매장지

1 강의의 주된 주제는 무엇인가?
　(A) 스톤헨지에서의 새로운 발견
　(B) 스톤헨지를 지은 유명한 건축가
　(C) 역사상 중요한 유적
　(D) 최근에 개장한 명소

2 교수에 따르면, 스톤헨지의 특징은 무엇인가?
　(A) 그것에는 상태가 좋은 돌들이 많이 있다.
　(B) 그것은 수백 개의 돌들로 이루어져 있다.
　(C) 그것에는 각기 다른 자세로 있는 돌들이 있다.
　(D) 그것에는 둥근 모양의 돌들이 포함되어 있다.

3 교수에 따르면, 스톤헨지의 목적에 대한 단서는 무엇인가?
　(A) 그것이 지어진 해
　(B) 그것이 향하는 방향
　(C) 그것의 돌들의 출처
　(D) 그것 주변에서 발견된 뼈들

강의의 일부를 다시 듣고 질문에 답하시오.
P: It would have required hundreds of people to move the stones. But, um, we can only imagine what happened. There are no documents about the construction.

4 교수는 왜 이렇게 말하는가:
   P: But, um, we can only imagine what happened.
   (A) 유적이 오래 전에 지어졌다는 것을 강조하기 위해
   (B) 건설에 대한 정보가 부족함을 나타내기 위해
   (C) 몇몇 의견이 비판받는 이유를 설명하기 위해
   (D) 다양한 이론이 있다는 것을 암시하기 위해

Vocabulary Review   본문 p.52

1 suitable   2 advanced   3 monument
4 produce   5 prepare for   6 purpose
7 consist of   8 ideal   9 analyze
10 (B)   11 (C)   12 (A)
13 (D)   14 (A)

CHAPTER 03
Function

Example   본문 p.55

A. (C)   B. (A)

A.

Note-taking

Professor's Request to Student
You've been working as a volunteer teacher.
→ Share your teaching[volunteer] experiences in one of my courses

Student's Response
Would like to help

Listen to a conversation between a student and a professor.

S: Hi, Professor Daniels. Did you want to see me about something?
P: Hello, Ellen. Yes, thank you for coming... Um, so you've been working as a volunteer teacher. Is that right?
S: Yes. I've been teaching English at an elementary school every Friday. It's been about a year now.
P: That is wonderful to hear.
S: Thank you, Professor. I've enjoyed it a lot.
P: Um, I'd like you to share your teaching experiences in one of my courses, Introduction to Education. You know, it would help the students understand the process of learning.
S: I welcome the opportunity. I've learned so much from your classes, so I'd really like to help.
P: Thank you, Ellen. I'll check the schedule and let you know.

학생과 교수 사이의 대화를 들으시오.

S: 안녕하세요, Daniels 교수님. 무언가에 대해 저를 보고 싶어 하셨다고요?
P: 안녕, Ellen. 그래, 와줘서 고맙단다... 음, 그래서 네가 자원봉사 선생님으로 일해 왔다면서. 그게 맞지?
S: 네. 저는 매주 금요일마다 초등학교에서 영어를 가르치고 있어요. 이제 약 1년 정도 됐고요.
P: 참 잘된 일이구나.
S: 감사해요, 교수님. 아주 즐겁게 해왔어요.
P: 음, 네가 내 수업 중 하나인 교육학개론에서 네 교육 경험을 함께 나눴으면 좋겠구나. 알다시피, 그것이 학생들이 학습 과정을 이해하는 데 도움이 될 거야.
S: 그 기회를 기꺼이 받아들일게요. 저는 교수님의 수업에서 아주 많이 배웠기 때문에, 정말로 돕고 싶어요.
P: 고맙구나, Ellen. 내가 일정을 확인하고 네게 알려주마.

work as ~으로 일하다   volunteer teacher 자원봉사 선생님
course 명 수업   process 명 과정
welcome 동 기꺼이 받아들이다; 환영하다   opportunity 명 기회
schedule 명 일정

대화의 일부를 다시 듣고 질문에 답하시오.
P: Um, I'd like you to share your teaching experiences in one of my courses, Introduction to Education. You know, it would help the students understand the process of learning.
S: I welcome the opportunity. I've learned so much from your classes, so I'd really like to help.

학생은 왜 이렇게 말하는가:
S: I welcome the opportunity.

(A) 수업을 수강하는 것에 대한 설렘을 표현하기 위해
(B) 그녀가 자신의 책임을 이해한다는 것을 보여주기 위해
(C) 그녀가 기꺼이 교수를 도울 의사가 있다는 것을 암시하기 위해
(D) 교수에게 시간을 내준 것에 대해 감사를 전하기 위해

B.

Note-taking

How Polynesians Navigated with Stars

1. Divided the sky into eight parts
2. Memorized the positions of hundreds of stars
→ Found the direction back to their islands this way

Listen to part of a lecture in an astronomy class.

P: If you are on a boat in the middle of the Pacific Ocean, it will be very difficult to know where you are. Of course, you can use advanced technology to help you. But, thousands of years ago, the Polynesian people didn't need it. Let's talk about how they were able to navigate with stars.

The Polynesians could travel thousands of miles across the Pacific Ocean and always find their way back home. They noticed certain stars always appear in the same positions in the sky at different times of the year. So, they divided the sky into eight parts. Each part had its own set of stars that moved together. Then, they memorized the positions of hundreds of stars. This helped them find the direction back to their islands.

천문학 강의의 일부를 들으시오.

P: 만약 여러분이 태평양 한가운데에 배를 타고 있다면, 여러분이 어디에 있는지 아는 것은 매우 어려울 것입니다. 물론, 여러분을 도울 첨단 기술을 사용할 수도 있겠죠. 하지만, 수천 년 전, 폴리네시아 사람들은 그것을 필요로 하지 않았습니다. 그들이 어떻게 별을 가지고 길을 찾을 수 있었는지 이야기해 봅시다.

폴리네시아인들은 태평양을 가로질러 수천 마일을 이동하고는 항상 집으로 돌아가는 길을 찾을 수 있었습니다. 그들은 특정 별들이 일 년 중 다른 시간대에도 항상 하늘에서 같은 위치에 나타나는 것을 알아차렸어요. 그래서, 그들은 하늘을 8개의 부분으로 나누었습니다. 각 부분은 함께 움직이는 별들의 집합으로 이루어졌죠. 그러고 나서, 그들은 수백 개의 별들의 위치를 외웠습니다. 이것이 그들이 섬으로 돌아가는 방향을 찾는 데 도움이 되었죠.

Pacific Ocean 태평양　advanced technology 첨단 기술
Polynesian (명) 폴리네시아인(폴리네시아의 원주민)
navigate (동) 길을 찾다; 항해하다
find one's way back 돌아가는 길을 찾다　notice (동) 알아차리다
certain (형) 특정한　appear (동) 나타나다　position (명) 위치
divide into ~으로 나누다　set of ~의 집합　memorize (동) 외우다
direction (명) 방향

강의의 일부를 다시 듣고 질문에 답하시오.
P: If you are on a boat in the middle of the Pacific Ocean, it will be very difficult to know where you are. Of course, you can use advanced technology to help you. But, thousands of years ago, the Polynesian people didn't need it.

교수는 왜 이렇게 말하는가:
P: But, thousands of years ago, the Polynesian people didn't need it.

(A) 폴리네시아인들에게 그들만의 항해법이 있다는 것을 나타내기 위해
(B) 폴리네시아인들이 여행을 자주 할 필요가 없었다는 것을 암시하기 위해
(C) 폴리네시아인들이 현대 기술을 좋아하지 않았던 이유를 설명하기 위해
(D) 첨단 기술 사용에 대한 문제점을 강조하기 위해

Listening Practice 1　　본문 p.57

1 (B)　　2 (C)　　3 (A)

Note-taking
Student's Problem
Having trouble with college[school/university] life
Counselor's Suggestion
Sign up for a photography club
→ A great opportunity to meet new people

Listen to a conversation between a student and a counselor at the University Counseling Center.

M: Hi, my name is Mason Conner. I had an appointment today.
W: Of course. Welcome, Mason. How can I help you?
M: ¹Well, I'm having trouble with, um, college life.
W: It's your first year here, right? What are you having difficulties with?
M: Actually, I come from a small town. There were only 180 people in my high school. And now, I'm in a place with thousands of students!
W: Going from high school to university is a big step in life. So, it can be a confusing experience for anyone.
M: ³You're exactly right. And also... Well... I guess I'm lonely, too. I'm shy, so it's hard to make new friends.
W: Don't worry. You're not the only one. Let's see... What are some of your interests or hobbies?
M: Uh, I love to take pictures.
W: ²Oh, did you know that the college has a photography club? How about signing up? It would be a great opportunity to meet new people. You can also do something you love.
M: That sounds like a great idea!

대학 상담 센터에서 학생과 상담원 사이의 대화를 들으시오.

M: 안녕하세요, 제 이름은 Mason Conner입니다. 오늘 예약이 있었어요.
W: 물론이죠. 어서 오세요, Mason. 어떻게 도와드릴까요?
M: 그게, 저는, 음, 대학 생활에 어려움을 겪고 있어요.
W: 이곳에서의 첫해예요, 그렇죠? 어떤 일로 어려움을 겪고 계시나요?
M: 사실, 저는 작은 마을 출신이거든요. 제 고등학교에는 180명밖에 없었어요. 그리고 지금, 저는 수천 명의 학생들이 있는 곳에 있고요!
W: 고등학교에서 대학교로 가는 것은 인생에서 큰 변화죠. 그래서 그것은 누구에게나 혼란스러운 경험이 될 수 있어요.
M: 정말 그래요. 그리고 또... 글쎄요... 외로운 것 같기도 해요. 저는 수줍음을 많이 타서, 새로운 친구를 사귀기가 힘들거든요.
W: 걱정하지 마세요. 학생만 그런 게 아니에요. 어디 봅시다... 관심사나 취미는 무엇인가요?
M: 어, 저는 사진 찍는 것을 좋아해요.
W: 아, 대학에 사진 동아리가 있다는 것을 알고 있었나요? 가입해 보는 건 어때요? 새로운 사람들을 만날 수 있는 좋은 기회가 될 거예요. 학생이 좋아하는 것도 할 수 있고요.

M: 좋은 생각인 것 같아요!

appointment 명 예약; 약속　come from ~의 출신이다
confusing 형 혼란스러운　guess 동 ~인 것 같다; 추측하다
interest 명 관심사, 흥미　hobby 명 취미
photography 명 사진 촬영, 사진술　sign up 가입하다

1 화자들은 주로 무엇을 논의하고 있는가?

(A) 대학 생활의 장점
(B) 학교 생활에 적응하는 방법
(C) 다양한 종류의 학교 프로그램
(D) 수업을 취소하는 방법

2 여자는 남자에게 무엇을 제안하는가?

(A) 새로운 취미를 찾기
(B) 온라인으로 사람들을 만나기
(C) 학교 동아리에 가입하기
(D) 학교 행사에 참여하기

대화의 일부를 다시 듣고 질문에 답하시오.

M: You're exactly right. And also... Well... I guess I'm lonely, too. I'm shy, so it's hard to make new friends.
W: Don't worry. You're not the only one.

3 여자는 왜 이렇게 말하는가:

W: Don't worry. You're not the only one.

(A) 남자의 기분이 나아지도록 하기 위해
(B) 남자의 실수를 바로잡기 위해
(C) 남자에게 서두르라고 말하기 위해
(D) 남자의 의견에 반대하기 위해

Listening Practice 2　　본문 p.59

1 (B)　　**2** (D)　　**3** (B)

Note-taking
Factors of Firenadoes

Firenadoes: Tornadoes made of gas, fire, and smoke
- A very hot fire, which needs a lot of fuel
- Wind

Listen to part of a lecture in an earth science class.

P: So... What are tornadoes? They are violent winds in the shape of a cone. But tornadoes can also be made of gas, fire, and smoke! ¹These are called fire tornadoes, or "firenadoes," and today I'd like to discuss how they form.

Well, fire tornadoes are very rare. You need very specific conditions. ²First of all, you must have a very hot fire. And for that, uh, you must have a lot of fuel. This can be dry wood, oil, hot gases in the air, or anything that can burn for a long time. Another factor is wind. If all of these conditions occur, it's possible to have a fire tornado.

Fire tornadoes often start from large fires. During a large fire, hot gases start to move the air around. This causes wind to move in different directions, and, uh, at different speeds. Occasionally, the fire will quickly rise up high into the air and... create a fire tornado.

So, let me give you an example... In 1926, an actual fire tornado happened at a storage facility in California. Lightning hit a big tank that was full of oil. This started a fire. Because of the huge amount of oil, the fire had enough fuel to last for several days. It grew so hot that hot gases moved the air around the fire and this created wind. ³So there was a lot of fuel, a very hot fire, and also a lot of wind. Because of this, many fire tornadoes formed. There were too many to count. Some were very tall and, uh, traveled up to five miles away from the original fire.

지구 과학 강의의 일부를 들으시오.

P: 자... 토네이도가 뭐죠? 그것들은 원뿔 모양의 격렬한 바람입니다. 하지만 토네이도는 가스, 불, 그리고 연기로도 만들어질 수 있어요! 이것들은 파이어 토네이도, 혹은 '파이어네이도'라고 불리는데, 오늘은 그것들이 어떻게 형성되는지를 논의하고 싶군요.

음, 파이어 토네이도는 매우 드뭅니다. 매우 구체적인 조건들이 필요하거든요. 우선, 매우 뜨거운 불이 있어야 합니다. 그리고 그러려면, 어, 연료가 많이 있어야 하는데요. 이것은 건조한 목재, 기름, 공기 중의 뜨거운 가스, 또는 오랫동안 탈 수 있는 거라면 무엇이든 될 수 있어요. 또 다른 요인은 바람입니다. 이 모든 조건들이 일어난다면, 파이어 토네이도가 생길 수 있습니다.

파이어 토네이도는 종종 큰 화재에서 시작됩니다. 큰 화재 동안, 뜨거운 가스는 공기를 이리저리 움직이기 시작합니다. 이것은 바람이 다른 방향으로 움직이게 하고, 그리고, 어, 다른 속도로도 움직이게 합니다. 가끔, 불은 빠르게 공중으로 높이 올라가서... 파이어 토네이도를 일으키죠.

자, 예를 하나 들어보겠습니다... 1926년에, 실제 파이어 토네이도가 캘리포니아에 있는 한 저장시설에서 발생했어요. 번개가 기름으로 가득 차 있던 큰 탱크를 내리쳤죠. 이것이 화재를 일으켰습니다. 엄청난 양의 기름 때문에, 그 화재는 며칠 동안 지속될 수 있을 만큼 충분한 연료가 있었죠. 그것은 너무 뜨거워져서 뜨거운 가스가 불 주위의 공기를 움직였고 이것은 바람을 만들었습니다. 그래서 많은 연료와 매우 뜨거운 불, 그리고 바람도 많이 있었습니다. 이것 때문에, 많은 파이어 토네이도가 형성되었어요. 셀 수 없을 정도로 많이요. 어떤 것들은 매우 컸는데, 어, 최초의 화재에서 5마일 떨어진 곳까지 이동하기도 했습니다.

tornado 명 토네이도, 회오리바람　violent 형 격렬한; 폭력적인
smoke 명 연기　rare 형 드문, 희귀한　specific 형 구체적인; 특정한
condition 명 조건; 상태　fuel 명 연료　burn 동 타다
factor 명 요인　occur 동 발생하다　occasionally 부 가끔
rise 동 올라가다　storage facility 저장시설　lightning 명 번개
last 동 지속되다　grow 동 ~하게 되다; 자라다　up to ~까지
original 형 최초의; 원래의

1 강의의 주된 주제는 무엇인가?

(A) 산불의 위험성
(B) 파이어 토네이도의 형성

(C) 산불을 통제하기 위한 노력
(D) 토네이도의 해로운 영향

2 교수에 따르면, 매우 뜨거운 화재에 필요한 것은 무엇인가?

(A) 매우 건조한 환경
(B) 강풍
(C) 뜨거운 온도
(D) 많은 양의 연료

강의의 일부를 다시 듣고 질문에 답하시오.
P: So there was a lot of fuel, a very hot fire, and also a lot of wind. Because of this, many fire tornadoes formed. There were too many to count.

3 교수는 왜 이렇게 말하는가:
P: There were too many to count.
(A) 학생들에게 숫자를 맞히라고 하기 위해
(B) 그녀가 한 주장을 강조하기 위해
(C) 화재가 위험하다는 것을 보여주기 위해
(D) 그녀가 소개한 조건을 재검토하기 위해

Listening Practice 3 본문 p.61

1 (C) 2 (B) 3 (B)

Note-taking

Student's Problem
Worried because her partner is not working hard

Professor's Suggestion
May be worth changing the topic of the project
→ Discuss it with Justin

Listen to a conversation between a student and a professor.

S: Umm... Professor Stone? May I speak with you about something?
P: Sure, Sarah. How can I help?
S: ¹It's about the group project. My partner is Justin, but, um... I'm worried because he's not really doing his work.
P: Oh, really? ²That's surprising. He was one of my most hardworking students last semester. It seems strange that he's not working hard.
S: That's what I thought, too. Um, I don't know what to do.
P: Maybe something about the project is bothering him. Hmm... Is the topic you chose too difficult?
S: ³No, but... Actually, Justin didn't seem to like the topic that much. He even talked about changing it two days ago, but I thought it would be too late.
P: It may be worth it. You have two weeks left.
S: Do you think that's enough time?
P: If you organize your time with a clear plan, well,

yes. You'll be able to finish it on time. Why don't you at least discuss it with Justin?
S: I will. Thanks for the advice, Professor Stone.

학생과 교수 사이의 대화를 들으시오.

S: 음... Stone 교수님? 얘기 좀 할 수 있을까요?
P: 물론이지, Sarah. 어떻게 도와줄까?
S: 조별 과제에 관한 건데요. 제 파트너는 Justin이에요, 그런데, 음... 자신의 일을 제대로 하고 있지 않아서 걱정이에요.
P: 오, 그래? 그거 놀랍구나. 그는 지난 학기에 가장 열심히 하는 학생 중 한 명이었거든. 그가 열심히 하고 있지 않다니 이상하구나.
S: 저도 그렇게 생각했어요. 음, 제가 어떻게 해야 할지 모르겠어요.
P: 아마도 그 과제에 대한 뭔가가 그를 신경 쓰이게 하고 있는 걸 수도 있어. 음... 너희가 선택한 주제가 너무 어렵니?
S: 아뇨, 그런데... 사실, Justin이 그 주제를 별로 좋아하지 않는 것 같았어요. 이틀 전에는 심지어 그것을 바꾸는 것에 대해서도 말했었는데, 저는 너무 늦었을 거라고 생각했거든요.
P: 그럴 만한 가치가 있을지도 모른단다. 2주가 남았잖니.
S: 그 정도면 충분한 시간이라고 생각하세요?
P: 만약 너희가 명확한 계획을 가지고 시간을 정리해본다면, 음, 그렇지. 제시간에 끝낼 수 있을 거야. Justin과 적어도 상의라도 해보는 게 어떠니?
S: 그럴게요. 충고 감사해요, Stone 교수님.

group project 조별 과제 hardworking 형 열심히 하는
semester 명 학기 seem 동 ~인 것 같다
bother 동 신경 쓰이게 하다 worth 형 ~할 가치가 있는
organize 동 정리하다; 준비하다 clear 형 명확한, 분명한
plan 명 계획 on time 제시간에 at least 적어도, 최소한
discuss 동 상의하다

1 학생은 왜 교수를 찾아가는가?

(A) 다른 과제를 요청하기 위해
(B) 조별 경연대회에 대한 정보를 얻기 위해
(C) 파트너에 대한 우려를 나타내기 위해
(D) 과제 성적을 변경하는 것에 대해 묻기 위해

2 교수는 왜 학생의 말에 놀라는가?

(A) 그는 과제에 대해 더 좋은 결과물을 기대했기 때문에
(B) 그는 한 학생이 열심히 할 것이라고 생각했기 때문에
(C) 그는 일부 학생들이 친한 친구였다는 것을 알고 있었기 때문에
(D) 그는 그 팀이 작업을 늦게 시작했다고 느꼈기 때문에

대화의 일부를 다시 듣고 질문에 답하시오.
S: No, but... Actually, Justin didn't seem to like the topic that much. He even talked about changing it two days ago, but I thought it would be too late.
P: It may be worth it. You have two weeks left.

3 교수는 이렇게 말함으로써 무엇을 의미하는가:
P: It may be worth it. You have two weeks left.
(A) 그는 그 조가 더 열심히 하기를 원한다.
(B) 그는 그들이 다른 주제를 선택해야 한다고 생각한다.

(C) 그는 그 과제가 의미 있다는 것에 동의한다.
(D) 그는 그 학생이 새로운 팀을 찾을 것을 제안한다.

Listening Practice 4
본문 p.63

1 (A) 2 (A) 3 (B)

Note-taking
Sculptures for Portraits
- Made of <u>family</u> members who died
- Made of the Roman <u>emperor</u>

Sculptures for Decoration
Appeared in public and private <u>gardens</u> and baths

Listen to part of a lecture in an art history class.

P: Let's get started. We discussed <u>the development of Greek sculpture</u> in the last class. Now, we're going to move on to Roman sculpture. ¹<u>Roman sculpture had a few interesting cultural functions.</u>

The most important one was for portraits, or uh, artworks of people. ²<u>Portrait sculpture was mainly for</u> the upper class. It was used to <u>honor family members and ancestors</u>. So, uh, upper class families hired artists to make sculptures of family members <u>who died</u>. Then, the sculptures <u>were placed</u> in the tombs of these dead family members.

But, uh, portraits were also made of <u>the Roman emperor</u>. As the Roman Empire spread, they put statues of the emperor in new territories. This way, people would <u>become familiar with</u> the appearance of the emperor. This had a couple of purposes. First, the people would <u>recognize the emperor's face</u>, which also appeared on Roman coins. Um, they would trade and pay taxes with these coins. Second, it would <u>display the emperor's power</u>. Typically, he would be wearing military armor, which <u>showed his strength</u> and authority.

Lastly... Sculptures were also <u>used for decoration</u>. They appeared in both public and private gardens and baths. Often, the subjects were gods or goddesses. Romans believed these sculptures <u>gave good luck and protection</u> to the home. ³Uh, and it did take some skill to produce these sculptures, but they weren't <u>as well-made as</u> the other types of statues. Let's just say they were <u>not intended for</u> museums.

미술사학 강의의 일부를 들으시오.

P: 시작해 봅시다. 우리는 지난 수업에서 그리스 조각상의 발전에 대해 논의했었죠. 이제, 우리는 로마 조각상으로 넘어갈 것입니다. 로마 조각상에는 몇 가지 흥미로운 문화적 기능이 있었어요.

가장 중요한 것은 초상화 혹은, 어, 인물을 담은 예술 작품에 대한 것이었습니다. 초상화 조각상은 주로 상류층을 위한 것이었어요. 그것은 가족 구성원과 조상들을 기리기 위해 사용되었죠. 그래서, 어, 상류층 가족들은 예술가들을 고용해서 죽은 가족 구성원들의 조각상을 만들었습니다. 그 다음, 그 조각상들은 죽은 가족 구성원들의 무덤에 놓였습니다.

하지만, 어, 초상화는 로마 황제로도 만들어졌어요. 로마 제국이 확장하면서, 그들은 새로운 영토에 황제의 조각상을 세웠는데요. 이렇게 해서, 사람들은 황제의 모습에 익숙해졌겠죠. 여기에는 두어 가지 목적이 있었습니다. 우선, 사람들이 황제의 얼굴을 알아보게 됐을 텐데, 이는 로마 동전에도 있었어요. 음, 그들은 이 동전들로 거래하고 세금을 냈을 겁니다. 둘째로, 그것은 황제의 권력을 보여줬을 거예요. 일반적으로, 그의 힘과 권위를 보여주는 군용 갑옷을 입고 있었을 것입니다.

마지막으로... 조각상들은 장식을 위해서도 사용되었습니다. 그것들은 공공 혹은 개인 정원과 목욕탕에 모두 있었습니다. 종종, 그 주제는 신이나 여신들이었습니다. 로마인들은 이 조각상들이 가정에 행운과 보호를 제공한다고 믿었어요. 어, 그리고 이 조각상들을 만드는 데는 약간의 기술이 필요하긴 했지만, 그것들은 다른 유형의 조각상들만큼 잘 만들어지지는 않았어요. 그냥 그것들이 박물관을 위해 만들어진 것이 아니었다고 해두죠.

---

sculpture 명 조각상   portrait 명 초상화   upper class 상류층
honor 동 기리다; 명 명예   hire 동 고용하다   emperor 명 황제
Roman Empire 로마 제국   spread 동 확장하다, 퍼지다
statue 명 조각상   territory 명 영토   appearance 명 모습, 외모
a couple of 두어 가지의, 둘의   recognize 동 알아보다
trade 동 거래하다, 교역하다   tax 명 세금
display 동 보여주다, 전시하다   military 형 군용의, 군사의
armor 명 갑옷   strength 명 힘   authority 명 권위
intended for ~을 위해 만들어진

1 강의는 주로 무엇에 관한 것인가?
(A) 로마 조각상의 기능
(B) 그리스와 로마 조각상의 비교
(C) 로마 조각상의 특징
(D) 로마 초상화의 시초

2 교수는 초상화 조각상에 대해 무엇이라고 말하는가?
(A) 그것은 친척들과 조상들을 기리기 위해 사용되었다.
(B) 그것은 주로 하류층을 위한 것이었다.
(C) 그것은 가장 비싼 종류의 조각상이었다.
(D) 그것은 새로운 영토에서는 덜 흔했다.

강의의 일부를 다시 듣고 질문에 답하시오.
P: Uh, and it did take some skill to produce these sculptures, but they weren't as well-made as the other types of statues. Let's just say they were not intended for museums.

3 교수는 이렇게 말함으로써 무엇을 암시하는가:
P: Let's just say they were not intended for museums.

(A) 개인 소유의 조각상은 항상 행운을 가져다주지는 않았다.
(B) 장식을 위한 조각상은 최상의 품질이 아니었다.
(C) 정원의 조각상은 공개적으로는 거의 전시되지 않았다.
(D) 박물관들에는 보통 그곳 고유의 조각가들이 있었다.

iBT Listening Test 1

본문 p. 65

1 (C) 2 (B) 3 (D) 4 (B)

Note-taking

Student's Problem
Has not received her pay

Employee's Response
- School's computer server broke down last week.
  → Some files were lost.
- Will call the school's IT department tomorrow

Listen to a conversation between a student and a university employee.

W: Hi, I talked to you on the phone yesterday. My name is Erin Parsons...

M: Oh, yes! You had a question about your part-time job?

W: Well, I work at the school library. ¹I was supposed to receive my pay last Friday, but I still haven't received anything.

M: Hmm... That's strange. Are you a new worker? It takes a while for the system to update new employee information.

W: ⁴I've been there since last semester. It's the first time this has happened. I checked with the bank, and there's no issue with my account.

M: Oh, I almost forgot! Actually, we had an unfortunate incident last week. ²Our computer server broke down and some files were lost. They included a list of employees and their pay.

W: Then what can I do now? When can I receive my money?

M: Um, I'm sorry, but you'll have to wait until the server is fixed. ³But I'll call the school's IT department tomorrow and let you know.

W: All right. I appreciate it.

학생과 교직원 사이의 대화를 들으시오.

W: 안녕하세요, 어제 통화했는데요. 제 이름은 Erin Parsons에요...

M: 아, 그래요! 학생의 아르바이트직에 대해 질문이 있으셨죠?

W: 음, 저는 학교 도서관에서 일하는데요. 지난 금요일에 급여를 받기로 되어 있었는데, 아직 아무것도 못 받았어요.

M: 흠... 그거 이상하네요. 새로운 직원이신가요? 시스템이 새로운 직원 정보를 업데이트하는 데 시간이 좀 걸리거든요.

W: 저는 지난 학기부터 그곳에 있었어요. 이런 일이 일어난 건 처음이에요. 제가 은행에 확인을 해봤는데, 제 계좌에는 문제가 없어요.

M: 아, 잊을 뻔했군요! 사실, 지난주에 유감스러운 일이 있었어요. 저희 컴퓨터 서버가 고장 나서 파일들이 몇 개 없어졌거든요. 그것들에는 직원 명단과 그들의 급여가 포함되어 있었어요.

W: 그럼 저는 이제 어떻게 하죠? 저는 언제 돈을 받을 수 있나요?

M: 음, 죄송하지만, 서버가 수리될 때까지 기다리셔야 할 거예요. 하지만 제가 내일 학교 IT 부서에 전화해보고 알려드릴게요.

W: 좋아요. 감사합니다.

---

part-time job 아르바이트(직)   receive 동 받다
pay 명 급여; 동 지불하다   account 명 계좌
unfortunate 형 유감스러운; 운이 없는   incident 명 일, 사건
break down 고장 나다   include 동 포함하다
fix 동 수리하다, 고치다   department 명 부서

1 화자들은 주로 무엇을 논의하고 있는가?
(A) 학생의 고장 난 컴퓨터
(B) 도서관에서의 일자리 공석
(C) 학생의 받지 못한 급여
(D) 학생이 하고 있는 학교 프로젝트

2 대화에 따르면, 일부 파일이 없어진 이유는 무엇인가?
(A) 직원이 실수를 했다.
(B) 컴퓨터 서버가 작동을 멈췄다.
(C) 한 부서에서 새로운 직원을 고용했다.
(D) 새로운 시스템이 도입되었다.

3 직원은 학생에게 무엇을 해주기로 하는가?
(A) 일부 계정 정보를 변경하기
(B) 교수님으로부터 서류에 서명받기
(C) 은행에 전화하기
(D) 학교 부서에 연락하기

대화의 일부를 다시 듣고 질문에 답하시오.

W: I've been there since last semester. It's the first time this has happened. I checked with the bank, and there's no issue with my account.

M: Oh, I almost forgot! Actually, we had an unfortunate incident last week.

4 직원은 이렇게 말함으로써 무엇을 암시하는가:
M: Oh, I almost forgot!
(A) 그는 학생의 은행 계좌를 확인했다.
(B) 그는 문제의 원인을 기억해냈다.
(C) 그는 방금 이전의 요청사항에 대해 들었다.
(D) 그는 할당된 일을 끝내지 못했다.

iBT Listening Test 2

본문 p. 68

1 (D) 2 (C) 3 (B) 4 (B)

Note-taking

The Pygmalion Effect
- Background: An ancient Greek story
  → Pygmalion truly loved the statue, and the goddess made his wish come true.
- Experiment: Robert Rosenthal's experiment with students
  → Those who were expected to do well performed the best.

Listen to part of a lecture in a psychology class.

P: Have you ever had a teacher who strongly believed in you? Or what about one who thought that you weren't good enough? ¹Think about which teacher helped you perform better. Well, this is related to today's topic. It's a psychological phenomenon called the Pygmalion Effect.

Now, um, the name Pygmalion comes from an ancient Greek story. It's a story about a sculptor named Pygmalion who fell in love with a statue he made. ²He asked Aphrodite, the ancient Greek goddess of love, to make the statue alive... Because Pygmalion truly loved the statue, the goddess made his wish come true. So the Pygmalion Effect describes a situation where wishing about something strongly can make it come true. In other words, positive expectations can have a positive effect on people. ³Um, when someone expects you to do well, there is a high chance that you will do well... This happens because people change their behavior based on expectations... So if your teacher thinks you're smart, you might study harder to become an actual smart student.

Anyway, in 1968, the psychologist Robert Rosenthal conducted an experiment to test the Pygmalion Effect. He made some elementary school students take an intelligence test at the beginning of the first semester. Then, he told the students' teachers which ones had a higher potential to be good students. However, the names given to the teachers were random. These were not related to the students' test scores... After eight months, he tested the students again. ⁴You can probably guess what he found. The students who were expected to do well actually performed the best. This shows the influence of the Pygmalion Effect.

심리학 강의의 일부를 들으시오.

P: 여러분은 여러분을 강력하게 믿어준 선생님이 있었나요? 아니면 여러분이 부족하다고 생각했던 분은요? 어떤 선생님이 여러분이 더 잘 해내도록 도움을 주셨는지 생각해보세요. 음, 이것은 오늘의 주제와 관련이 있거든요. 그것은 피그말리온 효과라고 불리는 심리 현상입니다.

자, 음, 피그말리온이라는 이름은 고대 그리스 이야기에서 유래되었어요. 그것은 자신이 만든 조각상과 사랑에 빠진 피그말리온이라는 조각가에 관한 이야기입니다. 그는 고대 그리스의 사랑의 여신인 아프로디테에 그 조각상을 살아있게 해달라고 부탁했어요... 피그말리온이 그 조각상을 진정으로 사랑했기 때문에, 여신은 그의 소원을 이루어 주었죠. 그래서 피그말리온 효과란 무언가를 강하게 바라면 그것이 이루어지도록 만들 수 있는 상황을 말합니다. 다시 말해, 긍정적인 기대는 사람들에게 긍정적인 영향을 미칠 수 있어요. 음, 누군가 여러분이 잘할 거라고 기대한다면, 여러분이 잘할 가능성이 높은거죠... 이것은 사람들이 기대에 따라 그들의 행동을 바꾸기 때문에 일어납니다... 그래서 만약 여러분의 선생님이 여러분이 똑똑하다고 생각한다면, 실제로 똑똑한 학생이 되기 위해 더 열심히 공부할지도 몰라요.

어쨌든, 1968년에, 심리학자 로버트 로젠탈은 피그말리온 효과를 실험하기 위해 한 실험을 수행했습니다. 그는 첫 학기 초에 몇몇 초등학생들에게 지능 검사를 받도록 했어요. 그 다음, 그는 학생들의 선생님들에게 어떤 학생들이 좋은 학생이 될 잠재력이 더 큰지 얘기를 해주었어요. 하지만, 그 선생님들에게 주어진 이름들은 무작위였습니다. 이것들은 학생들의 시험 점수와 관련이 없었어요... 8개월 후, 그는 학생들을 다시 테스트했습니다. 그가 무엇을 발견했는지 여러분은 아마 짐작할 수 있을 거예요. 잘할 것으로 기대되었던 학생들이 실제로 가장 잘했어요. 이것은 피그말리온 효과의 영향을 보여줍니다.

strongly (부) 강력하게; 튼튼하게　　perform (동) 해내다, 수행하다
be related to ~과 관련이 있다　　psychological (형) 심리의, 심리학적인
phenomenon (명) 현상
Pygmalion (명) 피그말리온(자신이 만든 조각상 Galatea를 연모한 조각가)
come from ~에서 유래되다　　sculptor (명) 조각가
Aphrodite (명) 아프로디테(사랑·미의 그리스 여신)
describe (동) 말하다, 설명하다　　positive (형) 긍정적인
expectation (명) 기대; 예상　　effect (명) 영향, 결과
chance (명) 가능성, 기회　　conduct (동) 수행하다, 처리하다
experiment (명) 실험　　intelligence test 지능 검사
potential (명) 잠재력, 가능성　　random (형) 무작위의
influence (명) 영향

1 강의의 주된 주제는 무엇인가?
   (A) 학생들에게 심리학에 대해 가르치는 가장 좋은 방법
   (B) 부정적인 생각이 학생들에게 미치는 영향
   (C) 스스로를 믿는 것의 힘
   (D) 심리 현상의 영향

2 교수에 따르면, 그리스 여신은 피그말리온을 위해 무엇을 했는가?
   (A) 그녀는 그에게 예술 작품을 주었다.
   (B) 그녀는 그를 신으로 만들었다.
   (C) 그녀는 조각상이 살아있게 했다.
   (D) 그녀는 그를 더 좋은 조각가로 만들어주었다.

3 교수에 따르면, 기대의 결과로 어떤 일이 일어날 수 있는가?
   (A) 학생들이 선생님들에게 더 자주 순종한다.
   (B) 학생들이 기대에 부응하기 위해 더 열심히 공부한다.
   (C) 학생들이 시험을 보는 것에 대한 부담을 덜 느낀다.
   (D) 학생들이 선생님들의 결정을 존중한다.

강의의 일부를 다시 듣고 질문에 답하시오.
P: You can probably guess what he found. The students who were expected to do well actually performed the best. This shows the influence of the Pygmalion Effect.

4 교수는 왜 이렇게 말하는가:
   P: You can probably guess what he found.
   (A) 학생들에게 이전 수업을 상기시키기 위해
   (B) 실험이 성공적이었다는 것을 암시하기 위해
   (C) 실험의 문제점을 지적하기 위해
   (D) 시험에 통과하기 쉬웠다는 것을 보여주기 위해

Vocabulary Review 본문 p. 72

1 authority 2 conduct 3 random
4 territory 5 appointment 6 worth
7 navigate 8 trade 9 original
10 (B) 11 (D) 12 (B)
13 (A) 14 (D)

CHAPTER 04
Attitude

Example 본문 p. 75

A. (B)   B. (B)

A.

Note-taking

Student's Problem
His essay grade is lower than he expected.

Professor's Solution
- Ask classmates to read the essay
- Use a program that checks the spelling and grammar

Listen to a conversation between a student and a professor.

S: Professor Evans, could I ask you about my essay? Um, my grade is lower than I expected, so...

P: Oh, well, you chose a good topic. However, um, the essay had a weak conclusion, and there were several grammar errors and spelling mistakes.

S: Oh, I'm sorry. I didn't check the essay carefully before I submitted it. Do you have any advice on how to avoid the same problems?

P: Well, you can ask your classmates to read your essay. Um, they can read it from a different point of view and tell you which parts of the essay are not clear... You should also use a program that checks the spelling and grammar.

S: Ah! I see... Thank you, Professor Evans. That's good advice.

P: You're welcome. I'm sure you'll do better next time, Kevin.

학생과 교수 사이의 대화를 들으시오.

S: Evans 교수님, 제 에세이에 대해 여쭤봐도 될까요? 음, 제 성적이 제가 예상했던 것보다 낮은데요, 그래서...

P: 아, 그래, 주제는 잘 골랐어. 하지만, 음, 에세이가 결론이 약했고, 몇 가지 문법 오류와 철자 실수들이 있었단다.

S: 아, 죄송합니다. 제가 에세이를 제출하기 전에 꼼꼼히 확인하지 않았어요. 같은 문제를 방지할 수 있는 방법에 대한 조언이 있으신가요?

P: 음, 동기들에게 네 에세이를 읽어달라고 부탁할 수 있겠지. 음, 그들이 다른 관점에서 그것을 읽고 에세이의 어떤 부분이 명확하지 않은지 알려줄 수 있을거야... 철자와 문법을 확인해주는 프로그램 또한 사용하는 게 좋겠구나.

S: 아! 그렇군요... 감사합니다, Evans 교수님. 좋은 조언이에요.

P: 천만에. 다음번에 네가 더 잘할 거라고 확신한다, Kevin.

expect 동 예상하다 conclusion 명 결론
spelling 명 (단어의) 철자, 맞춤법 carefully 부 꼼꼼하게, 신중하게
submit 동 제출하다 point of view 관점

학생의 친구들에 대한 교수의 의견은 무엇인가?
(A) 그녀는 그들의 에세이의 질에 놀랐다.
(B) 그녀는 그들의 의견을 물어보는 것이 도움이 될 것이라고 생각한다.
(C) 그녀는 그들이 더 좋은 성적을 받을 자격이 있다고 느낀다.
(D) 그녀는 그들이 수업 시간에 나아질 것이라고 확신한다.

B.

Note-taking

Why Emperor Penguins Are in Danger
Climate change → Less sea ice in Antarctica

How It Affects Chicks and Krill
- Sea ice is breaking up before the chicks learn swimming.
- Number of krill will decrease.

Listen to part of a lecture in a biology class.

P: So... Because of climate change, Antarctica has less sea ice than normal. This can cause many problems. For instance, the emperor penguins in Antarctica can become extinct.

You see, emperor penguins depend on sea ice to find safety from predators. They also use it to raise their chicks. However, as the temperature rises, the ice is breaking up before the chicks learn how to swim. As a result, many of them drown... Another problem is that krill are decreasing. Um, krill are a type of small sea animal that emperor penguins eat. If there is less ice, the number of krill will also decrease. So emperor penguins are not only harmed by the loss of sea ice, but they are also unable to get enough food. I really hope we can stop this situation.

생물학 강의의 일부를 들으시오.

P: 자... 기후 변화 때문에, 남극에는 해빙이 정상 상태보다 더 적죠. 이것은 많은 문제들을 야기할 수 있어요. 예를 들어, 남극에 있는 황제펭귄이 멸종하게 될 수 있습니다.

알다시피, 황제펭귄은 포식자들로부터 안전하기 위해 해빙에 의

존합니다. 그것들은 새끼들을 기르기 위해서도 그것을 이용하죠. 하지만, 온도가 올라감에 따라, 새끼들이 헤엄치는 법을 배우기도 전에 얼음이 부서지고 있습니다. 그 결과, 그것들 중 많은 수가 익사해요... 또 다른 문제는 크릴새우가 줄어들고 있다는 것입니다. 음, 크릴새우는 황제펭귄이 먹는 작은 바다 동물의 한 종류입니다. 만약 해빙이 더 적어지면, 크릴새우의 수 또한 줄어들 것입니다. 그래서 황제펭귄은 해빙의 손실로 인한 피해를 입을 뿐만 아니라, 충분한 먹이를 얻을 수도 없게 돼요. 저는 정말 우리가 이 상황을 멈출 수 있기를 바랍니다.

climate change 기후 변화   Antarctica 명 남극 대륙
sea ice 해빙   normal 명 정상(상태), 표준; 형 보통의
cause 동 야기하다   emperor penguin 황제펭귄
extinct 형 멸종된   depend on ~에 의존하다   predator 명 포식자
raise 동 (어린 동물을) 키우다   chick 명 (새의) 새끼, 병아리
break up 부서지다   drown 동 익사하다
krill 명 크릴새우(남극 근해에 사는 작은 새우를 닮은 갑각류)
decrease 동 줄어들다, 감소하다   loss 명 손실

강의의 일부를 다시 듣고 질문에 답하시오.
P: So emperor penguins are not only harmed by the loss of sea ice, but they are also unable to get enough food. I really hope we can stop this situation.

교수는 이렇게 말함으로써 무엇을 의미하는가:
P: I really hope we can stop this situation.

(A) 그녀는 동물들을 보호하기 위한 캠페인을 시작하고 싶어 한다.
(B) 그녀는 멸종 위기에 처한 동물들을 걱정한다.
(C) 그녀는 사람들이 기후 변화에 대해 신경 쓰지 않는다고 생각한다.
(D) 그녀는 기후 변화에 대한 생각을 듣고 싶어 한다.

Listening Practice 1   본문 p. 77

1 (C)   2 (B)   3 (A)

Note-taking

Student's Question
A course has been canceled.
→ What other courses can I take instead?

Employee's Answer
Take a similar course
→ Speak to the professor about it

Listen to a conversation between a student and a university employee at the registrar's office.

W: Good morning. ¹Um, I registered for one of the courses for psychology majors, but it's been canceled. May I ask what happened?
M: I see... According to our records, the course was canceled this semester because not enough students signed up for it. At least 10 students are needed for a course to continue.
W: That's a shame... Um, could you tell me what other courses I can take instead? Um, I need one more course to graduate...
M: ²Of course. If you're interested in something similar, I'd suggest Ethics in Psychology. There may be room for one more. But you'll have to speak to Professor Nichols about it first.
W: I guess I have no choice. So where can I find Professor Nichols?
M: ³She's in Bryan Hall, next to the Science Building. You can also e-mail her at s.nichols@franklin.edu. The class hasn't started yet, so I'm sure she will accept you. Still, you'd better hurry.
W: Thank you so much. I appreciate all your help.
M: No problem. Good luck!

학적과에서 학생과 교직원 사이의 대화를 들으시오.

W: 좋은 아침이에요. 음, 제가 심리학 전공 수업 중 하나를 신청했는데, 취소되어서요. 무슨 일이 있었는지 여쭤봐도 될까요?
M: 그렇군요... 저희 기록에 따르면, 그 수업을 신청한 수강생이 충분하지 않아서 이번 학기에 취소되었네요. 수업이 유지되려면 적어도 10명의 학생이 필요하거든요.
W: 아쉬운 일이군요... 음, 제가 대신 어떤 수업을 들을 수 있는지 알려주시겠어요? 음, 제가 졸업하려면 한 과목을 더 이수해야 해서요...
M: 물론이죠. 비슷한 것에 관심이 있으시다면, 심리학에서의 윤리를 추천해요. 한 명 더 들어갈 자리가 있을 수도 있어요. 하지만 Nichols 교수님과 먼저 이야기해 봐야 할 겁니다.
W: 선택의 여지가 없는 것 같네요. Nichols 교수님을 어디서 찾아뵐 수 있을까요?
M: 그녀는 과학 건물 옆에 있는, Bryan Hall에 계세요. s.nichols@franklin.edu로 이메일을 보낼 수도 있고요. 수업이 아직 시작되지 않았으니, 학생을 받아 주실 거라고 확신해요. 그래도, 서두르는 게 좋을 거예요.
W: 정말 고맙습니다. 많은 도움에 감사드려요.
M: 아니에요. 행운을 빌어요!

register 동 신청하다   course 명 수업   psychology 명 심리학
major 명 전공   record 명 기록; 동 기록하다   at least 적어도, 최소한
shame 명 아쉬운 일; 창피   graduate 동 졸업하다
ethics 명 윤리(학)   room 명 자리; 공간   accept 동 받아 주다

1 학생은 왜 학적과를 찾아가는가?
  (A) 그녀의 전공을 바꾸기 위해
  (B) 정식으로 항의하기 위해
  (C) 취소된 수업에 대해 문의하기 위해
  (D) 졸업에 대한 정보를 얻기 위해

대화의 일부를 다시 듣고 질문에 답하시오.
M: Of course. If you're interested in something similar, I'd suggest Ethics in Psychology. There may be room for one more. But you'll have to speak to Professor Nichols about it first.
W: I guess I have no choice. So where can I find Professor Nichols?

2 학생은 이렇게 말함으로써 무엇을 의미하는가:

W: I guess I have no choice.

(A) 그녀는 주제 선택에 대해 걱정하고 있다.
(B) 그녀는 수업을 수강하기로 결심했다.
(C) 그녀는 교수의 제안을 기꺼이 받아들이려고 한다.
(D) 그녀는 수업에 들어가는 것이 어려울 것이라고 생각한다.

대화의 일부를 다시 듣고 질문에 답하시오.
M: She's in Bryan Hall, next to the Science Building. You can also e-mail her at s.nichols@franklin.edu. The class hasn't started yet, so I'm sure she will accept you. Still, you'd better hurry.

3 직원은 왜 이렇게 말하는가:
M: I'm sure she will accept you.

(A) 학생이 교수와 이야기하도록 격려하기 위해
(B) 학생에게 교수가 기다리고 있다는 것을 알리기 위해
(C) 교수에 대한 잘못된 정보를 정정하기 위해
(D) 학생에게 교수가 친절하다고 말하기 위해

Listening Practice 2

본문 p.79

1 (C) 2 (D) 3 (B)

Note-taking

Formation of Fresh Water
Seawater turns into a gas → liquid again

Causes of Decrease in Fresh Water
- Pollution from factories
- Overuse of water
- Climate change

Listen to part of a lecture in an environmental science class.

P: Let's continue our discussion of the natural environment. ¹Our next topic is something plants and animals need to survive. But, we depend on it, too... I'm talking about fresh water.

When seawater is heated by the sun, it turns into a gas and rises into the atmosphere. During the process, salt is left behind because it's heavy. In the atmosphere, water cools and turns into liquid again. Then, it falls back to earth as fresh water, in the form of rain or snow. From there, it enters rivers and lakes...

And fresh water has many uses. It helps maintain biodiversity, which means the variety of plants and animals. ²Around 40 percent of all fish and 10 percent of all animals need fresh water. But it isn't just them... We use it to grow food, catch fish, and produce electricity. Of course, we also need it to drink, cook, and wash.

The problem is... fresh water supplies are in danger. Pollution from factories and other sources reduces the quality of fresh water and makes it unsafe to use. ³Another problem is, uh, overuse. Lots of water is wasted on farms and in homes. If we use too much, rivers and lakes dry up. Just think. The Colorado was once a powerful river... But, now, the amount of water there keeps decreasing... And, lastly, climate change can cause too much rain in some parts but too little in others. These are serious problems that threaten our health, our economies, and most life on the planet.

환경 과학 강의의 일부를 들으시오.

P: 자연환경에 대한 논의를 계속하죠. 우리의 다음 주제는 식물과 동물이 생존하기 위해 필요한 것입니다. 하지만, 우리도 그것에 의존한답니다... 저는 담수에 대해 얘기하고 있는 거예요.

바닷물이 태양에 의해 가열되면, 그것은 기체로 변해서 대기 중으로 올라갑니다. 그 과정에서, 소금은 무겁기 때문에 남겨져요. 대기 중에, 물은 냉각되어 다시 액체로 변합니다. 그러고 나서, 그것은 비나 눈의 형태로 담수로서 땅으로 다시 떨어져요. 거기에서, 그것은 강과 호수로 들어가게 됩니다...

그리고 담수는 용도가 다양합니다. 그것은 생물 다양성을 유지하는 데 도움이 되는데, 그건 식물과 동물의 다양성을 의미해요. 물고기의 약 40퍼센트와 동물의 10퍼센트는 담수를 필요로 합니다. 하지만 그것들만 그런 것이 아니에요... 우리는 그것을 식량을 기르고, 물고기를 잡고, 전력을 생산하기 위해 사용하죠. 물론, 우리가 마시고, 요리하고, 씻기 위해서도 필요하고요.

문제는... 담수 공급이 위기에 처해있다는 것입니다. 공장과 다른 원천들로부터 생긴 오염은 담수의 질을 떨어뜨리고 그것을 사용하기에 안전하지 않게 만듭니다. 또 다른 문제는, 어, 남용이에요. 많은 물이 농장과 가정에서 낭비돼요. 우리가 너무 많이 사용하면, 강과 호수가 말라 버립니다. 생각해 보세요. 콜로라도강은 한때 세찬 강이었어요... 하지만, 지금은, 그곳의 물의 양이 계속 줄어들고 있습니다... 그리고, 마지막으로, 기후 변화는 어떤 지역에는 비가 너무 많이 오게도 하지만 다른 지역에는 너무 적게 오게끔 할 수 있어요. 이것들은 우리의 건강, 경제, 그리고 지구상의 대부분의 생명체를 위협하는 심각한 문제입니다.

---

discussion 명 논의 natural environment 자연환경
fresh water 담수(염분의 함유량이 적은 보통의 물)
heat 동 가열하다 gas 명 기체 atmosphere 명 대기
leave behind (흔적·기록 등을) 남겨 두다 cool 동 냉각되다
turn into ~으로 변하다 use 명 용도 maintain 동 유지하다
biodiversity 명 (균형 잡힌 환경을 위한) 생물의 다양성
variety 명 다양성 electricity 명 전력 supply 명 공급
be in danger 위기에 처하다 pollution 명 오염
overuse 명 남용 waste 동 낭비하다
threaten 동 위협하다, 협박하다 economy 명 경제

1 교수는 주로 무엇에 관해 이야기하는가?
(A) 담수가 형성되는 과정
(B) 담수에 의존하는 식물과 동물들
(C) 담수 환경의 중요성
(D) 담수 자원의 다양한 용도들

2 담수에 대한 교수의 의견은 무엇인가?
(A) 그것은 장점보다 단점이 더 많다.
(B) 그것은 일부 동물들이 마시기에 위험하다.

(C) 그것은 주로 전력을 생산하는 데 사용되어야 한다.
(D) 그것은 인간과 다른 생물들 모두에게 필요하다.

강의의 일부를 다시 듣고 질문에 답하시오.
P: Another problem is, uh, overuse. Lots of water is wasted on farms and in homes. If we use too much, rivers and lakes dry up. Just think. The Colorado was once a powerful river...

3 교수는 왜 이렇게 말하는가:
P: Just think. The Colorado was once a powerful river...

(A) 물이 어디에서 나오는지 나타내기 위해
(B) 문제에 대한 실제 사례를 제공하기 위해
(C) 장소의 특징들을 묘사하기 위해
(D) 물 사용에 관한 정책들을 비판하기 위해

Listening Practice 3 본문 p. 81

1 (C) **2** (A) **3** (C)

Note-taking
Student's Request
Wants to take a swimming class for beginners at the school gym

Employee's Answer
Purchase a pass to take a class
→ Can use it for a semester

Listen to a conversation between a student and a university employee.

W: Excuse me... I saw on the website that the school gym is offering a swimming class for beginners.
M: That's right. Are you interested in joining?
W: Yes! I'm really impressed by how wide the pool is. I can't wait to swim in it.
M: ¹OK. Um, have you purchased a pass yet? You will need one to take a class.
W: Um, I thought I could use any facility in the gym with my student ID card.
M: Well, that's true. ²But if you want to take classes provided at the gym, you need to buy a gym pass... You know, we have to pay our instructors.
W: Oh, I didn't know that. Uh, so how much is the pass?
M: It's $15 and you can use it for a semester. You can then take any class you want.
W: Hmm... ³That's much cheaper than a regular fitness club membership. I'll try it for a semester and see how it goes.
M: OK. Here's the registration form.

학생과 교직원 사이의 대화를 들으시오.
W: 실례합니다... 제가 웹사이트에서 학교 체육관에서 초보자를 위한 수영 수업을 제공한다는 것을 보았거든요.
M: 맞아요. 가입하는 것에 관심이 있으신가요?
W: 네! 저는 수영장의 넓은 크기에 정말 놀랐거든요. 빨리 수영하고 싶어요.
M: 알겠습니다. 음, 정기권은 구입하셨나요? 수업을 듣기 위해서는 하나 필요하실 거예요.
W: 음, 전 학생증으로 체육관에 있는 어떠한 시설도 사용할 수 있다고 생각했는데요.
M: 음, 그건 사실이에요. 하지만 체육관에서 제공되는 수업을 듣고 싶다면, 체육관 정기권을 사야 해요... 알다시피, 저희가 강사에게 돈을 지불해야 해서요.
W: 아, 그는 몰랐네요. 어, 그래서 정기권은 얼마인가요?
M: 15달러이고 한 학기 동안 사용하실 수 있어요. 그러면 원하시는 어떤 수업이든 들으실 수 있어요.
W: 흠... 일반 헬스장 회원권보다 훨씬 더 저렴하네요. 한 학기 동안 해 보고 어떻게 되는지 볼게요.
M: 네. 여기 신청서입니다.

gym 명 (학교 등의) 체육관 offer 동 제공하다 beginner 명 초보자 purchase 동 구입하다 pass 명 정기권 facility 명 시설 instructor 명 강사 regular 형 일반의, 보통의 fitness club 헬스장 membership 명 회원권 registration form 신청서

1 화자들은 주로 무엇을 논의하고 있는가?
(A) 학생들을 위한 특별 할인
(B) 헬스 프로그램 일정
(C) 스포츠 수업을 듣기 위해 필요한 것
(D) 체육관 웹사이트의 변경 사항

2 대학은 왜 학생에게 비용 지불을 요구하는가?
(A) 선생님들에게 체육 수업료를 지불하기 위해
(B) 신축 건물의 건축비를 충당하기 위해
(C) 몇몇 오래된 장비를 교체하기 위해
(D) 체육관의 개장 시간을 연장하기 위해

학생은 정기권에 대해 어떻게 생각하는가?
(A) 그것은 충분할 만큼 유효하지 않다.
(B) 그것이 출입을 허용하는 시설이 적다.
(C) 그것의 가격은 합리적이다.
(D) 그것은 들을 수 있는 수업을 많이 제공한다.

Listening Practice 4 본문 p. 83

1 (A) **2** (C) **3** (B)

Note-taking
Girl with the Red Balloon
- Sent to auction → Destroyed itself
- Banksy's Intention
  : Art should not be an investment for rich people
  → Ironically, he increased its value.

CHAPTER 04 | Attitude 25

Listen to part of a lecture in an art class.

P: Modern Art is about creating something totally new or unique. ¹Well, today, I'm going to introduce a unique artist called Banksy and one of his most popular artworks. His works cause controversy because, um, they are often public graffiti, which is illegal. And, uh, they are usually about social problems.

Now, his most popular work is probably *Girl with the Red Balloon*. It shows a little girl, and she has lost her balloon. The red balloon is flying away, and the girl is trying to catch it. The painting contained the message, "There is always hope".

The artwork is loved by many people. I personally like the simple drawing with its positive message, too. ²People even wanted to own it, so it was sent to auction. And here comes the interesting part. When it was about to be sold, the painting started to go down and half of it was cut into pieces. The painting destroyed itself! It turned out that Banksy had installed a paper-shredding device inside the frame of the painting.

S: Why would he do that? I mean, destroy his own art...

P: ³Well, Banksy thought art should not be an investment for rich people. Also, he believed art should not be owned but shared. And this is quite ironic, if you think about it... By shredding the art, he actually increased its value. Later, the shredded work was sold in another auction with a new name called *Love is in the Bin*. Its price rose from $1.3 million to $24.5 million.

미술학 강의의 일부를 들으시오.

P: 현대 미술은 완전히 새롭고 독특한 무언가를 창조하는 데 목적이 있죠. 자, 오늘, 저는 뱅크시라는 독특한 화가와 그의 가장 인기 있는 미술품 중 하나를 소개하려고 합니다. 그의 작품들은 논란을 일으키는데, 음, 주로 불법인 공공 그라피티이기 때문이에요. 그리고, 어, 보통 사회 문제에 대한 것이라서요.

자, 그의 가장 인기 있는 작품은 아마도 '빨간 풍선을 든 소녀'일 것입니다. 그것에는 작은 소녀가 있는데, 풍선을 잃어버렸어요. 그 빨간 풍선은 날아가고 있고, 소녀는 그것을 잡으려고 하고 있죠. 그 그림은 "항상 희망은 있다"라는 메시지를 담고 있었습니다.

이 미술품은 많은 사람들에게 사랑을 받아요. 저도 개인적으로 긍정적인 메시지가 담긴 이 단순한 그림을 좋아하고요. 사람들은 심지어 그것을 소유하기를 원해서, 그것이 경매로 보내지기도 했습니다. 그리고 여기서 흥미로운 부분이 나오는데요. 그것이 막 판매되려고 할 때, 그림이 밑으로 내려가기 시작했고 그것의 절반이 조각조각 잘려나갔어요. 그림이 스스로 파괴된 것이죠! 알고보니 뱅크시가 그 그림의 액자 안에 종이 파쇄기를 설치했던 것이었어요.

S: 그가 왜 그랬을까요? 제 말은, 자신의 미술품을 파괴하다니...

P: 음, 뱅크시는 예술이 부자들의 투자 대상이 되어서는 안 된다고 생각했어요. 또한, 그는 예술은 소유되는 것이 아니라 공유되어야 한다고 믿었고요. 생각해 보면, 이건 꽤 모순적이죠... 그 미술품을 파쇄함으로써, 그는 사실상 그것의 가치를 높였거든요. 후에, 그 파쇄된 작품은 '사랑이 쓰레기통에 있다'라는 새로운 이름으로 다른 경매에서 판매되었어요. 130만 달러였던 가격이 2,450만 달러로 올랐답니다.

Modern Art 현대 미술 totally (부) 완전히 controversy (명) 논란
public (형) 공공의 graffiti (명) 그라피티(공공장소에 하는 낙서)
illegal (형) 불법의 social problem 사회 문제
contain (동) 담다, 함유하다 personally (부) 개인적으로
auction (명) 경매 cut into pieces 조각조각으로 잘리다
destroy (동) 파괴하다 paper-shredding device 종이 파쇄기
frame (명) 액자 investment (명) 투자 (대상) ironic (형) 모순적인
shred (동) 파쇄하다 value (명) 가치 bin (명) 쓰레기통

1 강의는 주로 무엇에 관한 것인가?
 (A) 유명한 예술가가 한 일
 (B) 현대 미술의 인기
 (C) 그라피티가 논란을 일으키는 이유
 (D) 현대 미술의 가치

강의의 일부를 다시 듣고 질문에 답하시오.
P: People even wanted to own it, so it was sent to auction. And here comes the interesting part. When it was about to be sold, the painting started to go down and half of it was cut into pieces. The painting destroyed itself!

2 교수는 왜 이렇게 말하는가:
P: And here comes the interesting part.
 (A) 그림에 담긴 메시지를 강조하기 위해
 (B) 경매의 분위기를 묘사하기 위해
 (C) 충격적인 사건을 소개하기 위해
 (D) 어떤 미술품의 질에 대해 논평하기 위해

강의의 일부를 다시 듣고 질문에 답하시오.
P: Well, Banksy thought art should not be an investment for rich people. Also, he believed art should not be owned but shared. And this is quite ironic, if you think about it... By shredding the art, he actually increased its value.

3 교수는 이렇게 말함으로써 무엇을 의미하는가:
P: And this is quite ironic, if you think about it...
 (A) 그는 뱅크시가 안타까운 실수를 했다고 생각한다.
 (B) 그는 뱅크시의 행동이 의도하지 않은 결과를 초래했다고 느낀다.
 (C) 그는 뱅크시의 미술이 더 가치가 있어야 한다고 믿는다.
 (D) 그는 뱅크시의 미술품에 대한 부자들의 반응에 실망했다.

iBT Listening Test 1
본문 p.85
1 (C)   2 (A)   3 (C)   4 (B)

Note-taking
Professor's Suggestion to Student
You are a candidate for a scholarship from the Zellman Foundation

Requirements

- Documents that prove how many hours you worked
- A report about your experience
- A letter of recommendation from a professor

Listen to a conversation between a student and a professor.

S: Hi, Professor Coleman. I'm here because I received your e-mail. You asked me to stop by your office.

P: Hello, Katherine. Yes, I was impressed with the paper you submitted about your volunteer work. ¹And, um, I want to let you know that you are a candidate for a scholarship.

S: Thank you, Professor. Um, I am? What kind of scholarship?

P: ²Yes, it's a community service scholarship. Um, the Zellman Foundation offers it to students who have done at least 100 hours of volunteer work in the local community.

S: ³I don't know what to say. Um, of course, I'm very pleased.

P: It's a wonderful opportunity. You will receive $3,000 if you are chosen.

S: Wow! I can use that to pay for college. Is there anything that I have to do?

P: ⁴Well, you'll have to provide documents that prove how many hours you worked. You should also give a report about your experience. The last thing is a letter of recommendation from a professor. But, obviously, you don't have to worry about this.

S: Thank you, Professor Coleman. I appreciate that.

학생과 교수 사이의 대화를 들으시오.

S: 안녕하세요, Coleman 교수님. 이메일을 받아서 이곳에 왔습니다. 사무실에 들르라고 하셨죠.

P: 안녕, Katherine. 그래, 네가 봉사 활동에 대해 제출한 보고서를 인상 깊게 봤단다. 그리고, 음, 네가 장학금 후보자라는 것을 알려주고 싶었어.

S: 감사합니다, 교수님. 아, 제가요? 어떤 장학금이요?

P: 그래, 그건 사회봉사 장학금이야. 음, Zellman 재단이 지역 사회에서 최소 100시간의 봉사 활동을 한 학생들에게 그것을 제공해.

S: 무슨 말을 해야 할지 모르겠네요. 음, 물론, 저는 정말 기뻐요.

P: 이건 정말 좋은 기회야. 선정되면 3,000달러를 받게 돼.

S: 와! 그것을 대학 등록금을 내는 것에 사용할 수 있겠어요. 제가 해야 할 일이 있을까요?

P: 음, 네가 몇 시간을 활동했는지 증명하는 서류를 제공해야 할 거야. 네 경험에 대한 보고서도 제출해야 하고. 마지막으로 교수의 추천서가 있어. 하지만, 말할 필요도 없이, 이것에 대해서는 걱정하지 않아도 된단다.

S: 고맙습니다, Coleman 교수님. 감사드려요.

---

volunteer work 봉사 활동   candidate 명 후보자
scholarship 명 장학금   community service 사회봉사
foundation 명 재단   local community 지역 사회
pleased 형 기쁜   document 명 서류   prove 동 증명하다
experience 명 경험   letter of recommendation 추천서, 추천장
obviously 부 말할 필요도 없이, 명백히

1 대화는 주로 무엇에 관한 것인가?
   (A) 최근 시험에서의 학생의 성적
   (B) 수업 수강을 위한 필요조건
   (C) 장학금을 받을 수 있는 학생의 기회
   (D) 지역 사회 기관의 활동들

2 교수는 Zellman 재단에 대해 무엇이라고 말하는가?
   (A) 그것은 자원봉사자들에게 재정적인 지원을 제공한다.
   (B) 그것은 최근에 많은 돈을 모금했다.
   (C) 그것은 일자리를 원하는 학생들을 찾고 있다.
   (D) 그것은 여러 자원봉사 프로그램을 운영하고 있다.

3 제안에 대한 학생의 태도는 무엇인가?
   (A) 그녀는 자원봉사자가 되는 것에 대해 들떠있다.
   (B) 그녀는 자신이 자격이 없을 것을 걱정한다.
   (C) 그녀는 고려되고 있다는 것에 기뻐한다.
   (D) 그녀는 답을 줄 수 없어서 미안해 한다.

대화의 일부를 다시 듣고 질문에 답하시오.
P: Well, you'll have to provide documents that prove how many hours you worked. You should also give a report about your experience. The last thing is a letter of recommendation from a professor. But, obviously, you don't have to worry about this.

4 교수는 왜 이렇게 말하는가:
   P: But, obviously, you don't have to worry about this.
   (A) 학생에게 그녀가 충분히 많은 시간을 활동했다고 말하기 위해
   (B) 그가 추천서를 제공할 것임을 암시하기 위해
   (C) 몇몇 서류들이 필요하지 않다는 것을 나타내기 위해
   (D) 신청 과정이 변경되었음을 암시하기 위해

iBT Listening Test 2   본문 p. 88

1 (C)   2 (A)   3 (D)   4 (D)

Note-taking

How Cartel Affects the Economy

Cartel: An organization formed by companies to control a market
- Companies: Work together to remove competition
- Countries: Formed OPEC, the Organization of Petroleum Exporting Countries
  → Increase or decrease oil production to control oil prices

Listen to part of a lecture in an economics class.

P: When you hear the word cartel, you might think of a large group of criminals. Well, um, in economics, it has a different meaning. ¹In general, an economic cartel is an organization formed by companies to control a market. Let's talk about how a cartel affects the economy.

Companies in a cartel work together to remove competition so that they can make profits more easily. ²Normally, competition is good for consumers like you and me. When companies compete, they have to work hard to improve their products and to sell them at reasonable prices. Sometimes, however, companies try to remove competition. That way, they have the power to control a market. They can also set high prices for products that people need for living. These companies know that customers have no other options and eventually have to buy products from them.

But, companies aren't the only ones that form cartels now. Countries do it, too. ⁴For example, OPEC, the Organization of Petroleum Exporting Countries, is a powerful cartel. It is a group of 13 countries that produce oil, including Iran, Iraq, and Saudi Arabia. And as you know, everyone needs oil. So, in 1960, countries that own oil formed OPEC, and they meet regularly to discuss oil prices and production. When they increase oil production, oil prices go down. ³But when they decrease oil production, oil prices go up as the production is smaller than the need. Um, 44 percent of the oil production in the world comes from countries in OPEC, so the decision affects many other countries. In this way, OPEC controls how much the world pays for oil.

경제학 강의의 일부를 들으시오.

P: 카르텔이라는 단어를 들으면, 여러분은 큰 범죄자 집단을 떠올릴지도 모릅니다. 자, 음, 경제학에서, 그것은 다른 의미를 가지고 있어요. 일반적으로, 경제상의 카르텔은 시장을 통제하기 위해 기업들에 의해 형성된 조직입니다. 카르텔이 어떻게 경제에 영향을 미치는지 이야기해 봅시다.

카르텔에 속한 기업들은 이익을 더 쉽게 낼 수 있도록 그들끼리 협력하여 경쟁을 없애려고 합니다. 일반적으로, 경쟁은 여러분과 저 같은 소비자들에게는 좋습니다. 기업들이 경쟁을 할 때, 그들의 제품들을 개선시키고 합리적인 가격에 판매하려고 노력하죠. 그러나, 때때로, 기업들은 경쟁을 없애려고 하는데요. 그렇게 해서, 그들이 시장을 통제할 힘을 갖는 것이죠. 그들은 또한 사람들이 생활을 위해 필요로 하는 제품들에 높은 가격을 책정할 수도 있어요. 이러한 기업들은 고객들이 다른 선택지가 없으니 결국 그들에게서 제품을 구입해야 한다는 것을 알고 있거든요.

하지만, 이제 기업들만이 카르텔을 형성하는 것은 아닙니다. 국가들도 하죠. 예를 들어, 석유수출국기구인 OPEC은 강력한 카르텔입니다. 그것은 이란, 이라크, 사우디아라비아를 포함하여, 석유를 생산하는 13개국으로 이루어진 집단입니다. 그리고 알다시피, 모든 사람은 석유가 필요하죠. 그래서, 1960년에, 석유를 보유한 나라들이 OPEC을 결성했고, 그들은 정기적으로 모여서 석유 가격과 생산량에 대해 논의합니다. 그들이 석유 생산량을 늘리면, 석유 가격은 내려갑니다. 그러나 그들이 석유 생산량을 줄이면, 생산량이 수요보다 적기 때문에 석유 가격이 올라가죠. 음, 세계 석유 생산량의 44%가 OPEC의 국가들로부터 나오기 때문에, 그 결정은 다른 많은 국가들에 영향을 미칩니다. 이런 식으로, OPEC은 세계가 석유에 얼마를 지불하는지를 통제합니다.

---

cartel 명 카르텔, 기업 연합 criminal 명 범죄자
economics 명 경제학 economic 형 경제(상)의, 경제적인
organization 명 조직 control 동 통제하다 market 명 시장
affect 동 영향을 미치다 competition 명 경쟁 profit 명 이익
consumer 명 소비자 reasonable 형 합리적인
set a price 가격을 책정하다 need 동 필요로 하다; 명 수요, 필요
Organization of Petroleum Exporting Countries 석유수출국기구
regularly 부 정기적으로 production 명 생산(량)
decision 명 결정

1 강의는 주로 무엇에 관한 것인가?
  (A) 범죄 집단이 어떻게 형성되는지
  (B) 불법 사업체들이 왜 해로운지
  (C) 조직들이 어떻게 시장을 통제하는지
  (D) 이익을 증가시킬 수 있는 전략들

2 경쟁에 대한 교수의 의견은 무엇인가?
  (A) 그것은 소비자들에게 이익이 된다.
  (B) 그것은 다른 회사들의 이익을 증가시킨다.
  (C) 그것은 제품 품질이 낮아지게 한다.
  (D) 그것은 기업들이 협업을 하도록 한다.

3 교수에 따르면, 석유 생산량이 줄면 왜 석유 가격이 상승하는가?
  (A) OPEC 국가들이 경쟁을 선호하기 때문에
  (B) OPEC이 다른 국가와 거래하는 것을 거부하기 때문에
  (C) 석유 생산에는 많은 돈이 필요하기 때문에
  (D) 석유에 대한 수요가 생산량보다 크기 때문에

강의의 일부를 다시 듣고 질문에 답하시오.
P: For example, OPEC, the Organization of Petroleum Exporting Countries, is a powerful cartel. It is a group of 13 countries that produce oil, including Iran, Iraq, and Saudi Arabia. And as you know, everyone needs oil.

4 교수는 왜 이렇게 말하는가:
  P: And as you know, everyone needs oil.
  (A) 학생들에게 이전 수업을 상기시키기 위해
  (B) 석유 생산 과정을 설명하기 위해
  (C) OPEC이 어떻게 형성되었는지를 보여주기 위해
  (D) OPEC이 왜 그렇게 강력한지를 언급하기 위해

Vocabulary Review

본문 p. 92

1 decrease 2 maintain 3 consumer
4 supply 5 carefully 6 extinct
7 left behind 8 caused 9 waste
10 (C) 11 (B) 12 (A)
13 (C) 14 (B)

CHAPTER 05
Organization

Example

본문 p. 95

A. (B) **B.** (C)

A.

Note-taking
Student's Request
Looking for a job on campus

Employee's Response
Computer lab is looking for a part-time assistant.
→ Help other students using the lab

Listen to a conversation between a student and a student center employee.

M: Hi. I'm looking for a job on campus. I need some extra money for books and other costs.
W: OK, but, um, it's a little bit late in the semester. Most of the jobs on campus have been taken already. What type of work are you interested in?
M: I'm not sure. Um, I'm a computer science major. Is there anything related to this?
W: Let me check… Oh, you're quite lucky. The computer lab is looking for a part-time assistant. You'll be helping other students using the lab. Students sometimes have trouble with things like connecting to the Internet or to a printer.
M: All right. So how do I apply?
W: Give me a minute. I'll get that information for you.

학생과 학생지원센터 직원 사이의 대화를 들으시오.

M: 안녕하세요. 저는 캠퍼스 내에 있는 일자리를 찾고 있어요. 책들과 기타 비용을 위해 여분의 돈이 좀 필요하거든요.
W: 알겠습니다, 그런데, 음, 학기 중에 조금 늦게네요. 캠퍼스 내 대부분의 일자리가 이미 다 찼어요. 어떤 종류의 일에 관심이 있으신가요?
M: 잘 모르겠어요. 음, 저는 컴퓨터 공학 전공이에요. 이것과 관련된 것이 있을까요?
W: 제가 확인해 볼게요… 오, 운이 꽤 좋으시네요. 컴퓨터실에서 시간제 조수를 찾고 있어요. 다른 학생들이 컴퓨터실을 이용하는 것을 도와주게 될 거예요. 학생들이 가끔 인터넷이나 프린터에 연결하는 것과 같은 것에 어려움을 겪거든요.
M: 좋아요. 그래서 어떻게 지원하나요?
W: 잠시만요. 제가 그 정보를 찾아드릴게요.

extra 휑 여분의, 추가의 cost 명 비용, 값 a little bit 조금
computer science 컴퓨터 공학 computer lab 컴퓨터실
part-time 휑 시간제의 assistant 명 조수
connect 통 연결하다 apply 통 지원하다, 신청하다

학생은 왜 자신의 전공을 언급하는가?

(A) 그가 들었던 몇몇 수업들을 설명하기 위해
(B) 일자리 추천을 받기 위해
(C) 그가 바쁜 일정이 있다는 것을 암시하기 위해
(D) 그가 일자리를 찾지 못하는 이유를 설명하기 위해

B.

Note-taking
Baroque Architecture in the Palace of Versailles
• Use of light
  e.g. Mirrors in the Hall of Mirrors
• Decorations with a repeating theme
  e.g. Louis XIV, the French king

Listen to part of a lecture in an architecture class.

P: Today, we're going to look at Baroque architecture. The Baroque style was popular in Europe during the 17th and 18th centuries. The Palace of Versailles represents this well.

Now, Baroque architecture is famous for the use of light. To create different shades, architects used paint and other materials. In the Palace of Versailles, they placed mirrors in a room called the Hall of Mirrors. This caused light to shine all around the room.

Another key element of Baroque architecture is decorations. These often have a repeating theme, such as a particular animal or, um, symbol. In the Palace of Versailles, the theme is Louis XIV, the French king who built the palace. His name and face can be seen throughout the palace, from the walls and ceilings to even the floors!

건축학 강의의 일부를 들으시오.

P: 오늘, 우리는 바로크 건축에 대해 살펴볼 것입니다. 바로크 양식은 17세기와 18세기 동안 유럽에서 인기가 있었죠. 베르사유 궁전이 이것을 잘 나타냅니다.

자, 바로크 건축은 빛의 사용으로 유명합니다. 다양한 명암을 만들기 위해, 건축가들은 페인트와 다른 재료들을 사용했어요. 베르사유 궁전에는, 거울의 방이라고 불리는 방에 그들이 거울들을 놓았습니다. 이것은 방 전체에 빛이 비치게 했어요.

바로크 건축의 또 다른 중요한 요소는 장식물입니다. 이것들은 종

종 특정한 동물이나, 음, 기호와 같이, 반복되는 주제를 가지고 있습니다. 베르사유 궁전에서는, 그 주제가 그 궁전을 지은 프랑스 왕인 루이 14세죠. 그의 이름과 얼굴을 벽과 천장에서부터 심지어 바닥에서까지, 궁전 곳곳에서 볼 수 있답니다!

Baroque [형] 바로크 양식의   architecture [명] 건축
Palace of Versailles 베르사유 궁전
represent [동] 나타내다; 대표하다   shade [명] 명암; 그늘
architect [명] 건축가   material [명] 재료
hall [명] (회의 등을 위한 큰) 방   element [명] 요소
decoration [명] 장식물   repeating [형] 반복되는
theme [명] 주제, 테마   particular [형] 특정한
symbol [명] 기호; 상징   throughout [전] 곳곳에, 도처에
ceiling [명] 천장

교수는 강의를 어떻게 구성하는가?

(A) 두 가지 유형의 건축 구조물들을 비교함으로써
(B) 여러 건축 양식들을 소개함으로써
(C) 건축 양식의 한 예시를 설명함으로써
(D) 유명한 건축물의 중요성을 강조함으로써

Listening Practice 1   본문 p. 97

1 (D)   2 (B)   3 (B)

Note-taking

Student's Problem
Other students are really noisy.
→ Wants to move into another building

Employee's Suggestion
- Waitlist
- Post a note on the board or wear earplugs

Listen to a conversation between a student and a university housing office employee.

M: Good morning. ¹Um, the other students in my dormitory are really noisy. Could I move into another building?
W: I'm sorry, but that isn't possible right now.
M: But why? I checked the university's website, and there's no rule against changing rooms.
W: That's true. But all of the dorms are currently full. I can put you on the waitlist, though.
M: The waitlist? Is that going to take several weeks? The midterm exams are next month. I won't be able to concentrate on studying for the exams with so much noise. ²Can't I get a new room sooner?
W: I'm afraid not. But there are some things you can do right away. Uh, try posting a note on the notice board in your dormitory. You could ask people to be quiet. If that doesn't work, maybe wear earplugs when you study.
M: I guess so. Um, I forgot to ask... ³How long is the waitlist?
W: Let me check... You will be number seven once I update it.
M: Really? That's not too bad. This might not take very long after all.

학생과 대학 기숙사 사무실 직원 사이의 대화를 들으시오.

M: 좋은 아침이에요. 음, 저희 기숙사에 있는 다른 학생들이 너무 시끄러워요. 제가 다른 건물로 옮길 수 있을까요?
W: 죄송하지만, 지금은 그게 가능하지 않아요.
M: 하지만 왜죠? 제가 대학 홈페이지를 확인해봤는데, 방을 바꾸는 것에 반하는 규정은 없어요.
W: 그건 맞아요. 하지만 모든 기숙사가 현재 만원이에요. 그렇지만, 제가 대기자 명단에 올려드릴 수는 있어요.
M: 대기자 명단이요? 그게 몇 주까지도 걸리는 건가요? 중간고사가 다음 달이에요. 저는 그렇게 큰 소음에서는 시험 공부에 집중을 할 수 없을 거예요. 새로운 방을 더 빨리 구할 수는 없나요?
W: 안 될 것 같아요. 하지만 학생이 바로 해볼 수 있는 것들이 있어요. 어, 기숙사에 있는 게시판에 메모를 게시해보세요. 사람들에게 조용히 해달라고 부탁해보는 거예요. 만약 그것이 효과가 없다면, 공부할 때 귀마개를 착용해볼 수도 있겠네요.
M: 그럴 수도 있겠네요. 음, 여쭤보는 걸 잊어버렸는데... 대기자 명단은 얼마나 긴가요?
W: 제가 확인해볼게요... 제가 업데이트를 하면 학생은 7번이 될 거예요.
M: 정말이요? 그렇게 나쁘진 않네요. 어차피 이게 그렇게까지 오래 걸리지 않을 수도 있겠어요.

dormitory [명] 기숙사   move into ~으로 옮기다
against [전] ~에 반(대)하여   currently [부] 현재는, 지금은
waitlist [명] 대기자 명단   concentrate on ~에 집중하다
right away 바로   post [동] 게시하다; (우편물을) 발송하다
notice board 게시판   work [동] (원하는) 효과가 있다; 일하다
earplug [명] (소음이나 물을 막기 위한) 귀마개   after all 어차피, 결국

1 학생은 왜 대학 기숙사 사무실을 찾아가는가?

(A) 대학 웹사이트에 대해 불평하기 위해
(B) 새 기숙사 규정에 대한 정보를 얻기 위해
(C) 대학 건물의 위치를 알아내기 위해
(D) 다른 기숙사로 옮기는 것에 대해 물어보기 위해

2 직원은 왜 게시판을 언급하는가?

(A) 학생에게 더 많은 정보를 어디에서 찾을 수 있는지 보여주기 위해
(B) 학생의 문제에 대한 해결책을 제안하기 위해
(C) 학생에게 공지사항에 관해 이야기하기 위해
(D) 명단이 이미 게시되었음을 확인해주기 위해

3 대기자 명단에 대한 학생의 의견은 무엇인가?

(A) 그는 그것이 더 자주 업데이트되어야 한다고 생각한다.
(B) 그는 그것의 대기 시간이 길지 않을 수도 있다고 생각한다.
(C) 그는 그것에 대해 더 일찍 들었다면 좋았을 것이라고 생각한다.
(D) 그는 그것이 더 나은 시스템으로 대체되기를 바란다.

Listening Practice 2 본문 p. 99

1 (C)   **2** (A)   **3** (B)

Note-taking
Shapes of Sand Dunes
- Crescent Dune
  → Looks like a moon that isn't full
  → Forms when wind blows in one direction
- Star Dune
  → Forms when wind blows in different directions

Listen to part of a lecture in a geology class.

P: So, I'm sure many of you have been to a beach. Or maybe you've seen pictures of famous deserts like the Sahara Desert in Africa. If you have, then you know what a sand dune is... ¹Now, let's talk about how different shapes of sand dunes are created.

Basically, sand dunes are hills made of sand... They form when wind continuously blows across a beach or a desert. Sand is light, so wind can move it easily. But wind doesn't always blow in one direction. Because wind blows in different directions, sand piles up in different ways. Um, that's why you have many shapes of sand dunes.

²The most common shape is the crescent. Um, try imagining what it looks like... Just like the name, it looks like the moon when it isn't full. This shape forms when wind blows in one direction. Anyway, crescent dunes can be very wide... even up to 100 meters long.

But what happens when the wind blows in different directions? Then, you get another common shape called the star. ²Try to guess what this one looks like. As the name suggests, it looks like a star. ³But it's also very tall. They can be quite impressive. Some of you might not know this, but we have one here in Colorado. It's 225 meters high, and it is the tallest dune in the country.

Now, let's look at images of some other sand dunes. See if you can guess how their shapes were formed.

지질학 강의의 일부를 들으시오.

P: 자, 여러분 중 대다수가 해변에 가본 적이 있을 거예요. 아니면 아마 아프리카의 사하라 사막과 같은 유명한 사막의 사진을 본 적이 있을 거예요. 만약 있다면, 그럼 여러분은 사구가 무엇인지 아는 겁니다... 이제, 다양한 형태의 사구가 어떻게 만들어지는지에 대해 이야기해 봅시다.

기본적으로, 사구는 모래로 만들어진 언덕이에요... 그것들은 바람이 해변이나 사막을 가로질러 계속해서 불 때 형성됩니다. 모래는 가벼워서, 바람이 그것을 쉽게 움직일 수 있죠. 하지만 바람이 항상 한 방향으로만 부는 것은 아닙니다. 바람이 여러 방향으로 불기 때문에, 모래도 다양한 방식으로 쌓이게 되죠. 음, 이것이 다양한 형태의 사구가 생기는 이유에요.

가장 흔한 형태는 초승달입니다. 음, 어떻게 생겼을지 상상해 보세요... 꼭 그 이름처럼, 그것은 만월이 아닐 때의 달처럼 생겼어요. 이 형태는 바람이 한 방향으로 불 때 형성됩니다. 어쨌든, 초승달 사구는 폭이 매우 넓을 수도 있어요... 심지어 100미터까지 될 수도 있죠.

하지만 바람이 여러 방향으로 불면 무슨 일이 일어날까요? 그러면, 별이라고 불리는 또 다른 흔한 형태가 생기게 됩니다. 이것이 어떻게 생겼는지 알아맞혀 보세요. 그 이름이 암시하듯이, 그것은 별처럼 생겼어요. 그런데 높이가 매우 높기도 합니다. 그것들은 꽤 인상적일 수 있죠. 여러분 중 몇몇은 모를 수도 있지만, 여기 콜로라도주에도 하나 있답니다. 그것은 높이가 225미터로, 이 나라에서 가장 높은 사구입니다.

이제, 다른 사구들의 사진들을 봅시다. 여러분이 그것들의 형태가 어떻게 형성되었는지를 추측할 수 있는지 한번 보세요.

Sahara Desert 사하라 사막   dune 명 사구, 모래 언덕   hill 명 언덕
continuously 부 계속해서, 연달아   blow 동 (바람이) 불다
across 부 가로질러; 건너서   pile up 쌓이다   crescent 명 초승달
full 형 만월(보름달)의; 가득한
guess 동 (추측으로) 알아맞히다; 추측하다   impressive 형 인상적인
Colorado 명 콜로라도주(미국 서부의 주)

1 강의의 주된 주제는 무엇인가?
  (A) 해변과 사막이 어떻게 비슷한지
  (B) 어떤 요소들이 모래가 형성되게 하는지
  (C) 사구가 어떻게 다양한 형태로 생길 수 있는지
  (D) 세계에서 가장 큰 사구는 어디에서 찾을 수 있는지

2 교수는 강의를 어떻게 구성하는가?
  (A) 학생들에게 그들의 상상력을 활용하도록 권함으로써
  (B) 학생들에게 사구의 사진들을 보여줌으로써
  (C) 실험의 결과에 대해 이야기함으로써
  (D) 유사점과 차이점을 설명함으로써

3 별 모양 사구에 대한 교수의 태도는 무엇인가?
  (A) 그는 그 명칭이 불명확하다고 생각한다.
  (B) 그는 그것들의 크기를 인상 깊게 여긴다.
  (C) 그는 더 많은 사람들이 그것들을 봐야 한다고 생각한다.
  (D) 그는 그것들을 더 쉽게 찾을 수 있기를 바란다.

Listening Practice 3 본문 p. 101

1 (D)   **2** (D)   **3** (A)

Note-taking
Student's Question
Should I write about how people feel about the presidential election?

Professor's Suggestion
- Focus on each candidate's campaign promises
- Make sure the opinions are true

Listen to a conversation between a student and a professor.

S: Are you busy, Professor Wilkins?
P: Well, I'm grading exams for another class, but I have a few minutes. What do you need, Eva?
S: ¹Um, at the end of yesterday's lecture, you told us to write an article about the upcoming presidential election. You said to include various points of view... Does this mean I should write about how people feel about the election?
P: Well, that might be too broad. I suggest focusing on each candidate's campaign promises... You know, what they promise to do when they become president.
S: Oh, I see. Um, then maybe I could interview a few students and ask if they agree or disagree with those promises. I could include their opinions.
P: Good idea. ²Just make sure the opinions are true. I had one student who lied about what someone said to make his article better. I gave him an F.
S: I'll keep that in mind. ³Oh, and I'm also thinking about interviewing professors, too.
P: Hmm... That would take a lot of time. Just doing student interviews would be enough.
S: OK, I'll do that. Thanks for your help.

학생과 교수 사이의 대화를 들으시오.

S: Wilkins 교수님, 바쁘신가요?
P: 음, 다른 수업의 시험을 채점하고는 있지만, 잠깐 시간이 있단다. 무엇이 필요하니, Eva?
S: 음, 어제 강의가 끝날 때, 교수님께서 저희에게 다가오는 대통령 선거에 대한 기사를 쓰라고 하셨잖아요. 다양한 관점을 포함하라고 말씀하셨는데요... 이게 사람들이 선거에 대해 어떻게 느끼는지에 대해 써야 한다는 뜻인가요?
P: 음, 그건 너무 광범위할 수도 있어. 각 후보들의 선거 공약에 초점을 맞추는 것을 추천한다... 그러니까, 그들이 대통령이 되면 하겠다고 약속한 것 말이야.
S: 아, 그렇군요. 음, 그럼 저는 몇몇 학생들을 인터뷰해서 그 공약들에 동의하거나 동의하지 않는지 물어볼 수 있겠어요. 그들의 의견들을 포함할 수 있겠네요.
P: 좋은 생각이야. 그 의견들이 사실이라는 것을 확실히 해두어야 한다. 자신의 기사를 더 좋게 만들기 위해서 누군가가 한 말에 대해 거짓말을 했던 한 학생이 있었거든. 나는 그에게 F 학점을 줬단다.
S: 명심할게요. 아, 그리고 저는 교수님들을 인터뷰하는 것도 생각하고 있어요.
P: 흠... 그건 시간이 많이 걸릴 거야. 학생 인터뷰를 하는 것만으로도 충분할 것 같구나.
S: 네, 그렇게 할게요. 도와주셔서 감사합니다.

grade 图 채점하다, 점수를 매기다   article 图 기사, 글
upcoming 图 다가오는   presidential election 대통령 선거
various 图 다양한   broad 图 광범위한
focus on ~에 초점을 맞추다, ~에 주력하다   candidate 图 후보
campaign promise 선거 공약   opinion 图 의견
keep in mind 명심하다

1 화자들은 주로 무엇을 논의하고 있는가?
  (A) 어려운 강의 주제
  (B) 다가오는 학생 선거
  (C) 최근의 중간고사
  (D) 새로운 수업 과제

2 교수는 정확한 의견의 중요성을 어떻게 강조하는가?
  (A) 실수를 방지하는 방법을 보여줌으로써
  (B) 인터뷰하는 방법을 설명함으로써
  (C) 여러 연구 자료를 제공함으로써
  (D) 또 다른 학생의 경험을 설명함으로써

3 교수들을 인터뷰하겠다는 생각에 대한 교수의 태도는 무엇인가?
  (A) 그는 그것이 오랜 시간이 걸릴 것이라고 생각한다.
  (B) 그는 그것이 하기 쉬울 것이라고 생각한다.
  (C) 그는 참여하는 것에 관심이 있다.
  (D) 그는 교수들이 충분히 있다고 확신한다.

Listening Practice 4   본문 p.103

1 (D)   2 (A)   3 (B)

Note-taking

English Words from French
- Come from French directly
  → Pronounced in a French way
  e.g. Café, cuisine, brunette, critique, and chic
- Feel like natural English words
  e.g. Surprise, effort, and police

Listen to part of a lecture in a linguistics class.

P: As you know, English is a very old language. It, uh, started in around AD 550. ¹In the beginning, it was influenced mainly by German and Latin. However, you may not realize that French also had a big impact on English.
For instance, consider how many words come from French directly. Some words are even used and spelled in exactly the same way. These include café, cuisine, brunette, critique, and chic, to name just a few examples. Phrases like en route, Déjà vu, and film noir are also equally common. However, these are often pronounced in a French way and spelled with unfamiliar accent marks. Nevertheless, none of these French words or phrases needs translation.
²In total, there are 1,700 words that English and French use in almost the same way. But not all of these have a French sound. ³Many words like surprise or effort or police do not sound like French words at all. They feel like natural English

words. And it feels that way because... well, they are. Many words like these became part of the English language over a thousand years ago. That was when the Normans, a powerful group of people from France, took over England. The Normans ruled England for centuries. During this period, over 10,000 French words entered the English vocabulary.

To this day, English and French still have many similar qualities. Um, I believe that the average English speaker can understand about 15,000 French words. That is true whether they can speak French or not.

언어학 강의의 일부를 들으시오.

P: 알다시피, 영어는 아주 오래된 언어입니다. 그것은, 어, 기원후 550년경에 시작됐죠. 초기에는, 그것은 주로 독일어와 라틴어의 영향을 받았습니다. 하지만, 여러분은 프랑스어 또한 영어에 큰 영향을 미쳤다는 사실은 알아차리지 못할 수도 있어요.

예를 들어, 얼마나 많은 단어들이 프랑스어에서 직접적으로 유래되었는지 생각해 보세요. 어떤 단어들은 심지어 완전히 동일한 방식으로 사용되며 같은 철자를 씁니다. 몇 가지만 예시를 말해보자면, 이것에는 *café, cuisine, brunette, critique,* 그리고 *chic*가 포함돼요. *en route, Déjà vu,* 그리고 *film noir*와 같은 어구들 또한 똑같이 흔하죠. 하지만, 이것들은 흔히 프랑스어의 방식으로 발음되기도 하고 철자를 낯선 강세 부호와 함께 쓰기도 합니다. 그럼에도 불구하고, 이러한 프랑스어 단어나 어구들 중 어떠한 것도 번역을 필요로 하지는 않아요.

전부 합해서, 영어와 프랑스어에서 거의 동일한 방식으로 사용하는 단어가 총 1,700개가 있습니다. 그러나 이 모든 것들이 프랑스어 발음을 가진 것은 아니에요. *surprise*나 *effort*나 *police*와 같은 많은 단어들이 전혀 프랑스어 단어처럼 들리지 않습니다. 그것들은 자연스러운 영어 단어들처럼 느껴져요. 그리고 그게 왜 그렇게 느껴지냐 하면... 음, 그것들이 그러니까요. 이것들과 같은 많은 단어들은 천 년도 더 전에 영어의 일부가 되었습니다. 그 때는 프랑스에서 온 강력한 부족인 노르만족이 영국을 점령했을 때였어요. 노르만족은 수 세기 동안 영국을 통치했죠. 이 기간 동안, 10,000개 이상의 프랑스어 단어들이 영어 어휘로 들어가게 됐습니다.

오늘날까지, 영어와 프랑스어에는 여전히 많은 비슷한 특성들이 있습니다. 음, 저는 영어권 사람이 평균 약 15,000개의 프랑스어 단어들을 이해할 수 있다고 생각해요. 그들이 프랑스어를 할 수 있든 할 수 없든요.

Latin 명 라틴어   realize 동 알아차리다, 자각하다
directly 부 직접적으로   cuisine 명 요리(법)
brunette 명 흑갈색   critique 명 평론, 비평한 글
chic 형 멋진, 세련된   phrase 명 어구   en route (어디로 가는) 도중에
Déjà vu 명 데자뷰, 기시감   film noir 누아르 영화(어둡고 긴장감 있는 영화)
equally 부 똑같이, 동일하게   pronounce 동 발음하다
accent mark 강세 부호   translation 명 번역
Normans 명 노르만족(1066년에 영국을 정복한 북유럽계 프랑스인 민족)
take over 정복하다   rule 동 통치하다; 규칙
century 명 세기, 100년   quality 명 특성; 질

1 강의의 주된 주제는 무엇인가?
 (A) 유럽 언어들의 공통된 특성들
 (B) 영어와 프랑스어의 차이점들
 (C) 영어가 널리 퍼진 이유들
 (D) 프랑스어가 영어에 미친 영향

2 교수는 프랑스어에 관해 무엇이라고 말하는가?
 (A) 그것은 영어와 1,000개 이상의 단어를 공유한다.
 (B) 그것에는 독일어처럼 들리는 단어들이 있다.
 (C) 그것에는 약 15,000개의 단어들이 있다.
 (D) 그것은 천 년 전에 바뀌기 시작했다.

3 교수는 왜 영국을 통치했던 노르만족에 대해 언급하는가?
 (A) 유명한 영어 어구의 유래를 보여주기 위해
 (B) 일부 프랑스어 단어들이 왜 자연스러운 영어로 느껴지는지 설명하기 위해
 (C) 프랑스인들이 매우 강력했다는 것을 암시하기 위해
 (D) 영국의 긴 역사를 강조하기 위해

iBT Listening Test 1
본문 p. 105

1 (A)   2 (B)   3 (D)   4 (B)

Note-taking
Organization of the Paper
1. Start with Gregor Mendel
 → Mention his main contribution first
2. Discuss the experiments with flowers
 → Write about how and why Mendel's ideas were not accepted at first

Listen to a conversation between a student and a professor.

S: ¹Hi, Professor Reed, I was, uh, wondering if you could give me some advice about my assignment. I'm writing a paper about the development of modern genetics.

P: Hi, Andrea. I like the topic, but, uh, it's very broad. ¹How do you plan to organize your paper?

S: ²Well, I want to start with Gregor Mendel since he's known as the father of modern genetics.

P: In that case, I would suggest that you mention his main contribution first... So, uh, talk about Mendel's Laws.

S: I agree... ³And then I was going to discuss his experiments with flowers.

P: They played an important role... But, um, I think you should also include some background information.

S: What do you mean by that?

P: It would be good to write about how and why Mendel's ideas were not accepted by other scientists at first... And then, uh, discuss how his work later got attention again.

S: ⁴I'm not familiar with that. I'd better do more research.
P: That would be wise. I can recommend some books if you like.
S: I'd appreciate that, Professor... Thank you!

학생과 교수 사이의 대화를 들으시오.
S: 안녕하세요, Reed 교수님, 저는, 어, 제 과제에 대해 조언을 좀 해주실 수 있는지 궁금합니다. 저는 현대 유전학의 발전에 관한 보고서를 쓰고 있어요.
P: 안녕, Andrea. 주제는 마음에 들지만, 어, 그건 너무 광범위하구나. 네 보고서를 어떻게 구성할 계획이니?
S: 음, 저는 그레고어 멘델이 현대 유전학의 아버지로 알려져 있기 때문에 그 이야기로 시작하고 싶어요.
P: 그렇다면, 그의 주요 공헌을 먼저 언급하는 것을 제안한다... 그러니까, 어, 멘델의 유전 법칙에 대해 이야기하는 거지.
S: 동의해요... 그러고 나서 저는 그가 꽃으로 한 실험들에 대해 얘기하려고 했어요.
P: 그것들은 중요한 역할을 했지... 하지만, 음, 내 생각엔 네가 배경지식도 좀 포함해야 할 것 같구나.
S: 그게 무슨 뜻인가요?
P: 멘델의 아이디어가 어떻게 그리고 왜 처음에는 다른 과학자들에 의해 받아들여지지 않았는지에 대해 쓰는 것이 좋을 것 같아... 그러고 나서, 어, 그의 연구가 어떻게 나중에 다시 관심을 받게 됐는지 얘기하렴.
S: 제가 그것에 대해서는 잘 알지 못해요. 더 조사를 해야겠어요.
P: 그게 현명하겠구나. 네가 원한다면 내가 몇몇 책들을 추천해 줄 수도 있단다.
S: 그렇게 해주신다면 감사하죠, 교수님... 감사합니다!

modern (형) 현대의 genetics (명) 유전학
contribution (명) 공헌; 기부금 Mendel's Laws 멘델의 유전 법칙
experiment (명) 실험 role (명) 역할
get attention 관심을 받다, 주의를 끌다
be familiar with ~에 대해 잘 알다, ~에 익숙하다
research (명) 조사, 연구 recommend (동) 추천하다

1 대화는 주로 무엇에 관한 것인가?
  (A) 보고서에 대한 아이디어를 어떻게 구상할지
  (B) 조별 과제에 대해 어떤 주제들을 선택할지
  (C) 좋은 연구 자료를 어디에서 찾을 수 있는지
  (D) 실험에 어떤 것을 포함할지

2 교수는 왜 멘델의 유전 법칙에 대해 이야기하는가?
  (A) 멘델이 어떻게 유명해졌는지 설명하기 위해
  (B) 과제를 어떻게 시작할지 제안하기 위해
  (C) 멘델의 중요성을 강조하기 위해
  (D) 학생에게 시험에 대해 무엇을 공부해야 하는지 상기시키기 위해

3 교수에 따르면, 멘델의 연구에서 중요한 역할을 한 것은 무엇인가?

  (A) 다른 과학자들의 도움
  (B) 그의 가족의 지원
  (C) 유전학에 관한 과거 연구
  (D) 꽃으로 한 실험들

대화의 일부를 다시 듣고 질문에 답하시오.
S: I'm not familiar with that. I'd better do more research.
P: That would be wise. I can recommend some books if you like.

4 교수는 이렇게 말함으로써 무엇을 의미하는가:
  P: That would be wise.
  (A) 그는 학생의 지식에 깊은 인상을 받았다.
  (B) 그는 학생이 더 많은 정보를 수집해야 한다고 생각한다.
  (C) 그는 일부 정보가 정확하지 않다는 것에 동의한다.
  (D) 그는 학생이 이전 강의를 복습하기를 원한다.

iBT Listening Test 2
본문 p. 108

1 (C) **2** (B) **3** (B) **4** (A)

Note-taking
1600s ~ 1700s
• Many Europeans decided to move to America.
• There were 13 British colonies in America.

Late 1700s
Colonies joined together and started the American Revolutionary War.
→ They signed the Declaration of Independence.

Listen to part of a lecture in a history class.
P: Today, America and Great Britain are considered great friends. However, 250 years ago, they were at war... ¹The Americans fought the British for independence. This is how the United States became a country.

²After the land of America was discovered, many Europeans like the Spanish, French, and British decided to move there. Um, most of them wanted to make money through trade. In 1607, the British formed a colony in Virginia. They grew tobacco there and sold it in Europe. This made them wealthy, so they formed more colonies. By the 1700s, there were 13 British colonies in America.

But, soon after, problems began. First, Britain was very far from America. At the time, it took about four months to get to America by boat. This made it hard for the British to control their American colonies... ³Another issue was taxes. You know, we pay taxes to the government to receive help from it. The people who lived in American colonies also paid taxes since these colonies were owned by the British. ³However, they got little help in return because of the long distance. Now, how would you feel if you did not get what you paid for?
S: I would feel angry...

P: Exactly. [4]And the colonies were certain that they could be more successful without the British. Uh, this makes sense, right? They were rich, after all. They owned land and natural resources. So, in 1775, the 13 colonies joined together and started the American Revolutionary War. This lasted until 1783. But in 1776, which was uh, before the war ended, the Americans signed the Declaration of Independence. This was the document that created the United States of America, and the 13 colonies became the first 13 states.

역사학 강의의 일부를 들으시오.

P: 오늘날, 미국과 영국은 좋은 친구로 여겨집니다. 하지만, 250년 전에, 그들은 전쟁 중이었습니다... 미국인들은 독립을 위해 영국인들과 싸웠어요. 이렇게 해서 미국은 국가가 되었습니다.

미국 대륙이 발견된 이후, 스페인인, 프랑스인, 그리고 영국인과 같은 많은 유럽인들이 그곳으로 이주하기로 결정했습니다. 음, 그들 중 대부분은 무역을 통해 돈을 벌고 싶어 했죠. 1607년에, 영국은 버지니아주에 식민지를 형성했습니다. 그들은 그곳에서 담배를 재배했고 그것을 유럽에서 판매했습니다. 이것은 그들을 부유하게 만들었기 때문에, 그들은 더 많은 식민지들을 형성했어요. 1700년대에는, 미국에 13개의 영국 식민지들이 있었습니다.

하지만, 곧이어, 문제가 시작되었습니다. 우선, 영국은 미국에서 매우 멀리 있었습니다. 그 당시에, 배를 타고 미국에 도착하는 데 약 4개월이 걸렸어요. 이것은 영국인들이 그들의 미국 식민지들을 통제하기 어렵게 만들었죠... 또 다른 문제는 세금이었습니다. 알다시피, 우리는 정부로부터 도움을 받기 위해 세금을 내죠. 이 식민지들은 영국에 의해 소유되었기 때문에 미국 식민지들에 살았던 사람들 또한 세금을 냈어요. 하지만, 그들은 먼 거리로 인해 도움을 거의 돌려받지 못했죠. 자, 만약 여러분이 돈을 지불한 것을 받지 못했다면 어떤 기분이 들었을까요?

S: 화가 났을 것 같아요...

P: 맞아요. 그리고 식민지들은 그들이 영국인들 없이 더 성공할 수 있다고 확신했어요. 어, 이건 말이 되죠, 그렇죠? 어쨌든, 그들은 부자였으니까요. 그들은 토지와 천연자원을 소유했어요. 그래서, 1775년에, 13개의 식민지들이 연합을 했고 미국 독립전쟁을 시작했습니다. 이것은 1783년까지 지속되었어요. 하지만 1776년에, 이때는 어, 전쟁이 끝나기 전인데, 미국인들은 독립 선언문에 서명을 했어요. 이것은 미합중국을 만든 문서였고, 13개의 식민지들은 최초의 13개의 주가 되었답니다.

be at war 전쟁 중이다   independence 명 독립
move 통 이주하다; 움직이다   colony 명 식민지
Virginia 명 버지니아주(미국 동부의 주)   tobacco 명 담배
wealthy 형 부유한   issue 명 문제; 주제   tax 명 세금
government 명 정부   own 통 소유하다   in return 보답으로
distance 명 거리   certain 형 확신하는, 확실한; 특정한
make sense 말이 되다, 타당하다   natural resource 천연자원
join together 연합하다   American Revolutionary War 미국 독립전쟁
Declaration of Independence 독립 선언문   state 명 (미국 등에서) 주

1 강의의 주된 주제는 무엇인가?

(A) 미국과 영국의 우정
(B) 미국인들이 부유해진 이유
(C) 미국의 기원
(D) 미국 대륙의 발견

2 교수에 따르면, 많은 유럽인들이 왜 미국으로 이주했는가?

(A) 전쟁에서 싸우기 위해
(B) 부자가 되기 위해
(C) 유럽 제품들을 판매하기 위해
(D) 그들의 종교를 전파하기 위해

3 교수는 세금에 관한 문제를 어떻게 설명하는가?

(A) 미국과 영국의 세금 체계를 비교함으로써
(B) 학생들에게 그들의 의견을 물어봄으로써
(C) 영국인들이 어디에 세금을 썼는지 설명함으로써
(D) 학생들에게 세금을 내는 방법을 보여줌으로써

강의의 일부를 다시 듣고 질문에 답하시오.

P: And the colonies were certain that they could be more successful without the British. Uh, this makes sense, right? They were rich, after all. They owned land and natural resources.

4 교수는 이렇게 말함으로써 무엇을 암시하는가:
P: Uh, this makes sense, right?

(A) 식민지들은 자신감을 가질 만한 충분한 이유가 있었다.
(B) 영국인들은 매우 성공적인 상인들이었다.
(C) 식민지들은 땅을 사기로 한 현명한 결정을 내렸다.
(D) 영국은 전쟁을 시작하는 실수를 저질렀다.

Vocabulary Review   본문 p.112

1 distance   2 opinion   3 chic
4 grade   5 contribution 6 represent
7 quality   8 connect   9 rule
10 (D)   11 (B)   12 (C)
13 (A)   14 (D)

CHAPTER 06
Connecting Contents

Example   본문 p.115

A. Yes: (B), (C) No: (A), (D)   B. (D)-(C)-(A)-(B)

A.

Note-taking
Student's Question
How can I make up a midterm exam?

Professor's Suggestion
- Can <u>double</u> the final test score
- Write a <u>paper</u> instead of a test

Listen to a conversation between a student and a professor.

S: Hello, Professor Hamilton. I'm here to ask how I can <u>make up my midterm exam</u>. As I told you before, I missed the exam because I <u>had an important interview</u> that day.

P: Hi, Rachel. ᴮWell, I can <u>double</u> your final test score to cover your midterm score. This way, you don't have to <u>take the midterm</u>.

S: Um, I'm not sure I'll <u>get a good grade</u> on the final... ᴬCan I take a test with different questions on another day?

P: Well, that would <u>be unfair to</u> the other students... Hmm... ᶜHow about <u>writing a paper</u> instead?

S: Could you <u>give me more details</u>?

P: You can <u>choose a topic</u> related to our class. It will be <u>a good chance</u> to review what you've learned.

S: Sounds interesting. I'd like to write a paper, then.

학생과 교수 사이의 대화를 들으시오.

S: 안녕하세요, Hamilton 교수님. 제가 중간고사를 어떻게 만회할 수 있는지 여쭤보려고 왔어요. 전에도 말씀드렸지만, 제가 그날 중요한 면접이 있었기 때문에 시험을 못 봤어요.

P: 안녕, Rachel. 음, 중간고사 점수를 대신하기 위해 네 기말고사 점수를 두 배로 곱할 수 있어. 이렇게 하면, 네가 중간고사를 볼 필요가 없지.

S: 음, 제가 기말고사에서 좋은 점수를 받을 수 있을지 잘 모르겠어요... 다른 날에 다른 문제들로 시험을 볼 수 있을까요?

P: 음, 그건 다른 학생들에게 불공평할 것 같구나... 흠... 대신 보고서를 쓰는 건 어떻니?

S: 좀 더 자세하게 말씀해 주시겠어요?

P: 우리 수업과 관련된 주제로 네가 선택해도 돼. 배운 것을 복습할 수 있는 좋은 기회가 될 거야.

S: 흥미로울 것 같네요. 그럼, 보고서를 써보겠습니다.

---

make up 만회하다, 보충하다　　double 두 배로 만들다; 두 배의
final test 기말고사　　cover 대신하다; 덮다　　take a test 시험을 보다
unfair 불공평한; 부당한　　review 복습하다, 재검토하다

다음의 항목이 중간고사를 만회하기 위해 학생이 할 수 있는 것으로 언급된 것인지를 표시하시오. 각 항목에 적절한 칸을 클릭하시오.

	예	아니오
(A) 중간고사를 다시 보기		V
(B) 기말고사만 보기	V	
(C) 주제 하나에 관해 보고서를 쓰기	V	
(D) 주제 하나에 관해 연설을 하기		V

B.

Note-taking
Process of Ancient Chinese Papermaking
1. <u>Collect</u> bark, and clean it in water
2. <u>Boil</u> or <u>steam</u> bark to release pulp
3. Beat bark with a <u>hammer</u> to get fibers, and mix them with <u>pulp</u> and water
4. Place the mixture on the <u>screen</u>, and let it dry

Listen to part of a lecture in a history class.

P: The process for <u>making paper</u> was invented around AD 150. Before then, people <u>wrote on pieces of wood</u>, but these were, uh, not convenient. Then, a Chinese man named Cai Lun made paper with the bark of trees.

ᴰTo make paper, the first step was to cut bark from a tree and <u>collect it into</u> a bundle. This bundle was cleaned in water. ᶜNext, the bark was boiled or steamed. This caused the bark <u>to soften</u> and <u>to release</u> a sticky liquid known as pulp. Then, the softened bark was beaten with a wooden hammer to <u>break it down into</u> fibers. ᴬThe fibers and pulp were <u>mixed with water</u>. ᴮFinally, a thin layer of the mixture was <u>placed on</u> a screen and <u>left in the sun</u> to dry. When the screen was removed, the paper was made.

역사학 강의의 일부를 들으시오.

P: 종이를 만드는 과정은 서기 150년경에 개발되었습니다. 그 전에는, 사람들이 나무토막에 글을 썼는데, 그것들은, 어, 편리하지 않았어요. 그 후, 채륜이라는 이름의 한 중국인이 나무껍질을 사용해 종이를 만들었습니다.

종이를 만들기 위해, 첫 번째 단계는 나무에서 나무껍질을 잘라 다발로 모으는 것이었어요. 이 다발은 물에 씻겨졌습니다. 다음으로, 나무껍질은 끓여지거나 쪄졌어요. 이것은 나무껍질을 부드럽게 하고 펄프라고 알려진 끈적거리는 액체를 발산하게 했습니다. 그러고 나서, 부드러워진 나무껍질은 나무망치로 두드려 섬유로 분해했어요. 섬유와 펄프는 물과 함께 섞였죠. 마지막으로, 이 얇은 층의 혼합물이 그물망 위에 놓였고 햇볕에 두어 건조되었어요. 그 그물망이 제거되면, 종이가 만들어졌습니다.

Cai Lun 채륜(蔡倫, 중국 후한 중기의 환관)　　bark 나무껍질
bundle 다발, 묶음　　boil (물이나 액체를) 끓이다
steam 찌다　　soften 부드럽게 하다
release 발산하다; 풀어 주다　　sticky 끈적거리는
pulp 펄프(목재 등에서 나온 섬유의 집합체)
beat 두드리다; 이기다　　break down into ~으로 분해하다
fiber 섬유　　mixture 혼합물　　screen 그물망, 스크린

교수는 고대 중국의 종이 제작 과정을 설명한다. 아래의 단계들을 올바른 순서대로 나열하시오. 각 답변을 해당하는 곳으로 끌어다 놓으시오.

단계 1	(D) 나무껍질이 모아져 물에 씻겨졌다.
단계 2	(C) 나무껍질이 끓여지거나 쪄졌다.
단계 3	(A) 섬유와 펄프가 물과 함께 섞였다.
단계 4	(B) 그물망이 햇볕에 건조되었다.

Listening Practice 1

본문 p. 117

1 (A) 2 (D) 3 Advantage: (A), (B), (C)
Not an Advantage: (D)

Note-taking

Student's Problem

Will be in a different country on the <u>orientation</u> day

What's Provided in the Orientation

- A <u>tour</u> of the campus
- Information about how to <u>sign</u> <u>up</u> for courses

Listen to a conversation between a student and a university employee.

M: Hi. ¹I heard that the orientation <u>will</u> <u>be</u> <u>held</u> next month.

W: That's right. Do you <u>have</u> <u>some</u> <u>questions</u> about it?

M: Um, I have a problem… ²My family will be <u>on</u> <u>holiday</u> in a different country <u>on</u> <u>the</u> <u>same</u> <u>day</u>. We've already <u>booked</u> <u>a</u> <u>flight</u>, so I'm not sure if we can <u>change</u> <u>the</u> <u>schedule</u>.

W: I see… Well, students <u>are</u> <u>not</u> <u>required</u> <u>to</u> <u>go</u> to the orientation, but I <u>strongly</u> <u>recommend</u> <u>you</u> <u>attend</u>.

M: Um… May I ask why? I don't know why it's so important.

W: Sure. ³ᴬFirst, there will be a <u>tour</u> <u>of</u> <u>the</u> <u>campus</u>. It would <u>be</u> <u>helpful</u> <u>to</u> <u>learn</u> where everything is.

M: Well, I guess I agree with that.

W: Right. ³ᴮIt will also provide information about how to <u>sign</u> <u>up</u> <u>for</u> <u>courses</u>. Many students are attending it <u>for</u> <u>this</u> <u>reason</u>.

M: I don't want to miss that, either. ³ᶜUm, and it <u>sounds</u> <u>like</u> <u>a</u> <u>great</u> <u>chance</u> to meet other students as well.

W: Good point. ³ᴰThere aren't any social activities, but you'd probably <u>make</u> <u>some</u> <u>new</u> <u>friends</u> anyway.

M: OK. I'll talk to my parents about this tonight.

학생과 교직원 사이의 대화를 들으시오.

M: 안녕하세요. 다음 달에 오리엔테이션이 열린다고 들었어요.

W: 맞아요. 그것에 대해 질문이 있나요?

M: 음, 문제가 있어요… 저희 가족이 그날 다른 나라에서 휴가 중일 거예요. 이미 비행기를 예약해놨기 때문에, 저희가 일정을 바꿀 수 있을지 잘 모르겠어요.

W: 그렇군요… 음, 학생들이 오리엔테이션에 반드시 갈 필요는 없지만, 저는 참석할 것을 강력히 권해요.

M: 음… 왜 그런지 여쭤봐도 될까요? 그게 왜 그렇게 중요한지 모르겠어요.

W: 물론이죠. 먼저, 캠퍼스 투어가 있을 거예요. 그건 모든 곳이 어디에 있는지 아는 데 도움이 될 거예요.

M: 음, 저도 그것에 동의하는 것 같아요.

W: 그래요. 그건 강의를 신청하는 방법에 대한 정보도 제공할 거예요. 많은 학생들이 이 이유로 참석한답니다.

M: 저도 그건 놓치고 싶지 않네요. 음, 그리고 다른 학생들을 만날 수 있는 좋은 기회일 것도 같고요.

W: 잘 말씀하셨어요. 사교 활동이 있지는 않지만, 그래도 아마 새로운 친구를 몇 명 만들게 될 거예요.

M: 알겠습니다. 오늘 밤에 저희 부모님과 이것에 대해 얘기해 봐야겠어요.

---

hold (동) 열리다; 개최하다 be on holiday 휴가 중이다
book a flight 비행기를 예약하다 require (동) ~이 필요하다
strongly (부) 강력하게 attend (동) 참석하다
sign up for ~을 신청하다 course (명) 강의, 수업
social activity 사교 활동 anyway (부) 그래도, 어쨌든

1 대화의 주된 주제는 무엇인가?

(A) 다가오는 학교 행사
(B) 여행 일정의 변경
(C) 공문서 양식에 대한 문제
(D) 몇몇 학교에 대한 투어

2 학생은 다음 달에 무엇을 할 계획이었는가?

(A) 교수와 대화하기
(B) 해외 유학하기
(C) 아르바이트직 찾기
(D) 가족 휴가 가기

3 다음의 항목이 오리엔테이션에 참석하는 것의 장점인지를 아래 표에 표시하시오. 각 항목에 적절한 칸을 클릭하시오.

	장점	장점 아님
(A) 캠퍼스 내 모든 곳이 어디에 있는지 보기	V	
(B) 강의를 신청하는 방법 배우기	V	
(C) 다른 학생들 만나기	V	
(D) 준비된 사교 활동에 참여하기		V

Listening Practice 2

본문 p. 119

1 (D) 2 (D) 3 Legends: (B), (D) Folktales: (A), (C)

Note-taking

Legends

- Based on <u>actual</u> events
- Have a <u>hero</u> as the main character

Folktales

- Passed down by word of <u>mouth</u>
- Changed because of the <u>preferences</u> of listeners

Listen to part of a lecture in a literature class.

P: As I mentioned earlier, folklore is a broad concept. It includes the stories and cultural traditions that belong to a particular group of people. ¹Now, I'd like to talk about two important parts of folklore... legends and folktales.

OK... All legends have two distinct features. ³ᴮFirst, they are based on actual events, although they sometimes include magical creatures like monsters or dragons. ³ᴰAnother characteristic of a legend is that it has a hero. The main character is always someone who can do what normal people cannot do. Um, an example with both of these characteristics is the Greek legend about the Minotaur... Does anyone know the story?

S: Um, it's about a monster that was half-man and half-bull.

P: That's right. According to the legend, the Minotaur was defeated by the hero Theseus, who would later become the king of Athens. Researchers believe that Theseus was a king in the 8th or 9th century BC. And they assume that monsters in legends were used to explain things that were hard to understand at that time, such as natural disasters.

So, what about folktales? Well, to begin with, folktales are generally passed down from person to person by word of mouth. ³ᴬThey are rarely written down. ³ᶜNext, they change as time passes. This is because people change the stories to match the preferences of listeners. ²Think about Little Red Riding Hood. In the earliest version of this story, Little Red Riding Hood was actually eaten by the wolf. However, in later ones, she was saved by the woodcutter.

문학 강의의 일부를 들으시오.

P: 앞서 언급했듯이, 민간전승은 넓은 개념의 단어입니다. 그것은 특정 집단의 사람들의 이야기와 문화적 전통을 포함해요. 이제, 저는 민간전승의 두 가지 중요한 부분에 대해 이야기할 건데요... 전설과 설화입니다.

자... 모든 전설에는 두 가지 뚜렷한 특징이 있어요. 먼저, 가끔 괴물이나 용 같은 마법의 생명체들이 포함되기도 하지만, 그것들은 실제 사건들을 기반으로 하죠. 전설의 또 다른 특징은 그것에 영웅이 있다는 것입니다. 주인공은 항상 평범한 사람들은 할 수 없는 것을 할 수 있는 인물이에요. 음, 이 두 가지 특징을 모두 가진 예시로 미노타우로스에 대한 그리스 전설이 있는데요... 그 이야기를 아는 사람이 있나요?

S: 음, 그건 반은 인간이고 반은 황소인 괴물에 관한 거예요.

P: 맞아요. 전설에 따르면, 미노타우로스는 후에 아테네의 왕이 되는 영웅 테세우스가 물리칩니다. 연구자들은 테세우스가 기원전 8세기 또는 9세기의 왕이었다고 생각해요. 그리고 그들은 전설 속의 괴물들이 자연재해와 같이 그 당시에는 이해하기 어려웠던 것들을 설명하기 위해 사용되었다고 추측합니다.

그러면, 설화는 어떨까요? 음, 우선, 설화는 일반적으로 사람에서 사람으로 구전으로 전해지죠. 그것들은 거의 기록되지 않습니다.

다음으로, 그것들은 시간이 지남에 따라 변합니다. 이것은 듣는 사람들의 취향에 맞춰 사람들이 이야기를 바꾸기 때문이죠. 빨간 모자에 대해 생각해 보세요. 이 이야기의 가장 초기 버전에서는, 빨간 모자는 사실 늑대에게 잡아먹혔어요. 하지만, 후기 작품들에서, 그녀는 나무꾼에 의해 구조됩니다.

folklore 명 민간전승, 민속   concept 명 개념
belong to ~의 것이다, ~에 속하다   legend 명 전설
folktale 명 설화   distinct 형 뚜렷한
be based on ~을 기반으로 하다   hero 명 영웅
Minotaur 명 미노타우로스(사람의 몸에 소의 머리를 한 괴물)
bull 명 황소   defeat 동 물리치다, 패배시키다
Theseus 명 테세우스(괴물 미노타우로스를 퇴치한 영웅)
natural disaster 자연재해   pass down ~을 전해주다
by word of mouth 구전으로   rarely 부 거의 ~하지 않는, 드물게
write down 기록하다, 적어놓다   match 동 맞추다
preference 명 취향, 선호   woodcutter 명 나무꾼

1 강의는 주로 무엇에 관한 것인가?
  (A) 여러 나라들에서 공유되는 이야기들
  (B) 전통적인 이야기들의 문화적 가치
  (C) 민간전승과 문화의 연관성
  (D) 두 종류의 민간전승의 특징들

2 교수는 왜 빨간 모자를 언급하는가?
  (A) 과거와 현재의 설화를 비교하기 위해
  (B) 설화가 어떻게 전해지는지 설명하기 위해
  (C) 설화의 가장 오래된 예시를 제공하기 위해
  (D) 설화의 이야기가 어떻게 변했는지 보여주기 위해

3 다음의 항목이 전설과 설화 중 어떤 것에 대한 설명인지를 표시하시오. 각 항목에 적절한 칸을 클릭하시오.

	전설	설화
(A) 그것들은 거의 기록되지 않는다.		V
(B) 그것들은 실제 사건들에 기반한다.	V	
(C) 이야기들이 청중이 무엇을 좋아하는지에 따라 달라진다.		V
(D) 이야기들에 영웅이 있다.	V	

Listening Practice 3

1 (B)   2 (D)   3 Included: (A), (C), (D)
Not Included: (B)

Note-taking
Student's Question
Could I get information about a field trip?

Activities at the Museum
- A dinosaur exhibition
- A session about the process of digging up fossils
- A talk by a researcher in archaeology

Listen to a conversation between a student and a professor.

S: Hi, Professor Lewis. I'm sorry I missed last Friday's class. Um, as I said in my e-mail, I couldn't attend it because I was ill.

P: That's fine, Greg. I understand your situation and it won't affect your grade.

S: Thanks. ¹Um, and I heard that there will be a field trip to the Museum of Natural History next week. Could I get more information about it?

P: Right. ³ᴬThere is a new dinosaur exhibition that I want everyone to see. ²As our midterm will be about dinosaurs and their fossils, things from the exhibition will be on the test.

S: OK. ³ᴮUm, then I guess there will be a curator's tour of the exhibition...

P: No, that won't be necessary. ³ᶜBut there will be a session on learning how to dig up fossils.

S: Wow. I've always wanted to see the process.

P: It should be interesting. ³ᴰUh, the field trip will end with a talk by Dr. Malcolm, one of the most influential researchers in archaeology.

S: I see... Thanks for organizing this. I'm really looking forward to it.

학생과 교수 사이의 대화를 들으시오.

S: 안녕하세요, Lewis 교수님. 지난 금요일 수업에 빠져서 죄송합니다. 음, 이메일에서 말씀드렸듯이, 제가 아파서 참석할 수 없었어요.

P: 괜찮아, Greg. 네 상황은 이해했고 그게 네 성적에 영향을 미치진 않을 거란다.

S: 감사합니다. 음, 그리고 다음 주에 자연사 박물관에 가는 현장 학습이 있다고 들었어요. 그것에 대해 더 많은 정보를 얻을 수 있을까요?

P: 맞아. 너희 모두 봤으면 하는 새로운 공룡 전시회가 있어. 중간고사가 공룡과 그 화석들에 관한 게 될 거니까, 전시회에서 나온 것들이 시험에 나올 거란다.

S: 그렇군요. 음, 그럼 전시회에 대한 큐레이터 투어가 있을 것 같네요.

P: 아니, 그건 필요하지 않을 거야. 하지만 화석을 발굴하는 방법을 배우는 시간이 있을 거야.

S: 와. 저는 항상 그 과정을 보고싶었어요.

P: 흥미로울거야. 어, 현장 학습은 고고학계에서 가장 영향력 있는 연구자 중 한 명인 Malcolm 박사님의 강연으로 마무리 될 거야.

S: 알겠습니다…이것을 준비해 주셔서 감사해요 정말 기대가 되네요.

miss a class 수업에 빠지다   ill 형 아픈; 나쁜
affect 동 영향을 미치다   field trip 현장 학습   exhibition 명 전시(회)
fossil 명 화석   curator 명 큐레이터(박물관 등의 전시 책임자)
necessary 형 필요한, 필수적인   session 명 (특정한 활동을 위한) 시간
dig up 발굴하다   talk 명 강연   influential 형 영향력 있는
researcher 명 연구자   archaeology 명 고고학
organize 동 준비하다; 정리하다   look forward to ~을 기대하다

1 학생은 왜 교수를 찾아가는가?
 (A) 그의 성적에 대한 변경을 요청하기 위해
 (B) 학교 현장 학습에 대한 정보를 얻기 위해
 (C) 그가 왜 수업에 늦었는지 설명하기 위해
 (D) 여행 참가에 대한 허가를 요청하기 위해

2 교수는 왜 중간고사를 언급하는가?
 (A) 수업에 빠지는 것이 성적에 영향을 미친다는 것을 나타내기 위해
 (B) 현장 학습이 왜 연기될 것인지 설명하기 위해
 (C) 학생이 더 열심히 공부해야 한다는 것을 암시하기 위해
 (D) 현장 학습의 중요성을 강조하기 위해

3 현장 학습에 어떤 활동들이 포함될 것인가? 다음의 항목이 포함되는 것인지를 표시하시오. 각 항목에 적절한 칸을 클릭하시오.

	포함됨	포함 안 됨
(A) 어떤 전시를 보는 것	V	
(B) 큐레이터의 안내를 받는 투어를 하는 것		V
(C) 화석을 발굴하는 방법을 배우는 것	V	
(D) 강연을 듣는 것	V	

Listening Practice 4 본문 p.123

1 (A)   2 (A)   3 Yes: (A), (C)   No: (B), (D)

Note-taking

The Silent Film Era
- Different types of songs were played live.
- Movies with large budgets had a soundtrack.

End of the Silent Film Era
Sound-recording technology allowed the recording of actors' voices, sound effects, and music.

Listen to part of a lecture in a film class.

P: Has anyone seen a silent film? If you have, raise your hand. Just a few of you... Well, silent films actually were not totally silent. ¹At the theater, there was music during silent films. And, uh, there were some changes in this form of music during the silent film era.

³ᴬUm, in this era, the music was played live during silent films. In the beginning, it was usually played by a single pianist. Pianists had to play different types of songs for different films and audiences. They would play classical songs or songs that were popular at that time, such as folk or jazz.

³ᶜGradually, silent films included bands and even entire orchestras. As this trend developed, the music changed too. People began writing musical scores just for films. Uh, a musical score is a written form of music. Then, around 1908, films

with soundtracks appeared. Now, does anyone know what a soundtrack is?

S: Uh, it's a collection of songs and sounds in a film.

P: Exactly! ²So, by 1915, movies with large budgets usually had soundtracks. The American film *The Birth of a Nation*, for example, included three music types. It used classical music, melodies from popular songs, and original music. By original music, I mean, music that was created just for this film.

³ᴰBut, soon, the silent film era ended when sound-recording technology was introduced. This technology allowed movie producers to record the sounds of actors' voices, sound effects, and music. Then, in a studio, these sound recordings were combined with the film. Audiences thought this combination gave a more realistic movie experience. ³ᴰTherefore, the silent film lost popularity.

영화학 강의의 일부를 들으시오.

P: 무성 영화를 본 적 있는 사람이 있나요? 있다면, 손을 들어주세요. 단 몇 명뿐이네요... 음, 무성 영화는 사실 완전히 소리가 없지는 않았어요. 극장에서, 무성 영화가 상영되는 동안 음악이 있었답니다. 그리고, 어, 무성 영화 시대 동안 이런 형태의 음악에는 몇몇 변화들이 있었어요.

음, 이 시대에는, 무성 영화가 상영되는 동안 음악이 라이브로 연주되었어요. 처음에는, 그것은 보통 한 명의 피아니스트에 의해 연주되었죠. 피아니스트들은 다양한 영화와 관객들을 위해 여러 종류의 노래들을 연주해야 했습니다. 그들은 클래식 음악이나 민요나 재즈처럼 그 당시에 인기 있었던 노래를 연주하고는 했어요.

점차적으로, 무성 영화에는 밴드와 심지어 오케스트라 전체가 포함됐습니다. 이러한 추세가 발전하면서, 음악도 바뀌었지요. 사람들은 영화만을 위한 악보를 쓰기 시작했어요. 음, 악보는 음악이 문서 형태로 된 것이죠. 그 후, 1908년경에, 사운드트랙이 있는 영화들이 등장했어요. 자, 사운드트랙이 무엇인지 아는 사람이 있나요?

S: 어, 그건 영화에 나오는 노래와 소리들의 모음집이에요.

P: 맞아요! 그래서, 1915년쯤에는, 많은 예산이 들어간 영화들은 보통 사운드트랙을 가지고 있었어요. 예를 들어, 미국 영화 '국가의 탄생'에는 세 가지 음악 유형이 포함되어 있었습니다. 그것은 클래식 음악, 인기곡들의 멜로디, 그리고 창작곡을 사용했습니다. 창작곡이라고 하면, 제 말은, 이 영화만을 위해서 만들어진 음악을 뜻하죠.

그러나, 곧, 녹음 기술이 도입되면서 무성 영화 시대는 끝이 났습니다. 이 기술은 영화 제작자들이 배우들의 목소리, 음향 효과, 그리고 음악 소리를 녹음할 수 있게 해주었어요. 그 후, 스튜디오에서, 이 녹음본들은 영화와 결합되었죠. 관객들은 이 조합이 좀 더 사실적인 영화 관람 경험을 제공한다고 생각했어요. 그래서, 무성 영화는 인기를 잃게 됐습니다.

silent film 무성 영화 raise 동 ~을 들다
silent 형 무성의, 소리가 없는; 조용한 era 명 시대
audience 명 관객, 청중 folk 명 민요

gradually 부 점차적으로, 서서히 trend 명 추세
musical score 악보 soundtrack 명 사운드트랙
collection 명 (노래 등의) 모음집 budget 명 예산, 비용
original 형 창작의, 독창적인; 최초의 sound-recording 명 녹음
producer 명 제작자, 생산자 sound effect 음향 효과
combine with 동 ~과 결합하다 combination 명 조합
realistic 형 사실적인, 현실적인 popularity 명 인기

1 강의의 주된 주제는 무엇인가?
   (A) 무성 영화 시대에서의 음악의 변화
   (B) 다양한 종류의 무성 영화들
   (C) 무성 영화 시대의 유명한 배우들
   (D) 초기 영화 역사상 인기곡들

2 교수는 왜 '국가의 탄생'을 언급하는가?
   (A) 사운드트랙이 있는 영화의 예시를 제공하기 위해
   (B) 미국 최초의 무성 영화를 소개하기 위해
   (C) 영화감독의 가장 유명한 작품을 강조하기 위해
   (D) 무성 영화가 돈이 많이 들었다는 것을 강조하기 위해

3 다음의 항목이 무성 영화 음악의 특징에 대한 설명인지를 표시하시오. 각 항목에 적절한 칸을 클릭하시오.

	예	아니오
(A) 음악이 라이브 공연으로 연주되었다.	V	
(B) 대부분의 음악은 영화감독이 썼다.		V
(C) 무성 영화에는 결국 밴드와 오케스트라가 포함됐다.	V	
(D) 녹음 기술은 무성 영화를 더 인기 있게 만들었다.		V

iBT Listening Test 1   본문 p.125

1 (D)   2 (B)   3 (B)   4 Yes: (A), (C), (D) No: (B)

Note-taking

Student's Problem
Trying to print a report, but keeps getting an error message

Librarian's Solution
- Apply for a printer card to use the printers
- Pay for the printing cost at the end of each month
- Put the card on the scanner, and enter your student ID number

Listen to a conversation between a student and a librarian.

M: Excuse me. ¹I'm trying to print a report, but I keep getting an error message on the computer.

W: Um, did you make a printer card? From last week, students can no longer print for free, and you have to apply for a printer card to use the printers. ²The school wants us to reduce spending, so we changed our policy.

M: Really? ³That doesn't seem like a fair decision. I mean, all of my friends' universities don't make students pay for printing.

W: I understand, but there's nothing I can do. ⁴ᴬUh, if you want to apply for a card, I have the form right here.

M: I guess I don't have a choice... ⁴ᴮUm, do I need to make a payment in advance?

W: No. You should pay for the printing cost at the end of each month. We'll send a text message about it.

M: Got it. Uh, so how do I use the card?

W: ⁴ᶜ/⁴ᴰJust put the card on the scanner next to the computer and enter your student ID number on its screen. After that, you'll be able to print your document.

M: I see... Thanks for explaining everything.

학생과 사서 사이의 대화를 들으시오.

M: 실례합니다. 제가 보고서를 인쇄하려고 하는데, 컴퓨터에 오류 메시지가 계속 떠서요.

W: 음, 프린터 카드를 만드셨나요? 지난주부터, 학생분들은 더 이상 무료로 인쇄를 할 수 없고 프린터를 사용하기 위해서는 프린터 카드를 신청해야 해요. 학교에서 지출을 줄이길 원해서, 저희가 정책을 바꾸게 됐어요.

M: 정말요? 그건 타당한 결정 같지 않은데요. 제 말은, 모든 제 친구들의 대학에서는 학생들이 인쇄비를 내지 않도록 하거든요.

W: 이해는 하지만, 제가 할 수 있는 것이 없어요. 어, 카드를 신청하고 싶으시면, 신청서는 여기에 있습니다.

M: 선택의 여지가 없는 것 같군요... 음, 제가 미리 결제해야 하나요?

W: 아뇨. 매달 말에 인쇄비를 내시면 돼요. 저희가 그것에 대해 문자 메세지를 보내드릴 거예요.

M: 알겠어요. 어, 그래서 제가 카드를 어떻게 사용하면 되나요?

W: 카드를 컴퓨터 옆에 있는 스캐너에 넣고 그 화면에 학생의 학생증 번호를 입력하시기만 하면 돼요. 그 후에, 학생의 문서를 출력하실 수 있을 거예요.

M: 알겠습니다... 모든 걸 설명해 주셔서 감사해요.

error message 오류 메시지   no longer 더 이상 ~ 않다
apply for ~을 신청하다, ~에 지원하다   spending 명 지출, 소비
policy 명 정책, 방침   fair 형 타당한; 공평한
make a payment 결제하다, 지불하다   in advance 미리, 사전에
scanner 명 스캐너   enter 통 입력하다; 들어가다   screen 명 화면

1 학생의 문제는 무엇인가?
 (A) 그는 노트북에서 인터넷에 접속할 수 없다.
 (B) 그는 도서관 웹사이트에 로그인할 수 없었다.
 (C) 그는 학교 과제를 위한 책을 찾을 수 없다.
 (D) 그는 문서를 인쇄할 수 없었다.

2 사서에 따르면, 정책이 왜 변경되었는가?

(A) 건물의 보안을 향상시키기 위해
(B) 돈을 절약하기 위해
(C) 컴퓨터 시스템을 업그레이드하기 위해
(D) 학생들의 불안에 대응하기 위해

3 학생은 학교의 부당한 결정에 대해 자신의 주장을 어떻게 강조하고 있는가?
 (A) 그의 친구들의 의견을 제공함으로써
 (B) 다른 대학들과 비교함으로써
 (C) 학교 방침에 대한 설명을 요청함으로써
 (D) 문서의 중요성을 언급함으로써

4 대화에서, 사서는 도서관에서 프린터를 사용하는 것에 대한 몇 가지 지시사항을 제공한다. 다음의 항목이 지시사항인지 아닌지를 표시하시오.
각 항목에 적절한 칸을 클릭하시오.

	예	아니오
(A) 신청서 작성하기	V	
(B) 카드 비용을 미리 지불하기		V
(C) 카드 스캐너 사용하기	V	
(D) 학생증 번호 입력하기	V	

iBT Listening Test 2   본문 p. 128

1 (B)   2 (C)   3 (A)   4 (C)-(D)-(B)-(E)-(A)

Note-taking
Five Stages of Grief
1. You deny reality.
2. The pain comes out and you feel angry.
3. You feel helpless and try to negotiate with yourself or with God.
4. You realize reality and experience depression.
5. You accept reality.

Listen to part of a lecture in a psychology class.

P: Have you ever lost someone important? You probably felt very sad. But did you have some other feelings at the same time? ¹Today, I'd like to talk about the five stages of grief. The five stages of grief are the steps people go through when they experience deep sadness. In 1969, psychiatrist Elisabeth Kübler-Ross wrote about them in her book, *On Death and Dying*. ²Um, let's explore each stage through an example...

So let's say that you've learned that you are dying. ⁴ᶜOf course, the news will be shocking. In response, you may try to deny that it's true. This gives you time to deal with the heavy emotions you're feeling. That's the first stage.

⁴ᴰWhen you can no longer deny the possibility of death, the pain you've been hiding comes out. And this causes you to feel angry. Like the first

stage, anger is another way to avoid dealing with grief directly.

Once you've overcome your anger, you start to feel helpless. This is when bargaining begins. ⁴ᴮWhen you bargain, you try to negotiate or reach an agreement with yourself or with God. You may say things like, "If I become a better person, then maybe God will let me live." Of course, that's impossible.

³/⁴ᴱThen, you will experience depression when you realize that you cannot avoid death. You will, um, find it difficult to think clearly and feel too weak to act. It may be useful to have a therapist's help at this stage.

⁴ᴬFinally, the last stage is accepting reality. Uh, this doesn't mean you are happy... It just means that you understand your grief and have found a way to continue living.

심리학 강의의 일부를 들으시오.

P: 여러분은 중요한 사람을 잃어본 적이 있나요? 여러분은 아마 매우 슬펐을 거예요. 하지만 동시에 다른 감정들도 가졌었나요? 오늘, 저는 슬픔의 다섯 단계에 관해 이야기하고자 합니다. 슬픔의 다섯 단계는 사람들이 깊은 슬픔을 경험할 때 겪는 단계들입니다. 1969년에, 정신과 의사 엘리자베스 퀴블러-로스가 그녀의 책인 '죽음과 죽어감'에 그것들에 대해 썼죠. 음, 각각의 단계를 예시를 통해 살펴보죠...

자, 여러분이 죽어가고 있다는 것을 알게 됐다고 가정해 보세요. 물론, 그 소식은 충격적일 것입니다. 이에 대해, 여러분은 그것이 사실이라는 것을 부정하려고 할 수도 있습니다. 이것은 여러분이 느끼고 있는 무거운 감정들에 대처할 시간을 줍니다. 그게 첫 번째 단계입니다.

더 이상 죽음의 가능성을 부정할 수 없을 때, 여러분이 그동안 숨겨왔던 고통이 나오게 되죠. 그리고 이것은 여러분을 화가 나게 합니다. 첫 번째 단계처럼, 분노는 슬픔에 직접적으로 대처하는 것을 피하는 또 다른 방법이에요.

분노를 극복하게 되면, 여러분은 무력하다고 느끼기 시작합니다. 이 때가 협상이 시작하는 때입니다. 협상을 할 때, 여러분은 여러분 자신 또는 신과 협상을 하거나 합의에 도달하려고 합니다. 여러분은 "만약 내가 더 나은 사람이 된다면, 아마도 신께서 나를 살게 해주실지도 몰라."와 같은 말들을 할 수도 있어요. 물론, 그것은 불가능하죠.

그 후, 죽음을 피할 수 없다는 것을 깨달았을 때 여러분은 우울증을 경험하게 될 것입니다. 여러분은, 음, 제대로 생각하는 것이 어렵고, 행동을 취하기엔 너무 나약하다고 느낄 것입니다. 이 단계에서는 치료사의 도움을 받는 것이 유용할 수 있어요.

마지막으로, 마지막 단계는 현실을 받아들이는 것입니다. 어, 이것은 여러분이 행복하다는 뜻은 아니에요... 단지 여러분이 슬픔을 이해하고 계속해서 살아갈 방법을 찾았다는 의미일 뿐입니다.

grief 명 슬픔, 비탄 go through 겪다, 경험하다
psychiatrist 명 정신과 의사 shocking 형 충격적인
deny 동 부정하다, 부인하다 deal with ~을 대처하다, 처리하다
emotion 명 감정 possibility 명 가능성 overcome 동 극복하다
helpless 형 무력한 bargain 동 협상하다, 흥정하다; 명 협상

reach an agreement 합의에 도달하다 depression 명 우울증
therapist 명 치료사 accept 동 받아들이다 reality 명 현실

1 강의는 주로 무엇에 관한 것인가?

   (A) 감정을 표현하는 다양한 방법들
   (B) 슬픔을 느끼는 과정
   (C) 어떤 요소들이 감정에 영향을 미치는지
   (D) 우울증을 피하는 방법

2 교수는 강의를 어떻게 구성하는가?

   (A) 그의 연구 논문을 읽음으로써
   (B) 개인적인 경험을 이야기함으로써
   (C) 학생들에게 상황을 상상하게 함으로써
   (D) 실험의 결과를 설명함으로써

3 교수에 따르면, 치료사가 사람들이 하도록 도울 수 있는 것은 무엇인가?

   (A) 우울감 극복하기
   (B) 인생의 의미를 이해하기
   (C) 다른 사람들의 말 듣기
   (D) 분노를 적절히 표출하기

4 강의에서, 교수는 사람들이 깊은 슬픔을 느낄 때 겪는 몇 가지의 단계들을 설명한다. 아래의 단계들을 올바른 순서대로 나열하시오. 각 답변을 해당하는 곳으로 끌어다 놓으시오.

단계 1	(C) 사람들이 슬픈 소식을 부정한다.
단계 2	(D) 사람들이 깊은 고통 때문에 화가 난다.
단계 3	(B) 사람들이 그들 자신 또는 신과 협상하려고 한다.
단계 4	(E) 사람들이 우울증을 경험한다.
단계 5	(A) 사람들이 상황의 현실을 받아들인다.

Vocabulary Review 본문 p. 132

1 deny   2 distinct   3 defeat
4 folklore   5 policy   6 attend
7 necessary   8 deal with   9 audience
10 (A)   11 (C)   12 (D)
13 (B)   14 (D)

CHAPTER 07
Inference

Example 본문 p. 135

A. (D)   B. (C)

A.

Note-taking

Student's Request
Noticed a small error in an article in the school newspaper

Advisor's Response
- Will write an apology notice and publish it
- A correction will be in next month's issue

Listen to a conversation between a student and a faculty advisor for the university newspaper.

W: Hello, I'd like to talk to you about an article. It was in this month's issue of the school newspaper.

M: All right... Which article did you want to discuss?

W: Well, it's the one on page six. It's about the school's history. I noticed a small error in one of the facts.

M: Really? Let me see that...

W: It's right here in paragraph three. It says that the school building was built on June 10, 1971, but, um, the correct date is June 20, 1971.

M: Oh, you're right! Thank you for pointing it out.

W: Um, I just thought you should know.

M: Absolutely. I'll write an apology notice immediately and make sure it gets published. There will also be a correction in next month's issue. I'll let you know when it comes out.

남자는 다음에 무엇을 할 것인가?

(A) 다음 달 기사 검토하기
(B) 편집자에게 편지 쓰기
(C) 약속 날짜 변경하기
(D) 사과의 글 준비하기

B.

Note-taking

Spanish in Spain and Mexico
- The same letter is pronounced with a different sound.
  e.g. Barcelona
- Different words are used to refer to the same objects.
  e.g. Potato, computer

Listen to part of a lecture in a linguistics class.

P: So one characteristic of language is variation. This, um, means that the same language can be spoken differently. It depends on where it is used... Let me give you some examples with Spanish. In Spain, words spelled with a c before an i or an e, like *Barcelona*, are pronounced with a th sound, as in *Bar-thelona*. However, in Mexico, the same letter is pronounced with an s sound, as in *Bar-selona*. Um, you'll also notice that different words may be used to refer to the same objects. For instance, a potato is *patata* in Spain, but *papa* in Mexico. Or, a computer is *ordenador* in Spain, but *computadora* in Mexico. Um, you might think this is confusing. However, Spanish speakers can understand each other just fine.

스페인어에 관해 추론할 수 있는 것은 무엇인가?

(A) 스페인어는 세계적인 영향 때문에 시간이 지나면서 변해왔다.
(B) 멕시코에서 쓰는 스페인어가 가장 다양성이 높다.
(C) 스페인어는 스페인과 멕시코에서 다르게 사용된다.
(D) 스페인어는 다양한 발음 때문에 어렵다.

Listening Practice 1

본문 p.137

1 (C)   **2** (A)   **3** (D)

Note-taking

Student's Request
Would like to <u>borrow</u> the books again

Librarian's Response
- Can't borrow a book another student has <u>requested</u>
- Use the copy that the library <u>keeps</u>

Listen to a conversation between a student and a librarian.

W: Hi. I, uh, borrowed these books for a school project. [1]The return date is today, but I'd like to borrow them again for two weeks.

M: You can borrow these two, but you'll have to return the other one.

W: Oh? That's strange. I've done this before. Why can't I extend the date for all of them?

M: [2]The library staff had a meeting, and we, uh, decided to change our policy. It used to be possible to extend the due dates for all books. Now, you can't borrow a book that another student has requested.

W: I see... But I really need all three books to finish my project. Don't you have other copies you could lend me? My project is due in two weeks.

M: Well, according to my computer, all of the copies are not here right now... [3]You can use the copy that the library keeps, but you'll have to use it here.

W: OK... I'll go look for it now.

학생과 사서 사이의 대화를 들으시오.

W: 안녕하세요. 제가, 어, 학교 과제 때문에 이 책들을 빌렸었어요. 반납일이 오늘인데, 2주 동안 이것들을 다시 빌리고 싶어서요.

M: 이 두 권은 빌리실 수 있지만, 나머지 한 권은 반납하셔야 할 거예요.

W: 어? 이상하네요. 전에도 이렇게 해본 적이 있거든요. 왜 제가 모든 책의 기한을 연장할 수 없는 건가요?

M: 도서관 직원들이 회의를 했는데, 저희는, 어, 방침을 바꾸기로 결정했어요. 예전에는 모든 책의 반납 예정일을 연장하는 것이 가능했었어요. 이제는, 다른 학생이 요청한 책은 빌릴 수 없어요.

W: 그렇군요... 하지만 제 과제를 끝내려면 세 권 모두 정말 필요해요. 저한테 빌려주실 수 있는 다른 책들은 없나요? 제 프로젝트는 2주 후 마감 예정이에요.

M: 음, 제 컴퓨터에 따르면, 모든 책들이 지금 여기에 없네요... 도서관에서 보관하는 책을 이용하실 수는 있지만, 이곳에서 이용하셔야 할 겁니다.

W: 네... 지금 그것을 찾아보러 갈게요.

return date 반납일   extend 동 연장하다, 확장하다   staff 명 직원   meeting 명 회의   decide 동 결정하다   policy 명 방침, 정책   due date 반납 예정일, 만기일   request 동 요청하다; 명 요청   copy 명 (같은 책·신문 등의) 책, 한 부   lend 동 빌려주다   due in ~에 마감 예정인   according to ~에 따르면   look for ~을 찾다; 기대하다

1 화자들은 주로 무엇을 논의하고 있는가?
(A) 도서관의 컴퓨터 시스템을 이용하는 것
(B) 연체된 책들에 대한 요금을 지불하는 것
(C) 책들을 더 오랫동안 빌리는 것
(D) 학생용 도서관 카드를 교체하는 것

2 사서는 왜 학생에게 직원 회의에 대해 말하는가?
(A) 방침이 변경된 이유를 설명하기 위해
(B) 도서관이 문을 닫는다는 것을 언급하기 위해
(C) 학생에게 나중에 돌아오라고 요청하기 위해
(D) 학생에게 직원들이 바쁘다고 말하기 위해

3 학생은 다음에 무엇을 할 것인가?
(A) 교수에게 마감 기한을 옮겨 달라고 요청하기
(B) 신청서를 작성하기
(C) 다른 학교의 도서관을 방문하기
(D) 책 한 권을 찾기

Listening Practice 2

본문 p.139

1 (C)   **2** Vertical pupils: (A)   Round pupils: (B), (C)   Horizontal pupils: (D)   **3** (B)

Note-taking

Pupils of Predators
- Vertical pupils: Help measure the <u>distance</u> to prey
- <u>Round</u> pupils   e.g. Tigers, eagles

Pupils of Prey
<u>Horizontal</u> pupils: Give a very <u>wide</u> view

Listen to part of a lecture in a biology class.

P: All right. So we know that meat-eaters like lions, bears, and sharks are predators. And we know that deer, rabbits, and other grass-eaters are prey. But what they eat isn't the only thing that determines this. [1]Eye pupils, uh, you know, the round, black holes in the center of your eyes... are also related to whether an animal is a predator or prey.

[2A]Let's consider the eyes of certain predators, like crocodiles or cats. They have vertical pupils. Their pupils are long and narrow. This is because it helps them accurately measure the distance to their prey. If they know how far away their prey is, they'll know the distance to jump. One interesting thing about vertical pupils, though, is that they are more common in predators that, um, hunt very close to the ground. [2B/2C]Other types of predators that are quite large, like tigers, or predators that chase their prey, like eagles, typically have round pupils just like people.

²ᴰNow, for grass-eaters… Think about what is important for them to survive. They must be able to detect predators, right? So, they need to see around themselves as widely as possible. A horizontal-shaped pupil allows light to enter from many directions. This gives those animals a very wide view. Then, they can see predators that approach them from many different angles. Also, they can roll their eyes to get even better view. ³So a sheep, for example, has to lower its head when it eats. But it can roll its eyes to get a full view of its surroundings. This way, it knows that it's safe while it eats.

생물학 강의의 일부를 들으시오.

P: 좋아요. 자, 우리는 사자, 곰, 상어와 같은 육식동물이 포식자라는 것을 알고 있죠. 그리고 우리는 사슴, 토끼, 그리고 다른 초식동물들이 피식자라는 것도 알고 있습니다. 하지만 그것들이 먹는 것만이 이것을 결정하는 것은 아닙니다. 눈의 동공, 어, 그러니까, 눈 중심에 있는 동그란, 검은자위도… 동물이 포식자인지 혹은 피식자인지와 관련이 있습니다.

악어나 고양이와 같은, 특정 포식자들의 눈을 생각해 봅시다. 그것들은 세로형 동공을 가지고 있습니다. 그것들의 동공은 길고 좁아요. 이것은 그것들이 먹잇감까지의 거리를 정확하게 측정할 수 있도록 하기 때문이에요. 만약 그것들이 먹잇감이 얼마나 멀리 있는지 안다면, 뛰어야 하는 거리를 알 수 있죠. 그런데, 세로형 동공에 대해 한 가지 흥미로운 점은, 땅 가까이에서 사냥하는 포식자들에게 더 흔하다는 것입니다. 호랑이와 같이 상당히 큰 다른 유형의 포식자들, 또는 독수리처럼 먹잇감을 뒤쫓는 포식자들은 보통 꼭 인간처럼 둥근 동공을 가지고 있습니다.

자, 초식동물의 경우… 그것들에게 생존하기 위해 무엇이 중요한지 생각해 보세요. 그것들은 포식자를 감지할 수 있어야만 해요, 그렇죠? 그래서, 그것들은 주변을 가능한 한 넓게 볼 수 있어야 합니다. 가로형의 동공은 빛이 여러 방향에서 들어올 수 있도록 해주는데요. 이것은 그 동물들에게 아주 넓은 시야를 줍니다. 그러면, 그것들은 여러 다양한 각도에서 그들에게 접근하는 포식자들을 볼 수 있겠죠. 또한, 그것들은 눈알을 굴려서 훨씬 더 좋은 시야를 얻을 수도 있습니다. 그래서 예를 들어, 양은 먹을 때 그것의 머리를 숙여야 해요. 하지만 눈알을 굴려서 주변에 대한 전면적인 시야를 가질 수 있어요. 이렇게 해서, 그것은 먹는 동안 안전하다는 것을 알 수 있습니다.

meat-eater ⑲ 육식동물   predator ⑲ 포식자
grass-eater ⑲ 초식동물   prey ⑲ 피식자, 먹잇감
determine ⑧ 결정하다; 알아내다   pupil ⑲ 동공, 눈동자
vertical ⑳ 세로의, 수직의   narrow ⑳ 좁은
accurately ㉨ 정확하게, 정밀하게   measure ⑧ 측정하다
chase ⑧ 뒤쫓다, 추적하다   typically ㉨ 보통, 일반적으로
detect ⑧ 감지하다, 발견하다   horizontal-shaped ⑳ 가로 모양의
view ⑲ 시야   approach ⑧ 접근하다, 다가가다   angle ⑲ 각도
roll ⑧ 굴리다; 구르다   surroundings ⑲ 주변, 환경

1 교수는 주로 무엇에 관해 논하는가?

   (A) 포식자가 피식자를 잡는 데 도움이 되는 요인들

   (B) 몇몇 동물들이 밤에 볼 수 있는 이유들
   (C) 포식자와 피식자 동공의 차이점들
   (D) 동물들의 눈 동공의 발달

2 이 동물들은 어떤 종류의 동공을 가지고 있는가? 각 동물의 동공 유형을 표시하시오. 각 항목에 적절한 칸을 클릭하시오.

	세로형 동공	둥근형 동공	가로형 동공
(A) 악어	V		
(B) 호랑이		V	
(C) 독수리		V	
(D) 양			V

3 교수는 풀을 먹고 있는 피식 동물들에 관해 무엇을 암시하는가?

   (A) 그것들은 포식자들에게 쉽게 죽임을 당한다.
   (B) 그것들은 먹으면서 동시에 포식자를 찾을 수 있다.
   (C) 그것들은 밤보다 낮에 더 많이 먹는다.
   (D) 그것들은 아래로 내려다봄으로써 포식자들을 피할 수 있다.

Listening Practice 3 본문 p. 141

1 (B)   2 Yes: (A), (B) No: (C), (D)   3 (A)

Note-taking

Student's Question
How can I get a new student ID?

Employee's Answer
- Fill out the request form and pay the $20 fee
- Make a temporary card

Listen to a conversation between a student and a university employee at the registrar's office.

W: Excuse me, I have a question… ¹I lost my student ID card. Could you tell me how to get a new one?

M: Yes, of course. ²ᴬJust fill out this request form, and pay the $20 fee.

W: Oh, uh, I don't have any cash right now… But I could bring some later this week.

M: That's OK. ²ᴮThen, I can make a temporary one for you. It's free. ²ᶜIt takes three weeks to make a new one, so you'll need it anyway.

W: All right. ²ᴰSo, um, how long can I use the temporary card?

M: You can use it for 60 days. If you still don't have a new ID card by then, you'll have to request another temporary one.

W: OK… But, uh, what happens if I find my old ID card?

M: Well, you can use your old ID card if you don't have a new one yet. Otherwise, you'll have to throw it away.

W: I see. Thanks for your help… ³I'll be back with the

CHAPTER 07 | Inference   45

$20.

학적과에서 학생과 교직원 사이의 대화를 들으시오.

W: 실례합니다, 질문이 있어요... 제가 학생증을 잃어버렸어요. 새 학생증을 얻을 수 있는 방법을 알려주시겠어요?

M: 네, 물론이죠. 이 신청서를 작성하시고 20달러의 요금을 내시기만 하면 됩니다.

W: 오, 어, 제가 지금 현금이 없어요... 하지만 이번 주 후반에는 가져올 수 있어요.

M: 괜찮아요. 그럼, 제가 임시 학생증을 하나 만들어 드릴 수 있어요. 이건 무료예요. 새것을 만드는 데 3주가 걸리기 때문에, 어쨌든 그게 필요하실 거예요.

W: 알겠어요. 그러면, 음, 제가 그 임시 카드를 얼마 동안 사용할 수 있나요?

M: 60일 동안 사용하실 수 있어요. 그때까지 새 학생증이 없으면, 또 하나의 임시 학생증을 신청하셔야 할 거예요.

W: 알겠습니다... 그런데, 어, 제가 이전 학생증을 찾으면 어떻게 되나요?

M: 음, 아직 새 학생증이 없다면 이전 학생증을 써도 돼요. 그렇지 않으면, 그것을 버려야 할 거예요.

W: 알겠어요. 도와주셔서 감사합니다... 20달러를 가지고 다시 올게요.

student ID card 학생증   fill out 작성하다
request form 신청서   fee 명 요금   cash 명 현금
temporary 형 임시의, 일시적인   free 부 무료의; 자유로운
anyway 부 어쨌든, 게다가
otherwise 부 (만약) 그렇지 않으면; 그 외에는
throw away (쓰레기 등을) 버리다

1 학생은 왜 학적과를 찾아가는가?

(A) 다른 학생의 학생증을 돌려주기 위해
(B) 잃어버린 신분증을 교체하기 위해
(C) 수업료를 지불하기 위해
(D) 수업에 대한 연체료에 대해 문의하기 위해

2 다음의 항목이 학생증에 대해 언급된 것인지를 표시하시오. 각 항목에 적절한 칸을 클릭하시오.

	예	아니오
(A) 새 카드는 만드는 데 20달러가 든다.	V	
(B) 임시 학생증은 무료이다.	V	
(C) 새 카드는 만드는 데 4주가 걸린다.		V
(D) 임시 학생증은 3개월 동안 사용될 수 있다.		V

3 학생에 관해 추론할 수 있는 것은 무엇인가?

(A) 그녀는 기꺼이 요금을 지불할 의향이 있다.
(B) 그녀는 잃어버린 물건이 어디에 있는지 기억해냈다.
(C) 그녀는 중요한 서류를 버렸다.
(D) 그녀는 또 하나의 카드를 신청해야 한다.

Listening Practice 4   본문 p.143

1 (B)   **2** (B)   **3** (D)

Note-taking
Propylaea and Its Three Parts
Propylaea: Entrance to the Acropolis
- Central Room: Provided the main pathway to the Acropolis
- Eastern Room: Had beautiful ceiling
- Western Room: Contained paintings of Greek battles

Listen to part of a lecture in a history class.

P: All right. So we've been learning about ancient Greece, and last time we discussed the Acropolis. [1]Uh, if you remember, the Acropolis is a high area on a rock above the city of Athens. It has many historical sites, and Propylaea is one of them. This sounds difficult, but in Greek, it means "before the gates." So, the Propylaea is basically the entrance to the Acropolis.

Construction of the Propylaea began in 435 BC. The structure was built to honor the goddess Athena. It was composed of three parts. First, it had a central room. This provided the main pathway to the Acropolis. Here, the room was mostly made of marble. Interestingly, however, the ground was not paved. It was just natural ground. This probably had some religious reason...

There were also eastern and western rooms. The eastern room was very famous for its ceiling. [2]It was painted blue with gold stars, so it must have been very beautiful... like the night sky! A Greek writer called Pausanias once said nothing was more beautiful than this ceiling. And this was 600 years after the construction of the room. The western room was also impressive. It contained paintings of important Greek battles. This showed Greece's military strength. So, uh, the Propylaea had both religious and political purposes.

[3]Anyway, before its construction was completed, a war between Athens and Sparta began. Afterward, people tried to continue building it. However, to this day, no one is sure what it was supposed to look like. We'll talk about this war next time...

역사학 강의의 일부를 들으시오.

P: 자. 그래서 우리는 고대 그리스에 대해 배워왔고, 지난 시간에는 아크로폴리스에 대해 논의했었죠. 어, 만약 여러분이 기억한다면, 아크로폴리스는 아테네시 위의 암석에 있는 높은 지역이죠. 그곳에는 많은 유적지가 있는데, 프로필레아는 그것들 중 하나입니다. 이것은 어렵게 들리지만, 그리스어로, 그것은 "문 앞에"를 의미해요. 그래서, 프로필레아는 기본적으로 아크로폴리스의 입구랍니다.

프로필레아의 건설은 기원전 435년에 시작되었습니다. 그 건축물은 아테나 여신을 기리기 위해 지어졌어요. 그것은 세 부분으로 구성되어 있었는데요. 먼저, 중앙의 방이 있었습니다. 이곳은 아

크로폴리스로 가는 주요 통로를 제공했어요. 이곳은, 방 대부분이 대리석으로 만들어졌습니다. 하지만, 흥미롭게도, 바닥은 포장되어 있지 않았어요. 그것은 그냥 자연 그대로의 땅이었죠. 이것에는 아마 종교적인 이유가 있었을 겁니다...

동쪽과 서쪽 방도 있었는데요. 동쪽 방은 천장으로 매우 유명했어요. 그것은 금색 별들과 함께 파란색으로 칠해져 있어서, 매우 아름다웠을 것입니다... 마치 밤하늘처럼요! 파우사니아스라는 그리스 저술가가 한 번은 이 천장보다 아름다운 것은 없다고 말했어요. 그리고 이것은 그 방이 건설된 지 600년이 지났을 때의 일이었죠. 서쪽 방 또한 인상적이었어요. 이곳에는 그리스의 중요한 전투에 대한 그림들이 있었어요. 이것은 그리스의 군사력을 보여주었죠. 그래서, 어, 프로필레아에는 종교적 그리고 정치적인 용도가 모두 있었어요.

어쨌든, 그것의 건설이 완료되기 전에, 아테네와 스파르타 사이에 전쟁이 시작되었어요. 그 후, 사람들은 건설을 계속해보려고 했어요. 하지만, 오늘날까지, 누구도 그것이 어떻게 생겼어야 하는지는 알지 못해요. 우리는 다음 시간에 이 전쟁에 대해 이야기할 거예요...

Acropolis 명 아크로폴리스(고대 그리스 도시의 성채)
Athens 명 아테네(그리스의 수도)   historical site 유적지
Propylaea 명 프로필레아(고대 그리스 · 로마 신전의 정문)
gate 명 문, 출입구   basically 부 기본적으로, 근본적으로
entrance 명 입구   structure 명 건축물; 구조
honor 통 기리다; 명예   composed of ~으로 구성된
pathway 명 통로, 좁은 길   marble 명 대리석
paved 형 포장된   religious 형 종교적인
Pausanias 명 파우사니아스(2세기 후반에 활약한 그리스의 저술가)
ceiling 명 천장   impressive 형 인상적인
military strength 군사력   political 형 정치적
Sparta 명 스파르타(고대 그리스의 도시 국가)

1 강의의 주된 주제는 무엇인가?

(A) 고대 그리스의 종교들
(B) 그리스의 역사적 유적지
(C) 아크로폴리스의 역사
(D) 고대의 건축 방식

2 교수는 왜 파우사니아스를 언급하는가?

(A) 유명한 방의 설계자를 밝히기 위해
(B) 방의 아름다움을 강조하기 위해
(C) 예술작품들이 종교적인 의미를 가졌음을 보여주기 위해
(D) 그리스의 위대한 군사 지도자들 중 한 명을 소개하기 위해

3 교수는 프로필레아의 원래 건설에 관해 무엇을 암시하는가?

(A) 그것은 군에 의해 설계되었다.
(B) 그것은 매우 빨리 지어졌다.
(C) 그것은 전쟁 이후에 완공되었다.
(D) 그것은 한 번도 완공되지 못했다.

iBT Listening Test 1

본문 p.145

1 (C)   2 (A)   3 (C)   4 (A)

Note-taking

Student's Problem
Having some trouble with the lessons

Professor's Response
- Find online videos on biology or read the articles mentioned in class
- Don't worry too much about your grade

Listen to a conversation between a student and a professor.

S: Excuse me, Professor Bennett? ¹I've never taken a biology class before, so, uh, I'm having some trouble with your lessons. Everyone else seems to be doing fine except me. So I'm, uh, worried about my grade...

P: Hi, Lawrence. I'm sorry to hear that you're having difficulties...

S: Thank you, but the thing is... ¹I don't want to give up the class. So I was wondering if you had any advice.

P: ²/³Hmm... You could find online videos on biology or read the articles I mentioned in class.

S: I'll try searching for some videos. Are there any specific ones you'd recommend?

P: Sure. ²I can send you links to some videos. They cover the same material we discuss in class.

S: That would be great, Professor Bennett.

P: Of course. And don't worry too much about your grade. ⁴I have another student like you in my other course. She's doing fine, so I'm sure you'll also do well.

S: Thanks for the encouragement, Professor.

학생과 교수 사이의 대화를 들으시오.

S: 실례합니다, Bennett 교수님? 제가 이전에 생물학 수업을 들어 본 적이 없어서, 어, 교수님 수업에 어려움이 좀 있어요. 저를 제외하고 다른 사람들은 다 잘하고 있는 것 같아요. 그래서 저는, 어, 제 성적이 걱정돼요...

P: 안녕, Lawrence. 네가 어려움을 겪고 있다니 안타깝구나...

S: 고맙습니다만, 문제는... 저는 수업을 포기하고 싶지 않아요. 그래서 교수님께서 조언이 있으신지 궁금했어요.

P: 흠... 생물학에 관한 온라인 동영상들을 찾아보거나 내가 수업 시간에 언급했던 논문들을 읽어볼 수 있을 것 같은데.

S: 동영상들을 좀 찾아볼게요. 구체적으로 추천해 주실만한 것들이 있을까요?

P: 그럼. 동영상들 몇 개의 링크를 보내 줄 수 있어. 그것들은 우리가 수업 시간에 논의한 것과 같은 내용을 다루고 있단다.

S: 그거 정말 좋겠네요, Bennett 교수님.

P: 물론이지. 그리고 네 성적에 대해 너무 걱정하지 마라. 다른 수업에도 너와 같은 학생이 또 있어. 그녀는 잘하고 있으니, 너도 잘할 거라고 확신한다.

S: 격려 감사드립니다, 교수님.

biology 명 생물학　　except 전 ~를 제외하고, ~ 외에는
sorry 형 안타까운, 안쓰러운　　search for ~을 찾다
specific 형 특정한; 구체적인　　cover 동 다루다; 씌우다
encouragement 명 격려

1 화자들은 주로 무엇을 논의하고 있는가?
　(A) 수업 프로젝트를 위해 필요한 것
　(B) 더 쉬운 수업으로 옮기는 것
　(C) 수업을 더 잘 이해할 수 있는 방법들
　(D) 학생이 안 좋은 성적을 받은 이유

2 교수는 학생을 어떻게 도와주는가?
　(A) 정보의 출처들을 추천해줌으로써
　(B) 개인 지도 프로그램을 소개함으로써
　(C) 자세한 수업 계획서를 제공함으로써
　(D) 수업에서 논의된 개념을 복습함으로써

3 교수는 왜 논문들을 언급하는가?
　(A) 주제에 대한 그녀의 지식을 보여주기 위해
　(B) 학생에게 과제에 대해 상기시키기 위해
　(C) 읽을 자료들을 추천해 주기 위해
　(D) 학생이 한 말을 정정하기 위해

4 교수에 관해 추론할 수 있는 것은 무엇인가?
　(A) 그녀는 현재 또 다른 수업을 가르치고 있다.
　(B) 그녀는 몇몇 연구 논문들을 썼다.
　(C) 그녀는 온라인 강의 동영상들을 올렸다.
　(D) 그녀는 다음 학기에 더 많은 강의들을 개설할 것이다.

iBT Listening Test 2
본문 p. 148

1 (C)　2 (D)　3 Bolshoi dancers: (B), (C)
Mariinsky dancers: (A), (D)　4 (A)

Note-taking
Bolshoi
- Tries to make a big impression
- Powerful[Strong] movements on the stage

Mariinsky
- Elegant and artistic
- Known as classical ballets
- Performed in front of the royal family

Listen to part of a lecture in a dance class.

P: Has anyone heard of Bolshoi or Mariinksy? They are famous Russian ballet companies. Both have a long history and dancers with excellent skills. ¹In fact, they are often compared to each other because they have contrasting styles. So what are the differences between them?

Well, in Russian, Bolshoi means "big." And Bolshoi tries to make a big impression. ³ᴮThe dancers are strong and athletic, so they use powerful movements on the stage. ³ᶜThe performances are also very emotional and dramatic. So the audience can easily feel the emotions of the characters.

In contrast, Mariinsky is elegant and artistic. Its ballets are known as classical ballet. ³ᴰThe dancers wear traditional ballet costumes. ³ᴬAnd, um, their movements are graceful and beautiful. Also, Mariinsky was originally known as the Imperial Russian Ballet. ²This is because its ballets were performed in front of the royal family. So, Mariinsky is more "upper class" than Bolshoi in that way.

Now, the two companies don't just have different styles. They also perform the same ballet in different ways. Let's use *Swan Lake* as an example. As you all know, *Swan Lake* is a story about a princess and a prince. Princess Odette is turned into a swan by an evil magician. She can be saved only by the love of the prince, Siegfried. Well, in the Bolshoi version, the ending is sad. The evil magician creates a bad storm. The storm keeps Odette and Siegfried away from each other. They never marry, and Odette dies. ⁴But in the Mariinsky performance, Siegfried fights and kills the evil magician. Then, he and Odette can be together.

무용학 강의의 일부를 들으시오.

P: 볼쇼이나 마린스키에 대해 들어본 사람이 있나요? 그들은 유명한 러시아 발레단이에요. 둘 다 오랜 역사와 뛰어난 기술을 가진 무용수들이 있죠. 사실, 그들은 종종 서로 비교되는데, 그들이 상반된 스타일을 가지고 있기 때문이에요. 그렇다면 그들 사이에는 어떤 차이점이 있을까요?

음, 러시아어로, 볼쇼이는 '크다'라는 뜻입니다. 그리고 볼쇼이는 큰 인상을 주려고 하죠. 무용수들이 힘이 세고 건장해서, 무대 위에서 힘찬 동작들을 구사합니다. 공연 또한 굉장히 감성적이고 극적이죠. 그래서 관객들은 등장인물들의 감정을 쉽게 느낄 수 있습니다.

대조적으로, 마린스키는 우아하고 예술적이에요. 그곳의 발레는 고전 발레로 알려져 있습니다. 무용수들은 전통적인 발레 의상을 입어요. 그리고, 음, 그들의 동작은 기품 있고 아름답습니다. 또한, 마린스키는 원래 황실 러시아 발레단으로 알려져 있었습니다. 이것은 그곳의 발레가 왕족들 앞에서 공연되었기 때문이에요. 그래서, 마린스키는 그런 면에서 볼쇼이보다 더 '상위급'인 거죠.

자, 두 발레단은 단지 다른 스타일만을 가진 것이 아닙니다. 그들은 같은 발레를 서로 다른 방식으로 공연하기도 해요. '백조의 호수'를 예로 들어보겠습니다. 여러분 모두 알다시피, '백조의 호수'는 한 공주와 왕자에 관한 이야기입니다. 공주 오데트는 사악한 마법사에 의해 백조로 변합니다. 그녀는 왕자인 지크프리트의 사랑에 의해서만 구해질 수 있죠. 음, 볼쇼이 버전에서는, 결말이 슬픕니다. 사악한 마법사는 심한 폭풍을 일으키는데요. 폭풍은 오데트와 지크프리트를 서로 떨어뜨려 놓죠. 그들은 결코 결혼을 하지 못하고, 오데트는 죽습니다. 하지만 마린스키 공연에서는, 지크프

리트가 사악한 마법사와 싸워서 죽입니다. 그 후, 그와 오데트는 함께 할 수 있게 되죠.

ballet company 발레단　**excellent** 형 뛰어난, 훌륭한
skill 명 기술　**compare** 동 비교하다
contrasting 형 상반된, 대조적인　**impression** 명 인상
athletic 형 건장한, 운동선수 같은　**movement** 명 동작
performance 명 공연　**emotional** 형 감성적인, 정서의
elegant 형 우아한, 고상한　**artistic** 형 예술적인
costume 명 의상　**graceful** 형 기품 있는, 우아한
royal family 왕실, 황족　**evil** 형 사악한, 악랄한
magician 명 마법사, 마술사

1 강의의 주된 주제는 무엇인가?

(A) 러시아 발레의 초기 역사
(B) 러시아 무용 스타일의 발전
(C) 두 발레단의 차이점들
(D) 러시아에서 발레 '백조의 호수'의 중요성

2 교수에 따르면, 마린스키를 볼쇼이보다 더 상위급으로 만든 것은 무엇인가?

(A) 그곳은 부호에 의해 창단되었다.
(B) 그곳은 볼쇼이보다 훨씬 더 오래되었다.
(C) 그곳은 발레를 제작하는데 많은 돈을 썼다.
(D) 그곳은 원래 왕족들을 위해 공연을 했다.

3 다음의 항목이 볼쇼이 무용수들 혹은 마린스키 무용수들 중 어떤 것과 관련 있는 지를 표시하시오.
각각의 설명에 맞는 칸을 클릭하시오.

	볼쇼이 무용수들	마린스키 무용수들
(A) 그들은 우아하고 기품 있는 동작을 가지고 있다.		V
(B) 그들은 힘 있고 대담한 동작을 구사한다.	V	
(C) 그들은 많은 감정을 보여준다.	V	
(D) 그들은 보통 전통 발레 의상을 입는다.		V

4 마린스키 버전의 '백조의 호수'에 관해 추론할 수 있는 것은 무엇인가?

(A) 그것은 행복한 결말을 갖고 있다.
(B) 그것에는 착한 마술사가 있다.
(C) 그것은 러시아 역사에 바탕을 두고 있었다.
(D) 그것은 시간이 지나면서 바뀌었다.

Vocabulary Review　본문 p. 152

1	approach	2	entrance	3	temporary
4	compare	5	refers to	6	requests
7	surroundings	8	extends		
9	Encouragement	10	(B)	11	(D)
12	(D)	13	(B)	14	(A)

Actual Test 1

PART 1. Passage 1　본문 p. 154

1 (B)　**2** (C)　**3** (A)　**4** (D)　**5** (A)

Note-taking

Student's Request
Not sure I can interview all <u>three</u> people
→ Can I interview <u>two</u> people instead?

Professor's Answer
Will change the <u>requirement</u> to interviewing only two people
→ Will <u>announce</u> the change to the class

Listen to a conversation between a student and a professor.

S: Professor Kane? Could I, uh, ask you about the assignment you gave us in class?

P: Of course. ¹You were supposed to interview three people about their jobs.

S: Yes, um, about that… ¹/²Well, the thing is I'm not sure I can interview all three people. One of them is out of the country and can't come. Is it OK if I interview two people instead?

P: I completely understand. Actually, other students have come to me with the same problem. Um, I think I will change the requirement to, uh, interviewing only two people.

S: Oh, wow! That's great, Professor Kane. ³It was really hard to find a third person to interview. Many people are busy with their jobs.

P: Yes, I see that now. ⁴I'll, uh, announce the change to the class later today.

S: Is it OK if I tell some of the students about this right away?

P: Yes… ⁴But they will still have to check the e-mail I send for details.

S: I'll make sure they know that. Um, can I ask you one more question?

P: Sure, but please make it quick. I have to finish grading some test papers.

S: ⁵Sorry. There's one more thing I have to ask you. I have a question about how long the report should be. Does it need to be at least 2,000 words?

P: It does, and that is not going to change… Anyway, I think you won't have trouble reaching that number.

S: All right, Professor. Thank you. I'll try to do my best.

Actual Test 1　**49**

학생과 교수 사이의 대화를 들으시오.

S: Kane 교수님? 제가, 어, 수업 시간에 내주셨던 과제에 대해 여쭤봐도 될까요?
P: 물론이야. 세 사람을 그들의 직업에 대해 인터뷰하기로 되어 있었지.
S: 네, 음, 그것에 대해서요... 음, 문제는 제가 세 사람 모두를 인터뷰할 수 있을지 잘 모르겠어요. 그들 중 한 명이 외국에 나가 있어서 올 수가 없거든요. 혹시 제가 대신 두 사람을 인터뷰해도 될까요?
P: 완전히 이해한다. 사실, 다른 학생들도 같은 문제로 나를 찾아왔었어. 음, 필요조건을, 어, 두 사람만 인터뷰하는 걸로 바꾸게 될 것 같구나.
S: 오, 와! 그러면 정말 좋겠어요, Kane 교수님. 인터뷰를 진행할 세 번째 사람을 찾는 것이 정말 어려웠어요. 많은 사람들이 일로 바빠서요.
P: 그래, 나도 그걸 이제 알았다. 어, 오늘 이따가 학생들에게 변경 사항을 알려야겠구나.
S: 혹시 제가 이걸 지금 바로 몇몇 학생들한테는 말해도 괜찮을까요?
P: 그래... 하지만 그래도 내가 세부 사항에 관해 보낸 이메일을 확인해야 할 거야.
S: 그들이 그걸 확실히 알도록 할게요. 음, 제가 질문 하나 더 해도 될까요?
P: 물론이야, 하지만 빨리해줬으면 좋겠구나. 몇몇 시험지를 채점하는 걸 마쳐야 하거든.
S: 죄송해요. 여쭤볼 것이 한 가지 더 있어요. 보고서가 얼마나 길어야 하는지에 대해 질문이 있어요. 최소한 2,000단어가 되어야 하나요?
P: 그래, 그리고 그건 바뀌지 않을 거야... 어차피, 그 분량에 이르는 데에는 어려움이 없을 것 같구나.
S: 알겠습니다, 교수님. 감사합니다. 최선을 다 해볼게요.

be supposed to ~하기로 되어 있다　interview 동 인터뷰하다
completely 부 완전히　requirement 명 필요조건
announce 동 알리다　details 명 세부 사항
make sure 확실히 ~하도록 하다　grade 동 채점하다, 점수를 매기다
at least 최소한　reach 동 ~에 도달하다

1 학생의 문제는 무엇인가?
   (A) 그는 과제를 끝낼 시간이 없다.
   (B) 그는 과제의 필요조건에 어려움을 겪고 있다.
   (C) 그는 어떤 수업 자료를 이해하지 못한다.
   (D) 그는 자신이 선택한 보고서 주제가 마음에 들지 않는다.

2 학생은 왜 인터뷰를 할 수 없는가?
   (A) 회사에서 그것을 진행하지 못하게 했다.
   (B) 그는 다른 과제들로 너무 바쁘다.
   (C) 그는 해외에 있는 사람을 만날 수 없다.
   (D) 인터뷰 날짜가 옮겨져야 한다.

3 학생은 왜 사람들의 일을 언급하는가?
   (A) 그가 인터뷰를 할 사람들을 찾을 수 없는 이유를 설명하기 위해
   (B) 특정 직업에 대한 그의 관심을 보여주기 위해
   (C) 다른 사람을 인터뷰하는 것에 허가를 요청하기 위해
   (D) 그가 조사를 했음을 나타내기 위해

4 교수에 관해 추론할 수 있는 것은 무엇인가?
   (A) 그녀는 학생에게 시간을 더 줄 것이다.
   (B) 그녀는 학생이 이메일을 보내기를 원한다.
   (C) 그녀는 경영학과에서 가르친다.
   (D) 그녀는 이메일을 통해 변경 사항을 알릴 것이다.

대화의 일부를 다시 듣고 질문에 답하시오.
S: Sorry. There's one more thing I have to ask you. I have a question about how long the report should be. Does it need to be at least 2,000 words?
P: It does, and that is not going to change... Anyway, I think you won't have trouble reaching that number.

5 교수는 왜 이렇게 말하는가:
   P: Anyway, I think you won't have trouble reaching that number.
   (A) 필요조건이 동일하게 유지될 것임을 강조하기 위해
   (B) 학생이 더 열심히 공부하도록 격려하기 위해
   (C) 보고서의 길이에 대한 이유를 설명하기 위해
   (D) 학생의 변경에 대한 요청에 동의하기 위해

PART 1.　Passage 2　　　본문 p. 156

6 (D)　7 (B)　8 (A)　9 (A)　10 (D)　11 (B)

Note-taking

Emily Brontë
- Poet and novelist in England in the 19th century
- Wrote with the name Ellis Bell
- Wrote *Wuthering Heights*, which expressed beliefs that were not popular at the time

J. K. Rowling
- Her real name is Joanne Rowling.
- Became incredibly successful

Listen to part of a lecture in a literature class.

P: Let's continue talking about women writers. ⁶Female authors used fake names for a long time... This is because many people in society believed that people would not purchase novels written by women... So many female authors used a fake name. We'll take a look at a couple of examples: Emily Brontë and J. K. Rowling.

First, let's start with Emily Brontë. She was a poet and novelist who lived in England in the 19th century. ⁷During that time, England was much more traditional and old-fashioned than it is today. Men were supposed to have jobs while women were supposed to stay home and take care of the family. So writing books was not considered suitable for women. But if a woman wanted to write a novel, what do you think she had to do?

S: Um, she had to hide her name?

P: Yes. So that's exactly what Emily Brontë did. ⁸She, uh, wrote with the name Ellis Bell so that no one would know she was a woman. ⁹Brontë wrote only one novel called *Wuthering Heights*, but it is a very good novel. I mean, critics did not like it at first, but I think that's mainly because they were shocked by its content. The novel expressed beliefs that were not popular at the time. And traditional England was not ready for its modern themes. However, later, the book became known as one of the greatest novels in the English language. And nowadays it is commonly taught in schools.

¹⁰Anyway, um, this trend of using fake names continued into the late twentieth century. By this time, more women were writing all kinds of books. Still, there were people who didn't think that women were good writers. I'm sure you all know J. K. Rowling. Her real name is Joanne Rowling. Her publishers believed that a story written by a woman would not interest readers. That's why she chose to use the name J. K. Rowling. ¹¹Well, um, as we now know, J. K. Rowling became incredibly successful... I mean, she wrote the Harry Potter series! So, uh, I think publishers will welcome more women writers in the future.

문학 강의의 일부를 들으시오.

P: 계속해서 여성 작가들에 대해 이야기해 봅시다. 여성 작가들은 오랫동안 가명을 사용했습니다... 이것은 사회의 대다수가 사람들이 여성들에 의해 쓰인 소설을 사지 않을 것이라고 믿었기 때문이에요... 그래서 많은 여성 작가들이 가명을 사용했어요. 에밀리 브론테와 J. K. 롤링, 이 두어 가지 예시들을 살펴보죠.

먼저, 에밀리 브론테부터 시작해 봅시다. 그녀는 19세기에 영국에 살았던 시인이자 소설가였습니다. 그 당시, 영국은 오늘날보다 훨씬 더 전통적이고 구식이었습니다. 남자들은 직업을 가져야 했던 반면, 여자들은 집에 머물면서 가족을 돌봐야 했어요. 그래서 책을 쓰는 것은 여성에게 적합하지 않다고 여겨졌죠. 하지만 만약 여성이 소설을 쓰고 싶어 했다면, 여러분은 그녀가 무엇을 해야 했다고 생각하시나요?

S: 음, 자신의 이름을 숨겨야 했을까요?

P: 그래요. 그래서 그게 바로 에밀리 브론테가 한 일이었어요. 그녀는, 어, 아무도 그녀가 여자라는 것을 알지 못하도록 엘리스 벨이라는 이름으로 글을 썼어요. 브론테는 '폭풍의 언덕'이라는 단 하나의 소설만을 썼지만, 그것은 매우 훌륭한 소설이에요. 제 말은, 비평가들이 처음에는 그것을 좋아하지 않았는데, 저는 주된 이유가 그들이 그것의 내용에 충격을 받았기 때문이라고 생각해요. 그 소설은 당시에는 유명하지 않았던 신념을 표현했습니다. 그리고 전통적인 영국은 그것의 현대적인 주제를 받아들일 준비가 되어 있지 않았죠. 하지만, 이후에, 그 책은 가장 위대한 영문 소설들 중 하나로 알려지게 되었답니다. 그리고 오늘날 그것은 학교에서 흔히 가르쳐지죠.

어쨌든, 음, 가명을 사용하는 이런 추세는 20세기 후반까지 계속되었어요. 이 무렵에는 더 많은 여성들이 온갖 종류의 책을 쓰고 있었죠. 그런데도, 여성들이 좋은 작가라고 생각하지 않는 사람들이 있었습니다. 저는 여러분 모두가 J. K. 롤링에 대해 알고 있을 거라고 확신해요. 그녀의 진짜 이름은 조앤 롤링이에요. 그녀의 출판사들은 한 여성이 쓴 이야기가 독자들의 관심을 끌지 못할 것이라고 생각했습니다. 그것이 그녀가 J. K. 롤링이라는 이름을 사용하기로 선택한 이유였죠. 자, 음, 우리가 지금 아는 것처럼, J. K. 롤링은 엄청나게 성공을 했습니다... 제 말은, 그녀는 해리포터 시리즈를 썼잖아요! 그래서, 어, 저는 출판사들이 미래에는 더 많은 여성 작가들을 환영할 것 같아요.

---

author 명 작가, 저자　fake 형 가짜의　society 명 사회
a couple of 두어 가지의, 둘의　poet 명 시인　novelist 명 소설가
traditional 형 전통적인　old-fashioned 형 구식의
consider 동 ~이라고 여기다　suitable 형 적합한, 적절한
novel 명 소설　critic 명 비평가　shock 동 충격을 주다
content 명 내용　belief 명 신념, 믿음　theme 명 주제
publisher 명 출판사, 출판인

6 강의는 주로 무엇에 관한 것인가?

　(A) 역사상 여성의 전통적인 역할들
　(B) 소설에서 여성 등장인물들이 어떻게 나오는지
　(C) 여성들에 의해 쓰인 현대 서적들
　(D) 여성 작가들이 가명을 쓴 이유

7 교수에 따르면, 19세기 영국에서 여성은 무엇을 할 것으로 기대되었는가?

　(A) 시 쓰기
　(B) 집에 있기
　(C) 학교에서 가르치기
　(D) 많은 자식들을 갖기

8 교수에 따르면, 브론테는 왜 엘리스 벨이라는 이름을 썼는가?

　(A) 그녀의 성별을 숨기기 위해
　(B) 다른 작가를 따라 하기 위해
　(C) 더 많은 관심을 받기 위해
　(D) 남성 작가들을 비판하기 위해

9 '폭풍의 언덕'에 대한 교수의 의견은 무엇인가?

　(A) 그것은 그 시대에 비해 매우 현대적이었다.
　(B) 그것에는 매우 현실적인 등장인물들이 있다.
　(C) 그것은 오늘날에도 여전히 충격적인 주제를 가지고 있다.
　(D) 그것은 여성에 의해 쓰인 최고의 소설이다.

10 교수는 왜 J. K. 롤링을 예시로 들었는가?

　(A) 현대적인 글쓰기와 전통적인 글쓰기를 비교하기 위해
　(B) 여성 작가들이 어떻게 발전해왔는지 설명하기 위해
　(C) 그녀가 가장 좋아하는 작가들 중 한 명을 학생들에게 이야기하기 위해
　(D) 작가들에 있어 성별이 얼마나 오랫동안 문제가 되어왔는지 보여주기 위해

강의의 일부를 다시 듣고 질문에 답하시오.

P: Well, um, as we now know, J. K. Rowling became incredibly successful... I mean, she wrote the Harry Potter series!

11 교수는 왜 이렇게 말하는가:

　P: I mean, she wrote the Harry Potter series!

(A) 학생들이 J. K. 롤링에 대해 조사하는 것을 권하기 위해
(B) J. K. 롤링의 성과를 강조하기 위해
(C) J. K. 롤링이 쓴 책을 추천하기 위해
(D) 그녀가 J. K. 롤링에 대해 잘 알고 있다는 것을 나타내기 위해

PART 2. Passage 1
본문 p. 158

1 (B)   2 (C)   3 (C)   4 (C)   5 (D)

Note-taking
Student's Question
What are the results of last week's interview for the student reporter position?

Editor's Answer
- Decided to hire you as a reporter
- Details about the position:
  - Starts on Monday with an orientation at 4 p.m.
  - Will meet the team and Allison, the leader of the team

Listen to a conversation between a student and a newspaper editor.

M: Hi, Ms. Lawson. I was on my way to class and, um, I decided to stop by your office. ¹I would like to ask about the results of last week's interview for the student reporter position.

W: Oh, hi, Robert! We planned to give applicants the results of their interviews this afternoon. I was going to send them by e-mail. But since you're here...

M: Is it good news?

W: Yes, actually. We've decided to hire you as a school newspaper reporter. ²We were really impressed with the sample articles you wrote.

M: Really? That's great. I wasn't sure you'd like them.

W: We did, and we'd like you to write more articles like those... Also, one of your samples will be in our next school newspaper.

M: ⁵I'm very pleased. I've wanted to become a reporter since I was 15.

W: You see, that's what I mean. We also chose you because you clearly enjoy the work.

M: Thank you... ³Um, is it OK if I ask for more details about the position?

W: Sure. You will start on Monday, and, um, you will need to be here at 4 p.m. There'll be an orientation.

M: All right. I can do that.

W: ³Afterward, I'll introduce you to the team. You'll meet Allison, the leader of your team. She will be giving you your first assignment.

M: I look forward to meeting her.

W: ⁴And one last thing... We need a photo of you for the website.

M: OK! I can take one on my phone right now and send it to you.

학생과 신문 편집자 사이의 대화를 들으시오.

M: 안녕하세요, Lawson씨. 제가 수업을 들으러 가는 길이었는데, 음, 당신의 사무실에 들르기로 했어요. 저는 학생 기자직에 대한 지난주 면접 결과에 대해 여쭤보고 싶어요.

W: 오, 안녕하세요, Robert! 저희가 오늘 오후에 지원자들에게 면접 결과를 전달할 계획이었어요. 그들에게 이메일로 전달하려고 했어요. 그런데 여기 계시니까...

M: 좋은 소식인가요?

W: 사실은, 맞아요. 저희는 학생을 학내 신문 기자로 채용하기로 결정했어요. 학생이 작성한 샘플 기사들에 정말 깊은 인상을 받았답니다.

M: 정말요? 잘 됐군요. 그것들이 마음에 드실지 확실하지 않았어요.

W: 마음에 들었어요, 그리고 저희는 학생이 그것들과 같은 기사들을 더 많이 작성해줬으면 좋겠어요... 또, 학생의 샘플 중 하나가 저희의 다음 학내 신문에 실릴 거예요.

M: 너무 기쁘네요. 저는 15살 때부터 기자가 되고 싶었거든요.

W: 그러니까, 제 말이 바로 그거예요. 저희가 학생을 선택한 이유는 학생이 분명히 일을 즐기기 때문이기도 해요.

M: 감사해요... 음, 제가 혹시 직책에 대해 좀 더 자세히 여쭤봐도 될까요?

W: 물론이에요. 월요일부터 시작될 거고, 음, 여기에 오후 4시에는 와야 할 거예요. 오리엔테이션이 있을 거거든요.

M: 좋아요. 할 수 있어요.

W: 그 후에, 제가 학생을 팀에 소개시킬 거예요. 학생은 팀의 리더인 Allison을 만날 거예요. 그녀가 당신에게 첫 번째 과제를 줄 겁니다.

M: 그녀를 만날 것이 기대돼요.

W: 그리고 마지막 한 가지 더요... 저희가 웹사이트에 올릴 당신의 사진이 필요해요.

M: 네! 지금 바로 핸드폰으로 한 장 찍어서 보내드릴 수 있어요.

on one's way ~하러 가는 길에   stop by ~에 들르다
interview ⑲ 면접, 인터뷰   reporter ⑲ 기자   position ⑲ 직책
applicant ⑲ 지원자   impress ⑧ 깊은 인상을 주다, 감명을 주다
clearly ⑨ 분명히   orientation ⑲ 오리엔테이션, 예비 교육
introduce ⑧ 소개하다   leader ⑲ 리더, 지도자
look forward to ~이 기대되다; ~을 기대하다

1 남자는 왜 여자를 찾아가는가?
(A) 기사의 오류에 대해 논의하기 위해
(B) 직책에 대해 알아보기 위해
(C) 모임에 관해 물어보기 위해
(D) 직원을 인터뷰하기 위해

2 남자에 대해 여자가 깊은 인상을 받은 것은 무엇인가?
(A) 그의 친절한 태도
(B) 그의 이전 경험

(C) 그의 예시 작업물들
(D) 그의 학교에 대한 지식

3 여자는 직책 정보를 어떻게 설명하는가?
(A) 서류를 제공함으로써
(B) 과제 목록을 준비함으로써
(C) 업무 첫날을 묘사함으로써
(D) 기사를 쓰는 방법을 설명함으로써

4 남자는 다음에 무엇을 할 것인가?
(A) 카메라 사기
(B) 기사를 하나 더 쓰기
(C) 사진 찍기
(D) 웹사이트 살펴보기

대화의 일부를 다시 듣고 질문에 답하시오.
M: I'm very pleased. I've wanted to become a reporter since I was 15.
W: You see, that's what I mean. We also chose you because you clearly enjoy the work.

5 여자는 왜 이렇게 말하는가:
W: You see, that's what I mean.
(A) 남자에게 제안에 대해 고마워하기 위해
(B) 기사가 재미있었다고 말하기 위해
(C) 남자의 생각에 동의하기 위해
(D) 남자가 왜 선택되었는지 설명하기 위해

PART 2. Passage 2 본문 p. 160

6 (B)　7 (C)　8 (C)　9 (C)　10 (B)
11 Mesopotamia: (A), (D)　Egypt: (C)　Indus: (B)

Note-taking
Mesopotamia
- Civilization that first began
- Developed the first <u>written</u> <u>language</u> called pictographs

Egypt
Used copper for making <u>tools</u> and <u>weapons</u>
→ Big <u>improvement</u> compared to the stone tools

Indus
- <u>Larger[Bigger]</u> than the two other civilizations
- First civilization to make an accurate <u>measuring</u> <u>system</u>

Listen to part of a lecture in an anthropology class.

P: Human societies were not always civilized. Originally, people, uh, moved around and hunted or gathered food. ⁶But around six thousand years ago, people began to create long-term settlements that we know as civilizations. We'll learn about the four earliest civilizations: Mesopotamia, Egypt, Indus Valley, and China.

One of their common features was agriculture. Uh, agriculture was important for civilization. ⁷Growing crops made the amount of food stable, so people could live in one place. And you need water to grow crops, right? Well, this is why all of these societies began near rivers. Rivers provided water for crops.

Civilization first began in Mesopotamia around the Tigris and Euphrates rivers. ¹¹ᴬSmall cities formed in the area, and they were controlled by a religious king. ¹¹ᴰAround 3,300 BC, the first written language appeared in Mesopotamia. Mesopotamian people wrote with signs and symbols, uh, which are called pictographs. The pictographs were carved into wet clay and then dried. ⁸They were used until around 100 BC. At this time, an alphabet was adopted, so the original writing system was abandoned.

Not far away, in Egypt, civilization was established around the Nile River, which is the longest in the world. ¹¹ᶜThe Egyptians used copper for making tools and weapons. Uh, this was a big improvement compared to the old method, uh, which was using stone tools. And they carved stones for the amazing pyramids with these advanced tools. ¹⁰But building the pyramids still required much work because of the size and the amount of the stones. The stones used in the Great Pyramid, for example, weigh 2.5 tons each. And there are more than two million of them! Just thinking about it makes me tired...

Then, there is the Indus culture, which is named after the Indus River. In the Indus civilization, people built large walls around the cities. These protected them from enemies and floods. ⁹Uh, one unique feature of the Indus civilization was its size. Although it started later, the Indus civilization was larger than the previous two. ⁹/¹¹ᴮAnother important feature is that, um, it was the first civilization to make an accurate measuring system for distances and weights.

Well, that's all the time we have today, class. Next time, we'll discuss the fourth ancient civilization... China.

인류학 강의의 일부를 들으시오.

P: 인간 사회가 항상 문명화된 것은 아니었죠. 원래, 사람들은, 어, 돌아다니면서 사냥을 하거나 음식을 모았습니다. 하지만 약 6천 년 전에, 사람들은 우리가 문명사회라고 알고 있는 장기적인 정착지를 만들기 시작했어요. 우리는 메소포타미아, 이집트, 인더스 계곡, 그리고 중국, 이 네 개의 초기 문명사회들에 대해 배워볼 거예요.

그것들의 공통점 중 하나는 농업이었어요. 어, 농업은 문명사회에 중요했는데요. 농작물을 재배하는 것은 식량의 양이 안정적이도록 해서, 사람들이 한곳에서 살 수 있었어요. 그리고 농작물을 재배하기 위해서는 물이 필요해요, 그렇죠? 음, 이것이 이 모든 사회들이 강 근처에서 시작했던 이유랍니다. 강은 농작물에 필요한 물을 공급했거든요.

문명사회는 티그리스강과 유프라테스강 주변에 있는 메소포타미아에서 처음 시작되었어요. 작은 도시들이 그 지역에 형성되었고, 종교적인 왕의 지배를 받았어요. 기원전 3,300년경, 메소포타미아에서 최초의 문자가 등장하였는데요. 메소포타미아 사람들은, 어, 상형문자라고 불리는 기호와 상징을 가지고 문자를 썼습니다. 상형문자들은 젖은 점토에 새겨진 다음 건조되었어요. 그것들은 기원전 100년경까지 사용되었습니다. 이때, 알파벳이 채택되어서, 원래의 문자 체계가 버려지게 됐습니다.

멀지 않은 곳인, 이집트에서는, 문명사회가 세계에서 가장 긴 강인 나일강을 중심으로 세워졌어요. 이집트인들은 도구와 무기를 만드는 데 구리를 사용했는데요. 어, 이것은 석기를 사용하던, 어, 예전 방식에 비하면 큰 발전이었어요. 그리고 그들은 이 발전된 도구들로 엄청난 피라미드를 위한 돌을 조각했죠. 그러나 피라미드를 짓는 것은 돌의 크기와 양 때문에 여전히 많은 작업을 필요로 했어요. 예를 들어, 대 피라미드에 사용된 돌들의 무게는 각각 2.5톤이에요. 그리고 그것들은 2백만 개가 넘게 있죠! 그것에 대해 생각하는 것만으로도 피곤해지는군요...

그리고, 인더스강에서 이름을 따온 인더스 문명이 있어요. 인더스 문명사회에서, 사람들은 도시 주위에 큰 벽들을 쌓았어요. 이것들은 그들을 적과 홍수로부터 보호해 주었답니다. 어, 인더스 문명사회의 한 가지 독특한 특징은 그것의 규모였어요. 비록 인더스 문명사회가 나중에 시작되었지만, 그것은 앞선 두 문명보다 더 컸어요. 또 다른 중요한 특징은, 음, 그것이 거리와 무게를 정확하게 측정하는 시스템을 만든 최초의 문명사회였다는 것입니다.

자, 오늘은 이 정도로 하겠습니다, 여러분. 다음 시간에는, 네 번째 고대 문명사회인 중국에 관해 얘기할 거예요.

civilize 동 문명화하다   settlement 명 정착지
civilization 명 문명(사회)   agriculture 명 농업   crop 명 농작물
stable 형 안정적인   religious 형 종교적인
pictograph 명 상형문자, 그림문자   carve 동 ~에 새기다, 조각하다
adopt 동 채택하다   abandon 동 버리다   establish 동 세우다
copper 명 구리   improvement 명 발전
compared to ~과 비교하여   advanced 형 발전된
accurate 형 정확한   distance 명 거리

6 강의는 주로 무엇에 관한 것인가?
   (A) 고대 교통수단의 발명
   (B) 초기 문명사회의 발전
   (C) 고대 문명사회의 농업
   (D) 문자의 기원

7 교수에 따르면, 초기 문명사회들의 공통점은 무엇인가?
   (A) 그것들은 인구가 적었다.
   (B) 그것들은 같은 농작물을 재배했다.
   (C) 그것들은 강 근처에서 시작됐다.
   (D) 그것들은 오래가지 못했다.

8 교수는 메소포타미아의 상형문자에 관해 무엇을 암시하는가?
   (A) 그것들은 왕족에게만 가르쳐졌다.
   (B) 그것들은 간단한 문장에만 유용했다.
   (C) 그것들은 기원전 100년 이후에는 사용되지 않았다.
   (D) 그것들은 다른 문명들에서 채택되었다.

9 교수는 인더스 문명사회를 어떻게 설명하는가?
   (A) 그것을 후기 문명사회와 비교함으로써
   (B) 그것이 어떻게 기원했는지 설명함으로써
   (C) 그것의 두 가지 주요 특징을 소개함으로써
   (D) 그것과 다른 사회들과의 관계에 대해 이야기함으로써

강의의 일부를 다시 듣고 질문에 답하시오.
P: But building the pyramids still required much work because of the size and the amount of the stones. The stones used in the Great Pyramid, for example, weigh 2.5 tons each. And there are more than two million of them! Just thinking about it makes me tired...

10 교수는 왜 이렇게 말하는가:
   P: Just thinking about it makes me tired...
   (A) 대 피라미드가 완성된 적이 없었다는 것을 지적하기 위해
   (B) 피라미드를 짓는 것이 힘든 일이었다는 것을 강조하기 위해
   (C) 그가 강의를 빨리 끝내고 싶다는 것을 암시하기 위해
   (D) 고대 석공들이 굉장히 숙련되었다는 것을 보여주기 위해

11 강의에서, 교수는 세 가지 고대 문명사회들의 특징을 언급한다. 다음의 항목이 메소포타미아, 이집트, 인더스 중 어떤 것의 특징인지를 표시하시오.
각 항목에 적절한 칸을 클릭하시오.

	메소포타미아	이집트	인더스
(A) 종교적인 왕에 의해 통치되었다.	V		
(B) 정확한 측정 시스템을 개발했다.			V
(C) 발전된 도구와 무기를 사용했다.		V	
(D) 최초의 문자를 발명했다.	V		

PART 2. Passage 3   본문 p. 162

12 (C)   13 (B)   14 (C)   15 (B)   16 (A)   17 (B)

Note-taking
Types and Causes of Colorblindness
- Types
  - Complete colorblindness: Blind to all colors
  - Red-and-green colorblindness: Cannot easily see the colors red and green
- Causes
  - Genetic
  - Diseases or injuries that affect eyes or brain
    e.g. Diabetes

Listen to part of a lecture in a physiology class.

P: Most of us see colors in a similar way. But, uh, some people have difficulty seeing colors. This condition is known as colorblindness. ¹²There are various types of colorblindness, and its causes can be different, too.

Uh, colorblindness occurs when there is a problem with cone cells in the eye. Cone cells allow us to see color. Normally, we have three kinds of cone cells: red, green, and blue. If all three cone cells are missing, then complete colorblindness occurs. This is when you are blind to all colors, so you see the world only in gray. [13]However, complete colorblindness is extremely rare. More commonly, people cannot distinguish certain colors as they have a problem with only one or two of the cone cells. For example, if red and green cells are missing or not working properly, then you can have red-and-green colorblindness. People with this type cannot easily see the colors red and green. [14]So let's say there is a Christmas tree with red decorations... These people will be able to see the shape of the decorations, but, uh, the decorations and the tree will appear the same color to them...

[15]Now, one of the causes of colorblindness is genetic. So, uh, if your family has colorblind people, your children might also be born with it. But, uh, you can also get it even if you are not born with it. People can become colorblind from diseases or injuries that affect their eyes or brain. [16]For example, diabetes can cause colorblindness. Recent studies indicate that 22 percent of people with certain kinds of diabetes have colorblindness. And, uh, there are at least 10 other well-known illnesses which can lead to colorblindness...

[17]Then, how common is colorblindness? It's more common than you might think. Believe it or not, we all know colorblind people. We just don't realize it. So, uh, I always assume there are colorblind people in every class here on campus. This is why I always use black and white in my visual presentations. This lets everyone in the class read the screen.

생리학 강의의 일부를 들으시오.

P: 우리 대부분은 비슷한 방식으로 색을 봅니다. 하지만, 어, 어떤 사람들은 색을 보는 데 어려움을 겪는데요. 이러한 상태는 색맹이라고 알려져 있죠. 색맹에는 다양한 종류가 있으며, 그것의 원인 또한 다를 수 있습니다.

어, 색맹은 눈에 있는 원뿔세포에 문제가 있을 때 발생해요. 원뿔세포는 우리가 색을 볼 수 있게 해주죠. 보통, 우리는 빨강, 초록, 그리고 파랑, 이 세 종류의 원뿔세포를 가지고 있어요. 세 개의 원뿔세포가 전부 없으면, 완전한 색맹이 발생해요. 이는 모든 색을 보지 못하게 되는 것이며, 따라서 여러분은 세상을 회색으로만 볼 것입니다. 하지만, 완전한 색맹은 극히 드물어요. 더 일반적으로, 사람들은 원뿔세포 중 하나 또는 두 개에만 문제를 가지고 있어서 특정 색을 구별할 수가 없죠. 예를 들어, 만약 빨간색과 초록색 세포가 없거나 제대로 기능을 하지 않는다면, 그럼 여러분은 적록색맹을 가질 수 있어요. 이런 유형의 사람들은 빨간색과 초록색을 쉽게 볼 수 없어요. 그러면 빨간 장식들이 있는 크리스마스트리가 있다고 해봅시다... 이 사람들은 장식들의 모양은 볼 수 있지만, 어, 장식과 트리가 그들한테는 같은 색으로 보일 거예요...

자, 색맹의 원인 중 하나는 유전적인 것입니다. 그래서, 어, 만약 여러분의 가족 중에 색맹인 사람들이 있다면, 여러분의 아이들도 그것을 가지고 태어날 수도 있습니다. 하지만, 어, 그것을 가지고 태어나지 않았을지라도 가지게 될 수도 있죠. 사람들은 눈이나 뇌에 영향을 주는 질병이나 부상으로 색맹이 될 수도 있습니다. 예를 들어, 당뇨병은 색맹을 일으킬 수 있어요. 최근의 연구는 특정 종류의 당뇨병을 가진 사람들의 22%가 색맹을 가지고 있다는 것을 보여줍니다. 그리고, 어, 색맹으로 이어질 수 있는 것으로 잘 알려진 질병이 적어도 10개는 더 있죠...

그렇다면, 색맹은 얼마나 흔할까요? 여러분이 생각하는 것보다 더 흔합니다. 믿거나 말거나, 우리 모두는 색맹인 사람들을 알고 있어요. 우리가 단지 그것을 깨닫지 못했을 뿐이죠. 그래서, 어, 저는 항상 여기 캠퍼스의 모든 수업에 색맹인 사람들이 있다고 가정해요. 이것이 제가 항상 시각적인 발표자료에 흑백을 사용하는 이유입니다. 이것은 수업의 모든 사람이 화면을 읽을 수 있게 하거든요.

---

difficulty 몡 어려움　colorblindness 몡 색맹
cone cell 원뿔세포, 원추세포　extremely 뷔 극히　rare 휑 드문
distinguish 동 구별하다　properly 뷔 제대로　genetic 휑 유전적인
diabetes 몡 당뇨병　illness 몡 병　assume 동 가정하다
visual 휑 시각의

12 강의의 주된 주제는 무엇인가?

　(A) 색맹을 갖고 사는 것의 어려움
　(B) 색맹의 원인이 되는 질병들
　(C) 색맹의 종류와 원인
　(D) 색맹을 극복하는 방법들

13 교수는 완전한 색맹에 관해 무엇이라고 말하는가?

　(A) 그것은 질병에 의해 발생한다.
　(B) 그것은 극히 드물다.
　(C) 그것은 하나의 사라진 원뿔세포에 의해 발생한다.
　(D) 그것은 노인에게 발생한다.

14 교수는 적록색맹을 어떻게 설명하는가?

　(A) 그것이 얼마나 독특한지 강조함으로써
　(B) 그것을 다른 증상과 비교함으로써
　(C) 친숙한 예시를 제공함으로써
　(D) 다양한 색이 있는 사진을 보여줌으로써

15 색맹에 관해 추론할 수 있는 것은 무엇인가?

　(A) 그것은 여성보다 남성에게 더 영향을 미친다.
　(B) 그것은 선천적으로 또는 후천적으로 일어날 수 있다.
　(C) 그것은 시간이 지날수록 더 나빠질 수 있다.
　(D) 그것은 완전한 실명으로 이어질 수 있다.

16 교수는 왜 당뇨병을 언급하는가?

　(A) 색맹의 가능성 있는 원인을 제공하기 위해
　(B) 유전적인 질병의 예시를 제시하기 위해
　(C) 얼마나 많은 사람들이 색맹을 가지고 있는지 설명하기 위해
　(D) 질병이 얼마나 심각할 수 있는지 나타내기 위해

강의의 일부를 다시 듣고 질문에 답하시오.

P: Then, how common is colorblindness? It's more common than you might think. Believe it or not, we all know colorblind people. We just don't realize it.

17 교수는 이렇게 말함으로써 무엇을 의미하는가:

　P: Believe it or not, we all know colorblind people.

　(A) 수업에 있는 학생들 중 누구도 색맹이 아니다.
　(B) 대부분의 사람들은 자신이 색맹인 사람들을 알고 있다는 것을

알지 못한다.
(C) 색맹은 대부분의 사람들이 생각하는 것보다 더 드물다.
(D) 보통의 시력을 가진 사람들조차도 색을 같은 방식으로 보지 않는다.

Actual Test 2

PART 1. Passage 1
본문 p. 164

1 (B) 2 (C) 3 (C)
4 Yes: (A), (D) No: (B), (C) 5 (C)

Note-taking

Student's Question
Is the student lounge going to be open during the winter break?
→ Could we ask for it to stay open?

Employee's Suggestion
- Use the library
  → Too expensive to keep the lounge open
- Study in the dormitory common areas

Listen to a conversation between a student and a university employee.

M: Excuse me. I have a question about the student lounge.

W: Did you want to know the hours? It's open from 9 a.m. to midnight every day. This information is also posted on the school's website.

M: Oh, thank you for that. However, my question isn't about the hours. ¹I want to know whether the lounge will be open during the winter break.

W: I see. ²Well, the lounge is normally closed in winter because there are fewer students on campus. Most students go home to be with their families for the holidays.

M: ⁵I understand, but some other students and I are staying during winter break. And, um, we want to use the student lounge for a group project. Could we ask for it to stay open?

W: I do apologize. But that simply won't be possible. ⁴ᴬHow about using the library?

M: I'll consider it, but it's hard to use the library as a group because you have to be quiet all the time. Is the student lounge really not an option?

W: I'm afraid not. You'll have to think of something else. It's too expensive for the school to keep the facility open. It has to pay for heating and for lights.

M: Oh, OK. I didn't know that.

W: Yes, the school is trying to save money. ³/⁴ᴮDo any of you stay in the dorms on the school campus? You could study in one of the dormitory common areas.

M: ⁴ᴮHmm... But my group members and I all live outside the campus. ⁴ᴰMaybe we can just use the cafeteria instead.

W: That sounds like a good solution as well.

M: Great. Thanks for your help. I'll discuss it with the others.

학생과 교직원 사이의 대화를 들으시오.

M: 실례합니다. 학생 휴게실에 대한 질문이 있어요.

W: 운영 시간을 알고 싶나요? 그곳은 매일 오전 9시부터 자정까지 운영합니다. 이 정보는 학교 웹사이트에도 게시되어 있어요.

M: 아, 고맙습니다. 하지만, 제 질문은 운영 시간에 관한 것이 아니에요. 저는 휴게실이 겨울방학 동안 열리는지를 알고 싶어요.

W: 그렇군요. 음, 교내에 학생들이 적어지기 때문에 휴게실은 보통 겨울에 문을 닫아요. 대부분의 학생들은 방학 동안 가족들과 함께 있기 위해 집에 가거든요.

M: 알아요, 하지만 몇몇 다른 학생들과 저는 겨울방학 동안 머물 거예요. 그리고, 음, 저희는 그룹 프로젝트를 위해 학생 휴게실을 사용하고 싶어요. 계속 열어두기를 부탁드려도 될까요?

W: 정말 죄송해요. 하지만 그것은 도저히 안 될 것 같아요. 도서관을 이용하는 게 어떨까요?

M: 그것을 고려해보겠지만, 내내 조용히 있어야 하기 때문에 도서관을 단체로 이용하는 것은 어려워서요. 학생 휴게실은 정말 선택지가 될 수 없나요?

W: 안 될 것 같아요. 다른 방법을 생각해 봐야 할 거예요. 학교가 그 시설을 계속 열어두기에는 너무 돈이 많이 들어요. 난방비와 조명비를 지불해야 해서요.

M: 아, 그래요. 그건 몰랐네요.

W: 네, 학교에서 돈을 절약하려고 노력하고 있어요. 여러분 중에 교내에 있는 기숙사에 머무는 사람이 있나요? 기숙사 공용 공간 중 한 곳에서도 공부를 할 수 있어요.

M: 흠... 하지만 그룹원들과 저 모두 교외에 살고 있어요. 어쩌면 저희가 교내식당을 대신 이용할 수도 있겠네요.

W: 그것도 좋은 해결책인 것 같네요.

M: 좋아요. 도와주셔서 고맙습니다. 다른 사람들과 논의해볼게요.

---

lounge 휴게실, 라운지 midnight 자정 break 방학
normally 보통 holiday 명절, 휴일
apologize 죄송하다, 사과하다 simply 도저히, 간단히
option 선택지 facility 시설 save 절약하다
common area 공용 공간 solution 해결책

1 대화는 주로 무엇에 관한 것인가?

(A) 학생 휴게실의 운영 시간
(B) 방학 동안 이용 가능한 학교 시설들
(C) 학교 건물의 입구를 어디에서 찾을 수 있는지

(D) 겨울방학 동안 공간을 예약하는 방법

2 직원에 따르면, 왜 겨울에 학생들이 더 적은가?

(A) 기숙사 방이 충분하지 않다.
(B) 겨울 프로그램들이 흥미롭지 않다.
(C) 학생들이 가족들과 함께 있기 위해 집에 간다.
(D) 교내에 교수들이 적어진다.

3 기숙사 공용 공간에 관해 추론할 수 있는 것은 무엇인가?

(A) 그곳들에는 먹을 수 있는 공간이 있다.
(B) 그곳들은 조용히 사용되어야 한다.
(C) 그곳들은 기숙사에 사는 학생들을 위한 것이다.
(D) 그곳들은 미리 예약을 해두어야 한다.

4 대화에서, 학생을 위한 몇 가지 선택지들이 논의된다. 다음의 항목이 학생이 고려해볼 선택지인지를 표시하시오.
각 항목에 적절한 칸을 클릭하시오.

	예	아니오
(A) 도서관을 이용하는 것	V	
(B) 기숙사 방에서 공부하는 것		V
(C) 강의실을 이용하는 것		V
(D) 교내식당을 이용해보는 것	V	

대화의 일부를 다시 듣고 질문에 답하시오.

M: I understand, but some other students and I are staying during winter break. And, um, we want to use the student lounge for a group project. Could we ask for it to stay open?
W: I do apologize. But that simply won't be possible. How about using the library?

5 직원은 이렇게 말함으로써 무엇을 의미하는가:
W: I do apologize.

(A) 학생은 요금을 지불해야 한다.
(B) 대학이 요청을 거절했다.
(C) 휴게실은 문이 닫힐 것이다.
(D) 도서관이 수리될 것이다.

PART 1. Passage 2   본문 p. 166

6 (C)　**7** (B)　**8** (B)　**9** (C)　**10** (C)　**11** (A)

Note-taking
Old Stone Age
- Lasted for <u>millions</u> of years
- <u>Hand axe</u>: Most significant invention

Middle Stone Age
- Made <u>surface</u> of tools smoother to cut through <u>animal skin</u> easily
- <u>Arrows</u> and spearheads → Could kill animals from far away

New Stone Age
- A wider variety of <u>materials</u>
- Improved tools such as a <u>smoother</u> hand axe and <u>advanced</u> farming tools
→ Led to the development of permanent <u>agricultural settlements</u>

Listen to part of a lecture in an archaeology class.

P: Let's talk about early humans. Uh, today, we have all kinds of technology that change very fast. Originally, though, progress was very slow. ⁶Early humans developed tools for thousands of years. And we can separate this tool-making process into three periods.

The first is the Old Stone Age. As the name suggests, people used stone tools during this period. ⁷However, we don't know exactly when the first stone tools were invented... Anyway, this period lasted for millions of years, from 3.4 million years ago to around 10,000 BC. So, uh, it was extremely long. Stone tools were quite simple. Some were like hammers. Stone Age people used them to hit surfaces and crush materials. Later, they used the stone hammers to break rocks. ⁸The most significant invention, though, was the hand axe. It, uh, had two sharp edges for chopping and cutting.

The next two thousand years, uh, from 10,000 to 8,000 BC, represent the Middle Stone Age. People continued making hammers and hand axes, but they also made smaller and sharper tools. They even made the surface of the tools smoother by rubbing them. ⁹The smoother surface let people cut through animal skin much easier. ¹⁰They also made arrows and spearheads with small, sharp, and smooth tips. They attached these to long sticks of wood. Now, they could throw or shoot weapons when hunting. This was a huge benefit because they could kill animals from far away. Before, hunters had to get close to animals, which sometimes caused injury or death.

OK, the next five thousand years, until around 3,000 BC, is known as the New Stone Age. Tool-makers used a wider variety of materials... Stone, bone, ivory, and even the horns of animals... Uh, in this period, improved tools made a huge impact on society. For example, a smoother hand axe was very effective for cutting trees, so people could remove trees from fields. ¹¹Similarly, the creation of advanced farming tools allowed people to prepare their fields for farming. You could even say that, uh, all of these New Stone Age tools led to the development of permanent agricultural settlements.

고고학 강의의 일부를 들으시오.

P: 초기 인류에 대해 이야기해 봅시다. 어, 오늘날, 우리는 매우 빠르게 변화하는 온갖 종류의 기술을 가지고 있죠. 하지만, 원래는, 발전이 매우 더뎠어요. 초기 인류는 수천 년 동안 도구를 개발했어요. 그리고 우리는 이 도구를 만드는 과정을 세 가지 시대로 나눌 수 있습니다.

첫 번째는 구석기 시대입니다. 이름에서 알 수 있듯이, 사람들은 이 시기에 석기를 사용했어요. 하지만, 우리는 정확히 언제 최초의 석기가 발명되었는지는 모릅니다... 어쨌든, 340만 년 전부터 기원전 10,000년까지, 이 시대는 수백만 년 동안 지속되었어요. 그래서, 어, 아주 긴 시대였죠. 석기는 매우 단순했어요. 어떤 것들은 망치 같았어요. 석기시대 사람들은 그것들을 표면을 때리고 물질들을 부수는 데 사용했어요. 후에, 그들은 돌을 부수는 데 그 돌망치를 사용했습니다. 하지만, 가장 중요한 발명품은 손도끼였어요. 그것에는, 어, 자르고 베기 위한 날카로운 날 두 개가 있었어요.

그다음 2천 년, 어, 기원전 1만 년에서 8천 년까지는, 중석기 시대에 해당합니다. 사람들은 계속해서 망치와 손도끼를 만들었지만, 더 작고 날카로운 도구들도 만들었어요. 그들은 도구들을 문질러서 표면을 더 매끄럽게 만들기도 했죠. 매끄러운 표면은 사람들이 동물의 가죽을 훨씬 더 쉽게 잘라낼 수 있게 해줬습니다. 그들은 또한 작고, 날카롭고, 매끄러운 끝을 가진 화살과 창두도 만들었어요. 그들은 이것들을 긴 나무 막대기에 연결시켰습니다. 이제, 그들은 사냥할 때 무기를 던지거나 쏠 수 있었죠. 그들이 먼 곳에서 동물들을 죽일 수 있었기 때문에 이것은 큰 이점이었습니다. 이전에는, 사냥꾼들이 동물들에게 가까이 다가가야 했는데, 이것은 때때로 부상이나 죽음을 초래했거든요.

자, 그다음 5천 년, 기원전 3천 년경까지는, 신석기 시대라고 알려져 있어요. 도구 제작자들은 더 다양한 재료들을 사용했습니다... 돌, 뼈, 상아, 심지어 동물의 뿔까지... 어, 이 시대에는, 발전된 도구들이 사회에 큰 영향을 끼쳤어요. 예를 들어, 더 매끄러워진 손도끼는 나무를 자르는 데 매우 효과적이어서, 사람들이 들판의 나무를 제거할 수 있게 됐죠. 마찬가지로, 발전된 농기구의 발명은 사람들이 농사를 위한 밭을 준비할 수 있게 해주었습니다. 심지어, 어, 이 모든 신석기 시대의 도구들이 영구적인 정착농업의 발전을 초래했다고 말할 수도 있겠습니다.

progress 명 발전, 진보   last 동 지속되다   surface 명 표면
significant 형 중요한   axe 명 도끼   edge 명 (칼 등의) 날, 모서리
chop 동 자르다   smooth 형 매끄러운   rub 동 문지르다
arrow 명 화살   spearhead 명 창두(=창의 머리)   tip 명 끝
benefit 명 이점   ivory 명 상아   horn 명 뿔   field 명 들판, 밭
permanent 형 영구적인   agricultural 형 농업의
settlement 명 정착(지)

6 강의의 주된 주제는 무엇인가?

(A) 농업 사회의 기원
(B) 초기 인류의 무기 사용
(C) 고대 도구의 발전
(D) 인류 최초의 정착지

7 교수는 최초의 석기에 관해 무엇이라고 말하는가?

(A) 그것들 중 몇 개는 꽤 복잡했다.
(B) 그것들의 정확한 발명 시기는 알려지지 않았다.
(C) 그것들은 기원전 10,000년경 전까지 개발되지 않았다.
(D) 그것들 중 대부분은 방어를 위해 사용되었다.

8 교수는 왜 손도끼를 언급하는가?

(A) 고대 인류에 의해 사용된 최초의 도구를 설명하기 위해
(B) 구석기 시대의 중요한 발명품을 소개하기 위해
(C) 뼈로 만들어진 흔한 도구를 보여주기 위해
(D) 구석기 시대의 기술의 부족함을 강조하기 위해

9 중석기 시대에 도구의 표면이 더 매끄러워진 것에는 어떤 결과가 있었는가?

(A) 더 작은 도구들을 만드는 것이 가능해졌다.
(B) 도구들을 잡기 더 쉬워졌다.
(C) 동물의 가죽을 잘라내는 것이 더 쉬워졌다.
(D) 돌망치가 더 이상 쓸모 없어졌다.

10 교수는 화살과 창두에 관해 무엇을 암시하는가?

(A) 그것들은 큰 동물들을 사냥하기에 효과적이지 않았다.
(B) 그것들은 사람 한 명이 혼자서 사냥을 할 수 있도록 했다.
(C) 그것들은 사냥을 덜 위험하게 만들었다.
(D) 그것들은 쉽게 부러졌다.

11 신석기 시대 도구들에 대한 교수의 태도는 무엇인가?

(A) 그녀는 그것들이 영구적인 농업 사회를 초래했다고 믿는다.
(B) 그녀는 그것들이 구석기 시대의 도구들과 비슷했다고 생각한다.
(C) 그녀는 그것들이 만들어진 지 2,000년이 채 안 되었다고 확신한다.
(D) 그녀는 그것들이 나무를 자르는 데 유용하지 않다고 생각한다.

PART 2. Passage 1   본문 p. 168

1 (B)   2 (D)   3 (B)   4 Yes: (A), (C), (D) No: (B)
5 (A)

Note-taking

Things to Include in the Application
- A copy of the academic record
- A letter of recommendation
- A statement of purpose: An essay that describes interests and achievements in school
- An official document about an internship

Listen to a conversation between a student and a professor.

S: Thanks for meeting with me, Professor Harris. ¹I really need some advice about what to include in my application for graduate school.

P: I'm happy to help, Monica. ⁴ᴬOK, the first thing you need to do is get a copy of your academic record. This must be included to show that you received good grades.

S: OK. I'll pick that up tomorrow morning.

P: Excellent. ⁴ᴮNow, I've already prepared a letter of recommendation, so you don't need to worry about that.

S: Thank you. ²/⁴ᶜUm, I saw on the university's website that I have to write a statement of purpose?

P: Right. This is like an essay that describes your

interests and achievements in school. It only has to be one page long. I can help you if you'd like.

S: I'd really appreciate that. Um, is there anything else?

P: Well... Have you done any internships?

S: ³Actually, I was a research assistant at a government facility last summer. That was my only internship experience.

P: That's OK. ⁴ᴰYou'll need to show an official document from the company that you worked at. Be sure to include that as well.

S: Um, one last thing. You were working in a company when you were in graduate school, right?

P: Yes. Why do you ask?

S: ⁵I was wondering how to manage going to school and working at the same time.

P: Well, it will be difficult, but you just have to be organized. I believe you are. It also helps if you take good notes and find classmates you can work with.

S: That's great advice. Thanks again, Professor Harris.

학생과 교수 사이의 대화를 들으시오.

S: 만나주셔서 감사합니다, Harris 교수님. 저는 제 대학원 지원서에 어떤 것을 포함해야 할지에 대한 조언이 정말 필요해요.

P: 기꺼이 도와줄게, Monica. 자, 네가 가장 먼저 해야 할 일은 학업 성적표 한 부를 얻는 거란다. 이것은 네가 좋은 성적을 받았다는 것을 보여주기 위해 포함되어야만 해.

S: 알겠습니다. 내일 아침에 그것을 찾아올게요.

P: 좋아. 자, 추천서는 이미 내가 준비했으니, 그것에 대해서는 걱정하지 않아도 된단다.

S: 감사합니다. 음, 제가 대학 홈페이지에서 봤는데 학업계획서를 써야 하나요?

P: 맞아. 이것은 학교에서 네가 관심있는 것과 성취한 것을 설명하는 에세이 같은 거야. 한 페이지 길이면 된단다. 네가 원한다면 내가 도와줄 수 있어.

S: 그렇게 해주시면 정말 감사하겠습니다. 음, 다른 것은 없나요?

P: 음... 인턴십을 해 본 적이 있니?

S: 사실, 저는 지난 여름에 정부 시설에서 연구 보조원으로 있었어요. 그게 제 유일한 인턴십 경험이었어요.

P: 괜찮아. 네가 근무했던 회사에서 받은 공식 서류를 보여줘야 할 거야. 그것도 반드시 포함되도록 하렴.

S: 음, 마지막으로 하나만 더요. 대학원을 다니실 때 회사에서 일을 하고 계셨죠?

P: 그래. 왜 그러니?

S: 저는 학교에 다니는 것과 일을 하는 것을 어떻게 동시에 해낼 수 있는지가 궁금했어요.

P: 글쎄, 어렵겠지만, 계획적이여야만 해. 난 네가 그렇다고 생각한 다. 만약 네가 필기를 잘 하고 같이 일할 동급생들을 찾는다면 그것도 도움이 될 거야.

S: 좋은 조언이네요. 다시 한번 감사합니다, Harris 교수님.

---

application (명) 지원서   graduate school 대학원
academic record 학업 성적표   pick up ~을 찾아오다
letter of recommendation 추천서, 추천장
statement of purpose 학업계획서   interest (명) 관심(사)
achievement (명) 성취한 것, 업적   assistant (명) 보조원
facility (명) 시설   organized (형) 계획적인, 조직적인
take notes 필기하다

1 대화의 주된 주제는 무엇인가?
   (A) 여름 인턴십 프로그램
   (B) 대학원에 어떻게 지원할 수 있는지
   (C) 더 좋은 점수를 받는 것에 대한 학습 조언
   (D) 학교에서 공식 서류를 어떻게 얻을 수 있는지

2 학생은 무엇에 대해 써야 하는가?
   (A) 그녀의 업무 경험
   (B) 그녀의 졸업 후 진로 계획
   (C) 그녀의 직업적 목표
   (D) 그녀가 좋아하는 것과 성취한 것

3 학생은 왜 정부 시설을 언급하는가?
   (A) 교수에게 그녀가 어디로 가는지 말하기 위해
   (B) 그녀가 과거에 어디에서 일했는지 나타내기 위해
   (C) 사무실의 위치를 묻기 위해
   (D) 그녀의 직업적 관심사를 보여주기 위해

4 다음의 항목이 학생이 해야 하는 것으로 언급된 것인지를 표시하시오. 각 항목에 적절한 칸을 클릭하시오.

	예	아니오
(A) 성적표 받기	V	
(B) 추천서 요청하기		V
(C) 학업계획서 쓰기	V	
(D) 인턴십의 공식 서류 포함하기	V	

대화의 일부를 다시 듣고 질문에 답하시오.
S: I was wondering how to manage going to school and working at the same time.
P: Well, it will be difficult, but you just have to be organized. I believe you are. It also helps if you take good notes and find classmates you can work with.

5 교수는 이렇게 말함으로써 무엇을 의미하는가:
   P: I believe you are.
   (A) 그는 학생이 계획적일 수 있다고 생각한다.
   (B) 그는 학생이 좋은 친구를 찾을 것이라고 확신한다.
   (C) 그는 학생이 훌륭한 교수가 될 것이라고 생각한다.
   (D) 그는 학생이 시험을 통과할 것이라고 확신한다.

PART 2. Passage 2
본문 p.170

6 (C) 7 (B) 8 (D) 9 (C) 10 (D)
11 Terrestrial Planets: (A), (D) Gas Giants: (B), (C)

Note-taking

Terrestrial Planets
- Four planets that are closest to the Sun: Mercury, Venus, Earth, and Mars
- Hard surfaces, made of rocks and metals
- Small in size and have secondary atmospheres

Gas Giants
- Jupiter, Saturn, Uranus, and Neptune
- Surfaces made up of gases
- Much bigger than terrestrial planets
- Have primary atmospheres

Listen to part of a lecture in an astronomy class.

P: Good morning, everyone. So, last time, we discussed the origin of the solar system or, uh, how the Sun and the planets formed. [6]Today, we will talk about the planets in more detail. In total, there are eight planets in our solar system. And we can divide them into two different classes.

Um, the first kind is terrestrial. [11A]The terrestrial planets are the four planets that are closest to the Sun. They are Mercury, Venus, Earth, and Mars. The word terrestrial means something is related to land. [7]So the terrestrial planets have hard surfaces... because uh, they are mostly made of rocks and metals. Of course, Earth has a lot of water on its surface too, but the other terrestrial planets have little or no water.

The structure of the terrestrial planets is similar. They are small in size and have secondary atmospheres. [11D]They are called secondary because the gases did not form together with the planets. They were created after the formation of the planets. [8]Um, volcanoes are one of the causes of the formation of the atmosphere. You know, volcanic activities release a lot of gases, so they help create the atmosphere.

Now, the other planets are called gas giants. These include Jupiter, Saturn, Uranus, and Neptune. [9/11B]Unlike the terrestrial planets, the gas giants do not have a solid surface. Instead, they are mostly made up of gases like, um, largely helium and hydrogen. So when we see the pictures of them, we can find giant clouds moving around on their surfaces.

[11C]As their name suggests, the gas giants are much bigger than terrestrial planets. For example, Earth is the largest of the terrestrial planets, but Jupiter, the largest gas giant, is 11 times bigger than Earth. Another feature of gas giants is rings. [10]You've probably seen images of Saturn's famous rings. But, uh, the other gas planets also have rings. They are just not clear enough for us to see easily. And one last thing... Uh, the gas planets have primary atmospheres. This means that their atmospheres were created at the same time when the solar system formed.

천문학 강의의 일부를 들으시오.

P: 좋은 아침입니다, 여러분. 자, 지난 시간에, 우리는 태양계의 기원, 또는 어, 태양과 행성들이 어떻게 형성되었는지에 대해 논의했죠. 오늘은, 행성에 대해 더 상세히 이야기할 거예요. 우리 태양계에는 총 8개의 행성이 있습니다. 그리고 우리는 그것들을 두 개의 다른 유형으로 나눌 수 있어요.

어, 첫 번째는 지구형이에요. 지구형 행성들은 태양에 가장 가까운 네 개의 행성들입니다. 그것들은 수성, 금성, 지구, 그리고 화성이에요. 지구형이라는 단어는 육지와 관련이 있다는 것을 의미하죠. 그래서 지구형 행성들은 단단한 표면을 가지고 있는데요... 왜냐하면, 어, 그것들은 대부분 돌과 금속으로 만들어졌기 때문이에요. 물론, 지구는 표면에 많은 물도 있습니다만, 다른 지구형 행성들은 물이 거의 없거나 아예 없습니다.

지구형 행성들의 구조는 비슷해요. 그것들은 크기가 작고 부(차적)대기를 가지고 있어요. 그것들이 부차적이라고 불리는 이유는 기체가 행성들과 함께 형성되지 않았기 때문이에요. 그것들은 행성의 형성 이후에 만들어졌어요. 음, 화산은 그 대기의 형성 원인들 중 하나입니다. 알다시피, 화산 활동은 많은 기체를 방출해서, 그 대기를 형성하는 데 일조하죠.

자, 다른 행성들은 거대 기체 행성(목성형 행성)이라고 불려요. 이것들은 목성, 토성, 천왕성, 그리고 해왕성을 포함합니다. 지구형 행성들과 달리, 거대 기체 행성들은 단단한 표면을 가지고 있지 않아요. 대신, 그것들은, 어, 대부분 헬륨과 수소 같은 기체들로 이루어져 있어요. 그래서 우리가 그것들의 사진을 볼 때, 거대한 구름들이 그것들의 표면 주변에서 움직이는 것을 발견할 수 있습니다.

그것들의 이름이 나타내듯이, 거대 기체 행성들은 지구형 행성들보다 훨씬 큽니다. 예를 들어, 지구는 지구형 행성들 중에서 가장 크지만, 가장 큰 거대 기체 행성인 목성은 지구보다 11배나 더 큽니다. 거대 기체 행성들의 또 다른 특징은 고리예요. 여러분은 아마 토성의 유명한 고리 사진을 본 적이 있을 것입니다. 하지만, 어, 다른 거대 기체 행성들 또한 고리를 가지고 있어요. 그것들은 단지 우리가 쉽게 볼 수 있을 만큼 충분히 뚜렷하지 않을 뿐이죠. 그리고 마지막으로 한 가지... 어, 거대 행성들은 원시대기를 가지고 있어요. 이것은 그것들의 대기가 태양계가 형성되었을 때 동시에 만들어졌다는 것을 의미합니다.

---

origin 명 기원   solar system 태양계   form 통 형성되다; 형성하다
class 명 유형   terrestrial 형 지구의, 육지의
secondary 형 부차적인, 2차의   atmosphere 명 대기
formation 명 형성   solid 형 단단한; 명 고체   helium 명 헬륨
hydrogen 명 수소   primary 형 원래의, 1차의

6 강의의 주된 주제는 무엇인가?

(A) 다양한 종류의 대기들
(B) 태양계의 형성
(C) 태양계의 두 종류의 행성들
(D) 행성들에 관한 두 가지 최신 과학 연구들

7 교수는 지구형 행성들에 관해 무엇이라고 말하는가?

(A) 그것들에는 물이 많이 있다.
(B) 그것들은 표면이 단단하다.
(C) 그것들은 모양이 다양하다.
(D) 그것들에는 바위와 금속이 거의 없다.

8 강의에서 교수는 왜 화산을 언급하는가?

(A) 태양계의 수수께끼에 대한 예시를 제공하기 위해
(B) 지구형 행성들이 어떻게 형성되었는지 보여주기 위해
(C) 지구의 몇몇 자연재해들을 강조하기 위해
(D) 부대기가 어떻게 만들어졌는지 설명하기 위해

9 교수는 거대 기체 행성들의 표면에 관해 무엇이라고 말하는가?

(A) 그것들은 낮에 뜨거워진다.
(B) 그것들은 먼지와 얼음으로 둘러싸여 있다.
(C) 그것들에는 주로 헬륨과 수소가 포함되어 있다.
(D) 그것들은 보통 뜨거운 액체로 구성되어 있다.

10 교수는 화성의 고리에 관해 무엇을 암시하는가?

(A) 그것들은 목성의 고리들보다 작다.
(B) 그것들은 행성 자체보다 더 오래되었다.
(C) 그것들은 망원경 없이는 보기 힘들다.
(D) 그것들은 다른 거대 기체 행성들의 고리들보다 더 뚜렷하다.

11 강의에서, 교수는 지구형 행성들과 거대 기체 행성들의 특징을 언급한다. 다음의 항목이 각 유형의 특징으로 언급된 것인지를 표시하시오.

각 항목에 적절한 칸을 클릭하시오.

	지구형 행성들	거대기체 행성들
(A) 그것들은 태양에 더 가깝다.	V	
(B) 그것들은 표면이 단단하지 않다.		V
(C) 그것들은 다른 유형보다 더 크다.		V
(D) 그것들의 형성 이후에 대기가 형성되었다.	V	

PART 2. Passage 3
본문 p. 172

12 (D)　13 (A)　14 (A), (D)　15 (B)　16 (C)　17 (B)

Note-taking

Mid-1950s
Thousands of East Germans had moved to West Germany.
→ A law in 1956 banned all travel to the West.

1961 ~ 1970s
Construction of the Berlin Wall began.
→ Secured the border with wire fences, concrete blocks, mines, etc.

1980s
People started the Peaceful Revolution.
→ East and West Germany united, and the wall was destroyed.

Listen to part of a lecture in a history class.

P: OK... Let's continue our discussion of the Cold War. Last class, we talked about how the Soviet Union got control of Eastern Europe. And, um, after this, Eastern Europe was separated from the rest of Europe. One city... Berlin... was the symbol of this division. One section was part of democratic West Germany, while the other was part of communist East Germany. And a giant barrier called the Berlin Wall was built in the middle of the city. ¹²Today, I want to focus on the history of the separation of Berlin by the Berlin Wall.

Now, after World War II ended in 1945, East Germans could easily move to West Germany for many years though the two countries were divided. In fact, by the mid-1950s, thousands of people had moved, and many of them were technicians and, um, engineers. ¹³East Germany was afraid of losing its educated workers, so the country's ruler passed a law in 1956 that banned all travel to the West. The construction of the Berlin Wall began in 1961 to make sure people followed this new law.

At first, they secured the border with wire fences. However, soon they added large concrete blocks. ¹⁴ᴬIn addition, there were mines, a type of bomb that exploded if anyone stepped on them. ¹⁴ᴰWatch towers with armed guards were there too. Um, the guards were ordered to shoot anyone who came too close to the wall. But this did not discourage some East Germans. ¹⁷Over 5,000 people escaped to West Germany. Some dug tunnels and others jumped from nearby buildings. A few of them even made hot-air balloons themselves and used these to escape. You know, these were all very dangerous activities. I'm not sure what I would have done...

¹⁵In the 1980s, there was an economic crisis in East Germany, and it weakened the government. ¹⁶Then people started the Peaceful Revolution. They marched in the streets of East Berlin on November 4, 1989. Five days later, the government announced that the border would be opened. After that, many Germans from both parts of the city gathered in front of the wall to celebrate. And they brought tools to destroy the wall. A few months later, East and West Germany were united as one country again, and the wall was completely destroyed.

역사학 강의의 일부를 들으시오.

P: 좋아요... 냉전에 대한 논의를 계속해 봅시다. 지난 수업에서, 우리는 소련이 어떻게 동유럽의 지배권을 얻었는지에 대해 이야기했습니다. 그리고, 음, 그 이후, 동유럽은 유럽의 나머지 지역으로부터 분리되었어요. 한 도시... 베를린이... 이 분단의 상징이었죠. 한 구역은 민주주의인 서독의 일부였고, 반면 다른 구역은 공산주의인 동독의 일부였어요. 그리고 베를린 장벽이라고 불리는 거대한 장벽이 도시의 중앙에 세워졌죠. 오늘, 저는 베를린 장벽에 의한 베를린의 분단의 역사에 집중하고자 합니다.

자, 1945년에 제2차 세계 대전이 끝난 이후, 두 나라가 분단되었음에도 불구하고 수년 동안 동독인들은 서독으로 쉽게 이주할 수 있었어요. 실제로, 1950년대 중반까지, 수천 명의 사람들이 이주했고, 그들 중 많은 사람들이 기술자들과, 음, 공학자들이었어요. 동독은 교육받은 노동자들을 잃는 것을 두려워했고, 그래서 그 나라의 지도자는 1956년에 서독으로의 모든 이동을 금지하는 법안을 통과시켰어요. 사람들이 이 새로운 법을 확실히 따르도록 하게 하기 위해 1961년에 베를린 장벽의 건설이 시작되었습니다.

처음에, 그들은 철조망 울타리로 국경을 통제했어요. 하지만, 곧 그들은 큰 콘크리트 블록들을 추가했죠. 게다가, 그곳에는 밟으면 폭발하는 폭탄의 일종인 지뢰도 있었어요. 무장한 경비원들이 있는 감시탑도 있었습니다. 음, 그 경비원들은 장벽에 너무 가까이 오는 사람은 누구든 쏘라는 명령을 받았죠. 하지만 이것은 일부 동독 사람들을 낙담시키지는 못했습니다. 5천 명 이상의 사람들이 서독으로 탈출을 한 것인데요. 몇몇은 터널을 팠고 다른 사람들은 근처 건물에서 뛰어내렸어요. 그들 중 몇몇은 심지어 직접 열기구를 만들어서 그것들을 사용해 탈출했습니다. 알다시피, 이것들은 모두 매우 위험한 행위였어요. 저라면 어떻게 했을지 잘 모르겠군요...

1980년대에, 동독에 경제 위기가 있었고, 그것은 그 정부를 약화시켰어요. 곧이어 사람들은 평화적인 혁명을 시작했습니다. 그들은 1989년, 11월 4일에 동베를린의 거리에서 행진을 했습니다. 5일 후, 정부는 국경이 개방될 것이라고 발표했어요. 그 후, 양쪽 도시에서 온 많은 독일인들이 기념을 하기 위해 성벽 앞에 모였습니다. 그리고 그들은 장벽을 파괴할 도구들을 가지고 왔죠. 몇 달 후, 동독과 서독은 다시 하나의 국가로 통일되었고, 장벽은 완전히 파괴되었답니다.

division 명 분단   democratic 형 민주주의의
communist 형 공산주의의   barrier 명 장벽
separation 명 분단   technician 명 기술자
educated 형 교육받은   ruler 명 지도자   ban 동 금지하다
secure 동 통제하다, 지키다   border 명 국경   mine 명 지뢰
explode 동 폭발하다   armed 형 무장한
discourage 동 낙담시키다   escape 동 탈출하다
economic crisis 경제 위기   weaken 동 약화시키다
revolution 명 혁명   march 동 행진하다   unite 동 통일하다

12 강의는 주로 무엇에 관한 것인가?

(A) 냉전의 원인
(B) 제2차 세계 대전을 끝낸 협정
(C) 동독의 형성
(D) 도시의 분단

13 교수에 따르면, 동독은 왜 장벽을 세웠는가?

(A) 사람들이 새로운 법을 확실히 따르게 하기 위해
(B) 서독에 있는 동독인들을 처벌하기 위해
(C) 서독인들이 동독에 살 수 있도록 하기 위해
(D) 소련으로부터 도시를 지키기 위해

14 교수에 따르면, 동독 국경을 통제하기 위해 사용된 두 가지 방법은 무엇인가?
2개의 답을 고르시오.

(A) 폭발하는 폭탄들
(B) 경비견들
(C) 깊은 터널들
(D) 감시탑들

15 교수에 따르면, 1980년대에 동독 정부를 약화시켰던 것은 무엇인가?

(A) 서독의 공격
(B) 경제적 문제
(C) 자연재해
(D) 새로운 무역 규정

16 교수는 국경 개방에 관해 무엇을 암시하는가?

(A) 그것은 모든 동독인들에 의해 반대되었다.
(B) 그것은 투표로 결정되었다.
(C) 그것은 평화적인 시위에 의해 야기되었다.
(D) 그것은 몇 달밖에 지속되지 않았다.

강의의 일부를 다시 듣고 질문에 답하시오.
P: Over 5,000 people escaped to West Germany. Some dug tunnels and others jumped from nearby buildings. A few of them even made hot-air balloons themselves and used these to escape. You know, these were all very dangerous activities. I'm not sure what I would have done...

17 교수는 왜 이렇게 말하는가:
P: I'm not sure what I would have done...

(A) 많은 사람들이 자유를 얻었다는 것을 보여주기 위해
(B) 탈출하려는 것의 위험성을 강조하기 위해
(C) 혁명에 대한 부정적인 의견을 표현하기 위해
(D) 개인적인 문제의 예시를 제공하기 위해

APEX LISTENING for the TOEFL iBT Basic

Answer Book